OUTPOST OF OCCUPATION

OUTPOST
OF
OCCUPATION

How the Channel Islands Survived Nazi Rule
1940–1945

BARRY TURNER

First published in Great Britain

2010 by Aurum Press Limited

7 Greenland Street

London, NW1 0ND

www.aurumpress.co.uk

A catalogue record for this book is available from the British Library.

ISBN 978 1 84513 512 6

1 3 5 7 9 10 8 6 4 2

2010 2012 2014 2013 2011

Text design by Richard Marston
Typeset by SX Composing DTP, Rayleigh, Essex
Printed by MPG Books, Bodmin, Cornwall

It would be impertinent for any country that has not suffered
occupation to pass judgement on one that did.
Anthony Eden

CONTENTS

INTRODUCTION

Every country has its own take on the fortunes and misfortunes of war. National pride wraps itself in a fabrication which inflates victories and minimises defeats. Britain is no exception. After seventy years, the morale-boosting legends attached to a world war fought and won are still as powerful, if not more powerful, than less palatable aspects of Britain's involvement. One such is the deeply ingrained myth of a nation that, come what may, would never have surrendered. Though Nazi rule embraced continental Europe, it could not have happened here. That it did happen in the Channel Islands, the only part of Britain to be occupied by German forces, has long vexed the myth makers.

Confronted by an overwhelming power, islanders accommodated themselves as best they could to an unwelcome reality. It was no easy ride. Deprivation and suffering there was in plenty, more than enough to match experiences on the mainland. For long periods, the ordinary necessities of life – food, fuel, clothing – were in desperately short supply. More than this, on small islands where there were few secluded spaces the inhabitants had to live for five years under constant surveillance and arbitrary directives, the deadening effects of which should not be underestimated. But the absence of a mass uprising or much in the way of violent resistance offended those, Churchill in particular, who made no concessions to the possibility of defeat.

In the aftermath of the fall of the Third Reich, opinion was divided on the Channel Islands. While the liberation and the fortitude of those who had stayed the course was celebrated, there was in some quarters, notably the intelligence services, a conviction that the islanders had wilfully allowed the Germans to walk all over them. As hitherto unpublished intelligence reports reveal, the lust for retribution, strongest among those who had spent most of the war behind Whitehall desks, encouraged and sustained belief in a traitorous cover-up. This ill-founded view took such hold that even today historians of otherwise impeccable credentials feel obliged to take a swipe at 'the Quislings' who held sway in the Channel Islands – a charge repeated in the latest volume of the *New Oxford History of England*.[1] Madeleine Bunting's full-length study, *The Model Occupation*,[2] also takes a harsh view, highlighting the rare cases of blatant collaboration, notably the rounding up, at German behest, of the tiny, fully assimilated Jewish population.

But this is by no means the whole story. At no time did leading islanders accept German authority other than by enforcement. The islands were surrendered without a fight on orders from London, where, in the wake of domino defeats across Europe, demilitarisation seemed the only practical option. Subsequently, while many mistakes were made, most of them, starting with an ill-conceived and poorly managed evacuation, originated with central government. In contrast to other occupied countries, the Channel Islands were denied the arms and agents deemed essential for a grassroots rebellion, surely a critical factor when it comes to judging the islanders' wartime behaviour.

Why then are one-sided and condemnatory judgements on the Channel Islands in wartime still common currency? Partly, they reflect a British failure to understand what occupation really means. In recent years, studies of the social and economic responses to arbitrary foreign rule have shown patterns that were remarkably similar across Nazi-dominated Europe. Hating what was happening to them, most people tried as best they could to get on with their lives. Heroes of the resistance were a tiny minority until the near certainty of German defeat gave a fillip to active opposition.

This was certainly true of France, but perhaps a closer comparison is provided by the occupation experiences of Denmark and Norway, small countries which had long since lost any military pretensions. As in the Channel Islands, occupation came as a profound cultural shock to the Nordic people, who found it hard to credit that a neighbouring country should choose to exercise its will by force of arms. But they, along with the rest of mainland Europe, had the advantage, if it could be so called, of living with the early crises caused by Hitler's territorial ambitions. To that extent, they were aware of Nazi Germany's capacity for power politics at the point of a gun.

The Channel Islands, on the other hand, were a society apart, isolated by geography from the big events and more concerned with farm and fishing prices than with the struggle for first place in the European pecking order. The islanders were a hardy people used to managing their own affairs within the tight rules of the nonconformist ethic. Crime was rare; violent crime almost unknown. Their last military encounters had been during the Napoleonic wars. To cope with an enemy at first hand was to enter another dimension.

There were brave individuals in the Channel Islands who risked the concentration camp or the firing squad to fight for basic freedoms. But while their stories are inspirational, equal credit must surely go to the politicians and administrators who tried to work the system in ways that held their societies together while making minimum concessions to the enemy. It was a dangerous game with often grave consequences.

When it was all over, accusations of collaboration were firmly discounted by senior ministers in Churchill's government. But Churchill himself was not so sure. Why? Was it because the wartime experience of the Channel Islands failed to live up to his portrayal of a country ready to face extinction rather than submit? Certainly, Churchill made no allowance for the practicalities of living with the enemy. Is it possible that he saw the islands as an embarrassment, a departure from his chosen norm that was best soon forgotten? What cannot be denied is that his refusal to speak out on behalf of the islanders, together with the malign preoccupation of the intelligence services who saw traitors at every turn of their inept investigations, left a legacy of suspicion and recrimination that is still with us. This book is an attempt to clean the slate.

1

A SHOCK TO THE SYSTEM

Everywhere the flags were flying, but this was no celebration. The improvised banners flapping in a summer breeze were a uniform white and the message they conveyed was the same for every house and farm in Jersey. The Germans were coming and there was absolutely nothing anyone could do about it.

The date was 1 July 1940. It had happened so quickly. Two months earlier Hitler's army had been poised but was yet to strike. In London, there was confident talk of defending the Channel Islands if, and this was judged to be highly improbable, a German invasion was threatened. Then, starting in April, events unfolded with dramatic suddenness. First Denmark and Norway were overrun. Belgium and Holland soon went the same way. On 4 June the last British soldier was lifted from the beaches of Dunkirk and two weeks later, on Monday, 17 June, France finally crumbled before the German military machine. The whole of the coastline of north-west Europe, from north of Norway to the Spanish frontier, was now in German hands.

The shock to the people of Jersey and Guernsey and of their smaller neighbours, Alderney and Sark, was profound. Living as they did closer to France than to England (Jersey is just fifteen miles off the French coast and Alderney even closer), many islanders were more familiar with St Malo, Granville and Cherbourg than Plymouth, Southampton and Bournemouth. Though their first loyalty was to the British crown and had been since 1066, even those who did not have friends and relatives across that narrow strip of water shared France's pain and humiliation. There was fear too. Gunfire could be heard; the smoke from blazing oil depots was clearly visible. How long would it be before the enemy was at the gate?

*

Between the world wars, the Channel Islands were the places to go to get away from it all. Sea, sand and sunshine appealed to British holidaymakers, who enjoyed a touch of *joie de vivre* without the trouble of passports and currency exchange. The travel guides were characteristically euphoric, promising 'spectacular coastlines, rugged cliffs, golden beaches, secluded coves and green hills' with 'warm, invigorating days from April until October'. As the largest of the islands, with a population of just over 50,000, Jersey's average daily sunshine was touted as higher than that of any other British resort. Conditions were thus eminently suitable for those 'of advanced years or of delicate constitution'. But to get there they had to endure a nine-and-a-half hour sea crossing from Southampton or Weymouth, often over choppy water. On one gale-swept occasion, the journey to St Helier, with stopovers in the Solent and at Guernsey took sixty-two hours.

Though Jersey airport was not opened until 1937 (with Guernsey's following two years later), air services began as early as 1933, with the newly created Jersey Airways using West Park Beach as an airstrip. This 'beach aerodrome' was said to be the first to be submerged twice a day and to have its timetable controlled by the tides. In the first year of operation over 20,000 passengers were carried. (Today, the figure is well over 1½ million.) By 1939, there were daily services to Jersey and Guernsey with an inter-island hop from Jersey to Alderney. On the main routes, the journey time was soon little over an hour, an advance in communication which promised a healthy expansion of tourism.

While English was the predominant language, French was still used by government and law, though the patois spoken by the farmers

(Jérriaise in Jersey, Guernesais in Guernsey and Sercquiaise in Sark) was incomprehensible to anyone schooled on the canons of the Académie Française. The image of gentle living, attractive to well-heeled retirees in pursuit of a low tax regime as much as to tourists and long-stay residents, was reinforced by the seasonal appearance of luxury produce on British tables – butter, cream and new potatoes from Jersey, flowers and tomatoes from Guernsey.

But for the citizens of the Channel Islands who had to make a living from the land and sea, the cosy rural idyll was not all that visitors cracked it up to be. Basic services such as electricity and piped water were restricted to the most prosperous homes. On the tiny island of Alderney there were just seven pumps to provide fresh water for around three hundred residents; the only generator was used to power dockside lifting gear. Life was less harsh on Jersey and Guernsey but to eke out a precarious living from the land many farmers took to their fishing boats from May to September, often crossing the Atlantic to share in the catch of Newfoundland cod. Motor vehicles were heavily outnumbered by horse-drawn traffic (even today no cars are permitted on Sark) and it was with no sense of irony that Guernsey adopted the donkey, used for dragging goods up the steep, cobbled streets of St Peter Port, as a national symbol.

Though attached to the British crown, the Channel Islands were almost entirely free from ministrations of the British government. For this unique state of affairs, the islanders had to thank the Duke of Normandy, their protector in 1066 when he made his successful bid to occupy the throne of England. When the Norman Kingdom broke away in 1204, the islands remained crown properties, appropriately known as 'peculiars'. Jersey and Guernsey had parliaments, known as The States, elected on a property franchise. Each was led by a bailiff who was also the chief magistrate. Alderney had its own government while Sark, though left largely to its own devices, was a dependency of Guernsey. The official channel of communication with London, responsible for diplomacy and defence, was between the Home Office and the relevant lieutenant-governor and commander in chief, both royal appointments, based in Jersey and Guernsey.

With duties that were more ceremonial than political, these officers of state with their grand titles seldom had reason to bother their masters in Whitehall. Their first point of contact was Charles Markbrieter, the assistant secretary at the Home Office responsible for Channel Islands affairs. Little is known of Mr Markbrieter but we can imagine him, a dedicated civil servant at the pinnacle of his modest career, trying to come to terms with the dramatic change of tone in the correspondence that routinely passed across his desk.

The lieutenant-governors wanted to know what action they were supposed to take to meet the possibility of a German attack, a reasonable inquiry which went unanswered until the pecking order between the Home Office and the War Office, both acutely conscious of status, had been clarified. In true bureaucratic tradition, this took some time, and it was several weeks before the two departments of state agreed that the War Office could talk directly with the lieutenant-governors without first seeking Home Office approval.

Not that this did much immediate good for the Channel Islands. In September 1939, a military shopping list including two coastal defence guns, four anti-aircraft guns and twelve Bren guns, ended up in a War Office pending tray, where it remained until the weapons were no longer needed. Meanwhile, on their own initiative, the lieutenant-governors did what they could to bolster the islands' defences by summoning able-bodied men to their local militias. Many of those who were eager to sign up subsequently volunteered for the British armed forces, while others were netted by conscription. This left the Royal Guernsey Militia and Jersey's Insular Defence Corps at a state of readiness equivalent to a Dad's Army with ancient weapons and a near absence of experienced officers. A Jerseyman on guard duty on the promenade at West Park found himself sharing a rifle with two comrades. They had five rounds of ammunition between them. 'It was a strange thought,' he recalled, 'that the Germans were a few miles away at St Malo, Granville, Carteret, that their Luftwaffe could have blown our island out of existence in a few minutes.'[1]

A few British troops did little to inspire confidence. Much against his will E.V. Clayton found himself posted to Alderney, the 2,000-acre island only ten miles from the French coast. He was billeted in Fort Albert, one of a series of fortifications built in the early nineteenth century to repel attacks by Napoleon's army. Nothing much had changed since then. Rooms were lit by hanging oil lamps, the walls were damp and iron-frame beds with straw mattresses defied sleep. Apart from some new Bren guns, all their weapons were of First World War vintage.[2]

In the early months of 1940, the question of how the Channel Islands fitted into the broader strategy of defending the entire country was still a source of contention and confusion. Since any surrender of territory was bound to damage morale, the vulnerability of the islands had to be taken seriously. But the chiefs of staff were at a loss to know what to recommend. Even in late May, when the fall of France became a real possibility, they seemed none too sure of the precise location of each of the islands or to know anything about their history. A briefing document tabled on 5 June led off with a lengthy account of how they came to be part of Britain, with a summary of their military contribution to long-past Gallic skirmishes. Thus educated, the chiefs of staff tried to read the German mind. The likelihood seemed to be that if the German army succeeded in taking the north coast of France, it would almost certainly make the jump over to the islands. Little could be done to stop this. However, the briefing note suggested, 'once in occupation . . . the difficulties of maintenance, though not insuperable, would make his position precarious'. The anticipated action was thus a raid by troop-carrying aircraft and fast motorboats followed by a strategic withdrawal.

This left open various counter-moves including a demilitarisation of the islands, the least favoured option while the French were still fighting: 'We might be accused of exposing the French Northern flank to a further scale of attack from bases in the islands'. The compromise, since 'measures to ensure the security of the islands against all possible scales of attack would not be justified', was to bolster existing defences, in themselves barely adequate for token resistance, with two infantry battalions, one stationed in Jersey, the other in Guernsey.[3]

The other major recommendation was 'the evacuation of all women and children on a voluntary and free basis'. The prospect of a total evacuation was discounted for three reasons – inability to provide air cover to a large number of ships, the difficulty of coping with reluctant evacuees and, thirdly, startling in the brutality of the language, 'we have already too many useless mouths in the United Kingdom'.[4] It was clear that the chiefs of staff were not likely to be swayed by sentiment.

The report was considered and approved by the War Cabinet on 12 June, with Neville Chamberlain, as Lord President of the Council, presiding.[5] The battalions were put on standby. But no sooner was the decision taken than it was challenged. Later the same day, when the War Cabinet reconvened, Churchill, who had become Prime Minister on 10 May, was in the chair but made no comment when Anthony Eden, Secretary of State for War, asked that the matter of sending two battalions to the Channel Islands be reconsidered. With the now near certainty that the French coast would soon be in enemy hands, the idea that the so far unbeatable Werhmacht could be deterred by a couple of hundred ill-equipped Tommies was clearly absurd. In any case, what precisely was being defended? The underwater telephone cable link to France would be of no further use when the Germans were listening on the other end of the line. As for their strategic value, the islands could play no significant role in the defence of Britain, while from the enemy's point of view they were, at best, a depot for attacks on the mainland. Fortunately, perhaps, neither Jersey nor Guernsey was in the forefront of modern communications. Their harbours were not equipped to receive a naval armada, while the airports were barely able to cope with tourist traffic.

But if the defence of the islands could not be justified, practical politics, let alone humanitarian considerations, ruled against simply abandoning fellow countrymen. More thought was given to declaring the islands a demilitarised zone, a strategy proposed by the chiefs of staff on 13 June and confirmed in a paper for the War Cabinet five days later.[6]

Meanwhile, the frustration of the lieutenant-governors was palpable. Their only firm instruction from London was to assemble a fleet of small boats to help in the evacuation of British troops from St Malo.

This they did with commendable speed and efficiency, with the major contribution coming from Jersey, as the island closest to the action. As troops stationed on the islands began to leave, the absence of any official announcement stretched the nerves of the civil population. Confusion was greatest in Alderney whose chief administrator, Judge Frederick French, had no direct link with London and only sporadic contact with Jersey and Guernsey. Adopting the advice of the senior army officer on the island, he concluded the Sunday church service by assuring the congregation that there was no need for alarm, that everything was under control. The departure of British troops and the arrival of exhausted and demoralised French soldiers and sailors, escapees from Cherbourg, suggested otherwise.

The islanders might have been a little comforted had they known that they were not the only victims of shambolic planning. At this point in the war, when bad news was a daily occurrence, the entire British military and civil command structure was in danger of collapse. General Sir Alan Brooke, soon to be Chief of General Staff, noted in his diary, 'History is repeating itself in a most astonishing way. The same string-pulling as in the last war, the same differences bctween statesmen and soldiers, the same faults as regards changing key posts at the opening of hostilities, and now the same tendency to start subsidiary theatres of war, and to contemplate wild projects!'[7]

Churchill was already prime minister but had still to assert his unassailable authority as war leader. Maybe the Channel Islands should be grateful that he was still feeling his way, for the view from 10 Downing Street was that British territory should be defended to the last man. 'It was repugnant,' he argued, 'to abandon British territory which had been in the possession of the Crown since the Norman Conquest.' It took an angry session of the War Cabinet and the persuasive powers of the Vice-Chief of Naval Staff to prove to Churchill that to do battle over the islands was to invite a massive loss of ships, planes and civilian lives.[8]

Churchill gave way, enabling the War Office to reveal its plans for demilitarisation. But it did so half-heartedly. German intentions were still unclear, and any action on the Channel Islands might have been seen as premature. On 19 June orders were sent to the lieutenant-governors to prepare for their own imminent departure and of what was left of their military establishments, but no one thought fit to inform the citizenry or, more to the point, to tell the Germans that the islands were undefended. This omission was later rationalised as a delaying tactic to deter the enemy from moving in before a civilian evacuation had been organised. In reality, the problem was one of communication between the three departments of state – Home, War and Foreign – each claiming an interest in the immediate future of the islands.

Ordered to stay at their posts, the two bailiffs, Victor Carey on Guernsey and Alexander Coutanche on Jersey, were now in sole charge. It must have been an awesome moment for both when they realised the weight of responsibility thrust upon them. Coutanche was best prepared for the ordeal. A politician and lawyer in his prime, he kept his nerve. Carey was a weaker character, used to being a figurehead more than an active leader. Though holding on to his title, he was soon to be supplanted.

The last of the troops based on Guernsey and Jersey left by midday on 20 June, and the lieutenant-governors followed the next day. As they departed, work started on cutting the cable to the French mainland. A press announcement on demilitarisation, prepared by the Home Office, was ready for release on 22 June but held back, probably by the Foreign Office, on instructions from Downing Street. Instead, a message from Buckingham Palace was sent to the bailiffs, assuring them and 'my people in the islands' that their best interests were being served by the withdrawal of armed forces. The King had no doubt that the islanders 'will look forward with the same confidence as I do to the day when the resolute fortitude with which we face our present difficulties will reap the reward of victory'.

This ringing declaration of sympathy and support might have had more impact if it had not been accompanied by a letter from the Home Secretary urging discretion, on grounds of national security, in publicising the sentiments of the head of state. Since neither of the bailiffs had been told that demilitarisation was still a state secret, they had no idea what to make of this. Victor Carey had the letter read out over a loudspeaker from the office of the *Guernsey Evening Press*, expecting that those within hearing distance would spread the news.

The confusion was compounded by ill-thought-out preparations for evacuation, a repeat of what had already happened on the mainland. The mass exodus of mothers and young children from London and other cities had started immediately after war was declared in September 1939. In all, one and a half million people migrated to the rural areas thought to be safe from air attacks. But when the widely anticipated convoys of German bombers bringing death and destruction on an unprecedented scale failed to materialise, there was an inevitable drift back to familiar surroundings. Another migration began in the spring of 1940 as Germany began its assault on its European neighbours.

Government propaganda made out that all this was handled in good order. The reality was muddle and confusion. In Folkestone, only twenty miles by ferry from Boulogne, the news that the Germans had reached the Channel caused widespread panic. 'Families literally got up from the breakfast table and went. There was terrible looting.'[9]

Scenes like this, soon to be repeated on the Channel Islands were, as much as anything, prompted by bureaucratic incompetence. As early as 10 June, Jersey's lieutenant-governor was reporting to Markbrieter at the Home Office on 'the beginning of a fuss about the evacuation of children'. This failed to elicit a response while the question of demilitarisation was still under discussion. If there was to be no defence of the islands and thus no casualties, why evacuate? Well, as Coutanche patiently explained to Markbrieter in a telephone conversation on 14 June, the islanders themselves might have views on the matter. But he agreed that a decision should be held off until the War Cabinet had made up its mind on the military priorities.

In Guernsey, Victor Carey allowed his attorney-general, Ambrose Sherwill, to take the initiative. But though a more assertive character, used to speaking his mind, Sherwill had no better luck than Coutanche in forcing a decision. That had to wait until 18 June, when Edgar Dorey, holding the ancient office of Jurat in Guernsey, had returned from a meeting in London with Home Office officials. The Home Secretary had accepted that in addition to men of military age some 30,000 women and children should be offered the chance to leave for the mainland.

While the naval authorities at Portsmouth were casting about for spare shipping, prospective evacuees from Jersey and Guernsey were urged to register with their parish constable. It was the moment of truth. Up to now, some assurance had been gained from official 'business as usual' pronouncements, including encouragement for hotels to continue taking holiday bookings. No longer. The idea that tourists would soon be arriving in large numbers was clearly ludicrous.

For islanders, the decision to go or stay was made more difficult by instructions that were anything but precise. Additions to the original categories qualifying for evacuation were made almost by the hour so that before long just about everyone believed they had a claim to a place on one of the rescue ships. Appeals for calm were met with cynicism, though a brave display of patriotism was staged in Jersey's Royal Square where a large crowd, having heard Coutanche declare that he and his family had no intention of leaving, joined him in a rousing chorus of the National Anthem. About half of Jersey's population gathered at the Town Hall to register for evacuation. The administration collapsed under the strain with the result that when, on 20 June, the first transports of women and children were waved off from St Helier, nobody seemed to bother if evacuees were registered or not. Arthur Kent recorded his first-hand impressions in his diary:

> What overwhelming, heart-aching scenes there were in those next few hours! The boats were due early next morning. Imagine it if you can! Twelve hours in which to decide whether you would leave behind the home and work of a lifetime and, with just a few articles of clothing, join the melee in England or stick to your native soil to face the problems and uncertainties of the future as stoically as possible. I will never forget that day, its confusion, its tears. Everyone was waiting for the local newspaper for official information about the evacuation. When it came out there were

big 'Women and Children First' headlines, and the confusion became chaos! Relatives hastened to confer with each other – on all sides friends and strangers were asking 'What are *you* going to do?' The Post Office was swamped with telegrams to relatives and friends on the mainland, requesting permission to be 'put up' for a while. Most deeply one felt for parents with tiny children, for those who had invalid or aged fathers and mothers, grandparents and for those sick in the hospitals who could not go away.[10]

A few days after she and her family had moved in with relations in Hove, Sussex, Mrs Harman wrote to her father who had stayed in Jersey.

I am still completely at sea as to whether we really should have stayed. Everything was such a frightful nightmare those two days. I wish to God there had been more time to think before we came away . . . Audley spent two hours at the Town Hall in the evening trying to register, and then from 4 a.m. to 11 the next morning and after all that we might just as well not have registered at all as nothing whatever was asked for. Just imagine that ghastly, panicky crowd on the quay and me with Rosemary in her Karricot, and as much of our belongings as we had managed to get into two small cases and a rucksack. I'd never even contemplated such a quandary in all my life.[11]

The panic was greater in Guernsey, where officials gave contradictory advice while urging restraint. In St Peter Port, the town crier walked the streets spreading the word as far as his voice would carry, but there was little in the newspapers to enlighten the public. Guernsey Attorney-General, Ambrose Sherwill, who was soon to play a leading role in the Occupation, recalled:

Official notices were misread, words of advice completely mis-interpreted and the most grotesque rumours passed for truth. There was a run on the banks, one evacuating publican gave away his entire stock of liquor. One official, at his own expense, had posters with 'Keep Your Heads. Don't be Yellow' printed in black on a yellow ground put up all over the town. He then suddenly remembered that he ought to go and did so, without telling anyone in his department.[12]

A vociferous doctor was of the opinion that mass starvation could only be averted by total evacuation. His colleague disagreed and persuaded him otherwise, but not before his views had become widely known. Essential services were put at risk. Reg Blanchford, who was in charge of ambulances, was told by a senior officer to 'burn all records, cripple the ambulances and look after ourselves'. He refused: 'It was our duty to stay.'[13]

In the rush for places on the boats, the youngest took priority, if not always with the happiest results. Dr Alistair Rose recalled 'wretched little school children standing for hours in queues on St Julian's Avenue waiting to be evacuated, and in some cases they had to make their way home at night perhaps five or six miles away'.[14]

Three-year-old Jill Harris was parted from her family on the quayside. The circumstances were bizarre.

Armed with our boarding passes and one small suitcase each, Aunt Ethel came to fetch us all in her car and we duly arrived on the quay. Unfortunately so had hundreds more with no means of getting away. During a long, hot day my Aunt and my mother's imagination got somewhat overheated. 'You should come with us Ethel,' my mother urged her sister. Ethel thought perhaps she ought to, which would have come as a severe shock to Uncle Tom, at home and patiently waiting for his wife to get his lunch! 'You will never get on the boat without a child in your arms!' my mother announced dramatically. Ethel was inclined to agree and I was duly handed over.

At that moment the *Stork*, which until very recently had been used for transporting cattle, manoeuvred to the quayside, the gang planks were let down and the rush was on. Swept away in the tide of humanity, Aunt Ethel fetched up against the customs office wall still clutching me. When she had recovered her dignity and her hat she was startled to hear a boat's siren and looking round saw to her horror that the *Stork* was already in the harbour mouth and heading for England.[15]

The war years were not at all bad for the infant Jill. Cared for by her aunt and uncle, she was centre of their lives. But 'my war started when my real family came back in 1946. A family I did not know.'

A young Malcolm Woodland, who was thrilled to be leaving the island, was one of those set for a disappointment, but not for any shortage of berths.

My mum had had a letter about what we had to take, so a small case was packed, and we had to go to school in the morning. We were going to go on a boat to England, and we would be billeted; and my parents would join us later. So we went off to school . . . carrying sandwiches for the journey! We were supposed to leave about 10 o'clock in the morning but nothing happened, so come midday we started to eat our lunch. We were told that we should not eat it all as we might need some for the journey. Any rate about 3 o'clock all the lunches had been eaten! I think they tried gas mask drill, we had assemblies in the playground, and about 4 o'clock we were told the boats weren't in fact coming until much later. So I went home, went to bed, and the next morning when I woke up, it was sunshine, a lovely day, 'right, we're off back to school again, where's this boat?'

'Well,' Mum said, 'sorry, you're not going.'

'What!'

I was furious, I'd got my case packed, I was all labelled ready to go with my friends! And she said, 'No, they phoned at 4 o'clock in the morning and I went to look for you and you were sound asleep and I didn't have the heart to disturb you.'

I didn't talk to her for the whole morning.[16]

No wonder some boats sailed without a full complement. According to Dr Rose, the *Princess Astrid*, with space for several thousand refugees, returned to the mainland with less than two hundred on board.

With so many leaving in such a hurry, parts of the islands began to look like ghost settlements. In the rush to get away, houses were left open with food on the dining tables waiting to be cleared away, domestic animals ran wild and cars were abandoned on the dockside with keys in the ignition. Nobody knew how long they would be away. One Guernsey family, optimists to the last, left a saucer of milk and some food in a side passage for their cat. In the event, it was five years before they returned.[17]

Some houses were left open, beds unmade and the remains of a hurried morning meal on the table. Other houses were so securely locked that men authorised soon afterwards to collect perishable food from abandoned houses had difficulty in entering. A tobacconist gave away his entire stock before closing his premises and a publican before leaving invited his neighbours to go into his bar and help themselves to the liquor there. Panic is bad enough when the panickers are otherwise sober, but panic inflamed by drunkenness degenerates into sheer madness.[18]

The chaos was at its worst in Alderney, where smoke from the fires on the Cherbourg docks drifted over the island. Through binoculars, the Wehrmacht could be seen moving down the Cotentin peninsula towards Cap de la Hague. Immediate authority was vested in Judge French though, technically, he was subject to orders from Guernsey. With, at best, sporadic contact between the islands, the way was open to misunderstandings. On 21 June a letter from French arrived in Guernsey, addressed to the lieutenant-governor. Since that officer had departed the island and the Bailiff had gone home, the letter was handed to Attorney-General Ambrose Sherwill. Told that it contained an urgent request for supplies, he naturally took it as his duty to be next in line as correspondent and opened the letter. It was short and to the point: Alderney needed a quantity of yeast.

Not bothering to question this eccentric request, Sherwill made sure that a package of yeast was delivered to the waiting boatman and returned to more pressing responsibilities. The next he heard from Alderney was a broadside from French accusing him of tampering with his mail without authority and of deserting Alderney in its hour of peril. Sherwill was stung into action, but in the time he was calling for ships to be sent to Alderney, French appealed directly to the Admiralty for a rescue operation for whoever among the thousand or so citizens wanted to leave. That turned out to be just about everybody.

On the morning of 23 June, six ships were lined up offshore ready for boarding. By midday, all but twenty of the islanders had embarked. Later, many of the evacuees said that they had been ordered to abandon their homes. This was not strictly true, but it can well be imagined that in the general confusion, under pressure to decide quickly whether to stay or go, islanders had felt they were no longer their own masters.

With Alderney all but deserted, Guernsey farmers realised that high-grade cows and pigs had been left to fend for themselves. A flotilla of small crafts set off on a recovery mission.

Alf Martel was one of the men who went to Alderney. He was a big man, tall, very strong, daring, and completely fearless. His dark skin was usually unshaven, he had a loud gruff voice and a louder laugh. When the party of men left Alderney for home Alf decided to stay on alone. 'I'll be King of Alderney.' His brothers in Guernsey were anxious when they heard the story, so they boarded one of the boats and went to look for him. They found him lying fully dressed on a luxurious bed in one of the hotels and surrounded by bottles of whisky. It was with difficulty that they persuaded him to come home![19]

2

AWAY FROM HOME

Meanwhile, the migration from Jersey and Guernsey was continuing apace with more than its fair share of human drama. Betty Harvey was one of the small children who made the crossing.

On the day of leaving . . . our animals had been turned loose to fend for themselves – my black labrador, some cats, chickens and rabbits. At the harbour everyone was weeping, wives and husbands were being separated and older children were leaving without their parents. We crossed the Channel in a cargo boat, and there were cattle in the hold. The crossing was very rough and many people were seasick. I think there must have been about a dozen of us crammed into a small crewman's cabin. My mother was six months pregnant and I can remember a nurse popping in to check her several times during the crossing. . . . We arrived at Weymouth and were met by my mother's youngest brother George. At Weymouth my mother was approached by a radio reporter who referred to us as 'refugees' which my mother did not like at all. 'We are not refugees, we are evacuees, and we shall be going back as soon as we can.' Sadly this did not happen; my mother died when I was 13 and it was to be 60 years before I was able to make the trip back.[1]

The risk from German submarines was real. There were only around sixty enemy U-boats operating in or close to British coastal waters, but since the outbreak of war they had already disposed of 800,000 tons of merchant shipping. There were other dangers closer to home, which, for Polly Burford, had tragic consequences.

Sylvia, seven years older than myself, had been rather ill after a tonsillectomy. She was really too ill to travel and it should never have been allowed but sail she did and with her school; my mother had not been allowed to be with her. She kept calling for her parents and wondering why they didn't come. She was prone to stomach upsets and the boats had no stabilisers on them like they do today. During her sea sickness, and of course the aftermath of the operation, she haemorrhaged and became dangerously ill. She died in hospital in Weymouth two days after landing.[2]

Prevarication reigned until the last evacuee ship had sailed – and beyond. One man, having insisted that his wife should seek safety in England, was so miserable after she left that he departed on the next boat. Meanwhile, after a couple of days in England, the wife thought, 'What am I doing here? I'm going back to my home.' She managed to get on the last boat to Guernsey. 'When the Germans landed the following day she was on the island and her husband was in England.'[3]

Some of those who at first opted for evacuation were persuaded by patriotic neighbours to change their minds. Accusations of cowardice were hard to ignore unless there were children or other vulnerable family members involved. Material considerations also played a part. Recently married, Zilma Roussel had built a new house in the north of Guernsey, 'One that was modern for those days. I had a baby son just three weeks old. My parents had decided to stay. My two brothers had also decided to stay. My wife's parents who were farmers and had one of the best herds of Guernsey cattle in the island naturally decided to stay.'[4]

Maurice Hill, who was seventeen when war broke out, had no doubts when he registered for evacuation from Jersey along with his mother, sister and grandmother. But then, faced with the prospect of being ferried across in a coal boat and fearing for the health of an elderly relative, 'we decided to go back because they said that there'd probably be bigger boats coming over at the weekend. But no more boats came . . . my mother had had her dog put down, I'd sold my bike, well given my bike away actually, and then of course we had to start all over again. Fortunately, our flat hadn't been taken over by anybody, so it was just a matter of sitting back and waiting for the Germans to arrive.'[5]

A letter from a twenty-one-year-old woman with a seriously ill mother in Jersey, published in a British newspaper, brought home to readers on the mainland the agonies of decision created by the evacuation.

After we had finally decided not to cross, mother slept properly for the first time in three weeks. She certainly would not have survived the journey.

Conditions were appalling – women and children – some separated – were packed in the holds and on the decks of trawlers, potato-boats and even a coal boat. Several boats were only 30 ft long and expected to be at sea 55 hours and even those that went to Weymouth took over 24 hours, as we know from telephone calls by people who travelled.

Women with day-old babies and women who were expecting within 24 hours travelled in these conditions . . . There was no food or drink, except ship's biscuit and water. . . . Those of us who remain live in a world of suspense.[6]

Among the hardest hit were the women who had been left alone to look after young families after husbands and brothers had signed up. To stay or to leave was a decision they had to take for themselves. Josephine Ginns lived with her mother and baby sister in her grandparents' house on Jersey's Belvedere Hill. Her father was one of the lucky ones who escaped from Dunkirk, but in June 1940 he was with his unit somewhere in England, out of contact if not out of mind. A family debate tipped the scale in favour of leaving the island. So it was that Josephine, her entire family and their next-door neighbours joined the crowd of would-be evacuees on the St Helier dockside where they queued all day in the hot sunshine. In late afternoon, they got away in a cement boat. It took fifteen hours to reach Weymouth. 'It was all a bit hair raising because there were warnings of German submarines.'

At journey's end, the Salvation Army was on hand with cups of tea. The arrivals were given a quick medical – taps on the chest to test for tuberculosis – before being issued with luggage labels so that they had something tied to them to show who they were. Then it was off to Exeter where Josephine's aunt had the surprise of her life when, at ten-thirty at night, her sister and two children, 'dirty, hungry and dishevelled', turned up on her doorstop.[7]

Among those most eager to escape were the temporary workers who had come to the Channel Islands to help get in the potatoes and tomatoes. For Jack and Ada Willmot it was their third harvest in Jersey. The journey *from* Southampton had been scary enough.

> The barrage balloons were all up round the docks when we boarded the ship. We got underway at 12 midnight, it was very dark. They told us to try our lifejackets on. We had our five-year-old son with us, there was nothing for the children, but they said if the worst came to the worst they would do the best they could. Part way over the Channel everything went quiet, the engines had stopped, they told us not to make a sound, as enemy planes were passing overhead. After a while we started up again, reaching Jersey at 8 a.m., glad to be off the sea.

It wasn't long before they were on the way back, this time in the infamous coal boat, the *Suffolk Coast*. Ada decided that she and her son would stay on deck throughout the night.

My husband brought us tea to keep us warm. We arrived at Weymouth in the early hours of the morning and had to wait until daybreak for them to let us in. They were very good to us, gave us food and drink, examined us, put a ticket on each of us, and we were refugees. The Salvation Army paid for us to get home to Wisbech, Cambridgeshire, as we had no money.[8]

The young people who stood their ground were liable to find themselves promoted beyond their years. When, in Jersey, Bob Le Sueur turned up at his insurance office there was only one person there, 'a nineteen-year-old typist who was due to leave at the end of the month'. She had been left in charge of the keys. Meanwhile, there were customers to serve.

It was pandemonium, there were people asking the daftest things. There was somebody demanding a typewritten receipt that he had paid his last life insurance premium. Whether he thought that he would be able to raise money out of that I don't know. Nobody was thinking clearly. There was even one man wanting to arrange baggage insurance for going on one of the evacuation boats.

At the end of a hectic day, Le Sueur managed to telephone his branch office in Southampton to report that he was without a manager or, indeed, any senior staff. He was told to stay at his post until he was relieved, an instruction that remained in force nearly five years. 'So I became acting manager overnight. The first thing I did was to put up my wages.'[9]

Between 20 and 28 June 1940 up to 25,000 Channel Island evacuees landed at Weymouth. Alderney was all but abandoned, while most of those in Sark opted to stay. For this Ambrose Sherwill gave credit to Sybil Hathaway, the formidable Dame of Sark, who exercised her constitutional rights as a benevolent dictator: 'We had offered them a ship to bring away those wishing to leave. Our offer was declined. Scarcely anyone left or sought to leave. Such is the effect of leadership.'

The refugees who had nowhere else to go were put onto trains heading north. It was a mystery tour. Most of the passengers were unloaded in Lancashire or Yorkshire, with some travelling on as far as Glasgow – anywhere, in fact, where temporary accommodation was on offer.[10] Up to twenty towns and cities, ranging from Barnsley and Bradford to Huddersfield and Halifax, were busily preparing themselves for an influx of strangers. Few of the islanders had any idea where they were; arriving in Manchester, sixteen-year-old Gwenda Smith was convinced she was in Canada.[11]

The very young were confused by everything they saw. Few had even seen a train before, let alone travelled on one. And there were all those people, crowds of them. It was so easy to get lost. Five-year-old Margaret le Poiderin held on tight to her mother.

I have no idea how long we were travelling but we eventually arrived at Stockport in Cheshire. We were taken along with hundreds of other families to places like the town hall, church rooms and schools. We spent three to four days at the town hall. We slept on mattresses on the floor and meals were dished out from emergency kitchens. After the first few days, we were moved to a school hall. The arrangements were still the same for eating and sleeping but the children had the chance to get outside into the playground. Shortly afterwards we were given somewhere to live. In actual fact, it was mum's cousin who was able to rent the house as her husband was in the army. . . . We all moved in together into a house which had an old shop beside it. It was on the corner of two streets. The household consisted of eight children, two mothers and the grandmother and we stayed together right through the war.[12]

It was easy for families to be separated but much harder for them to be reunited. Antoinette Duperouzell's mother caught up with her in Burnley but it took longer to trace her two sons who were living in Glasgow and, as it happened, none too keen to move away. Then Antoinette went down with diphtheria and had to be put on a train to

Southport where she spent a month in a convalescent home. Finally reunited, the family had to bear the hardest blow.

> When we left Guernsey my father made the decision to remain there to run his antique business. During the occupation he died of TB, my mother received a letter from the Red Cross telling her of his death.[13]

If evacuees were confused, so too were those who were responsible for looking after them. Unloaded at Rochdale, one Guernsey family caused surprise among local people, who had been expecting them to be black. Another more common misapprehension was visited on a group from Jersey.

> We arrived in Barnsley in the early hours of the morning, and of course we didn't know where we were. And on top of that we'd never even heard of Barnsley. And then we walked along these cobbled streets, so uneven. And we went to this Methodist Church and we all slept on the pews because we had no identity cards. So we stayed at this church, and we weren't allowed out. We were confined to the church. People used to walk up and look at the refugees, and bring up bars of chocolate and things like that. They were very good, the Barnsley people. This chap got on the pulpit, and in broad Yorkshire he asked 'Do any of you speak English?' He'd never heard of Jersey.[14]

Whole schools from Guernsey had to be relocated. The boys of Elizabeth College were taken first to Oldham, where they were put up in an assembly hall owned by the local co-operative society. In the days following some of the children were collected by parents who had managed to leave Guernsey and by relatives, but the majority remained in the care of their teachers. Not knowing whether his parents were alive or dead, fourteen-year-old Michael was desperately unhappy. 'He sobbed quietly in the refuge of the lavatory and mopped his eyes with toilet paper because he had not brought a handkerchief in the confusion of the flight.'[15]

It was not long before Elizabeth College was again on the move, this time to a collection of holiday homes, corrugated iron huts, belonging to the Unitarian Church at Great Hucklow, a village west of Sheffield.

The accommodation was fairly primitive. An outhouse which was called a 'bathroom' contained only a tin bath, a copper for heating water and a few wash-basins. When bathing was in progress the hot water was poured into the bath and the boys were not allowed more than three minutes in the water before they were rinsed with cold water thrown over them by the next in the queue.[16]

The girls of the Ladies' College were more fortunate. They were taken in by Howell's School in north Wales, where the educational standards were high. The problems were in finding suitable billets in town and providing diversions in the holidays. The youngest children had the hardest time. Margaret Brehaut, aged five, was taken with the Amherst Infants' School (St Peter Port) to Glasgow. The one toy she was allowed to take was a favourite doll and she lost this on the long train journey. Margaret Stedman remembers her confusion when, separated from an elder sister and a cousin, she was 'crammed on a boat with lots of other children being sick'. She too went to Glasgow where her strongest memory is of an older girl saying to a group of Guernsey children, 'The Germans are in Guernsey and they've shot dead all your mummies and daddies.'[17]

Betty Moore was nearly ten when she was billeted with a young couple in Irby near Birkenhead. On her second day in the small house she was given a red ball to celebrate her birthday. 'By now,' she remembered, 'I realised my parents would not be coming, and often I cried myself to sleep. A few months later my brother (aged 20) who was stationed in Wales, came to see me. He was in army uniform and had grown a moustache. I didn't recognise him.'[18]

When Betty's foster mother became pregnant, a new billet had to be found. Betty moved to Heswall where she had a two-mile walk to school. At night she heard the bombs falling on Liverpool. When houses close by were hit, her latest foster parents decided to move and Betty was billeted yet again, this time with a woman and her elderly mother who treated her as an unpaid servant. Her last change of address in the war years took her to a farm at Barnston where, at last, she settled into a happy family.

Other young evacuees were less fortunate. It was not uncommon for foster parents to assume that the young people who landed on their doorstep represented little more than free muscle power. Many of those who today would be in full-time education ended up as farm labourers or domestic skivvies.

Some protection was provided by the Channel Islands Refugee Committee (how the word 'refugee' was hated by those who saw themselves as evacuees – they were, after all, part of the same country as those extending a helping hand). The Committee was chaired by Lord Justice du Parcq, a Jerseyman. Back-up came from local committees set up wherever there was a sufficient number of islanders in close proximity. A hardship appeal raised £25,000 along with a collection of second-hand clothing valued at some £20,000. But the CIRC could barely keep up with the requests for help which, at the start, were pouring in at the rate of a thousand letters and personal inquiries a day. Moreover, there was little to be done to help those worried about their property and businesses soon to be in German hands. Appeals for compensation were referred to the Home Office where a standard letter was ready for dispatch.

Sir/Madam,
    With reference to your letter of . . . regarding your property in the CIs, I am directed by the Sec. of State to say that he regrets that the Government cannot undertake any liability in respect of such property and that no machinery exists for registering it.
    I am, Sir/Madam,
    Your obedient servant,
    A. Maxwell

Little of this was known to the British public, but in the House of

Lords the charge that the mother country had abandoned the Channel Islands was frequently debated. Leading the debate was Lord Portsea, a Jerseyman who, as Bertram Falle MP, had represented Portsmouth North for sixteen years up to 1934, and has not been given sufficient acknowledgement for his championing of the islanders. By the time he took up cudgels in the House of Lords on behalf of his compatriots, he was already eighty. But age had not stunted his energy. His first concern was the evacuees, particularly those who were short of funds but were unable to draw on their bank accounts.

> The reason given them is that the territory from which they came is in the hands of the enemy. What are these poor people to do? It is no fault of theirs. In the case of the poorer people, there is no 'dole', there are no guardians, and they must beg from the Public Assistance Committee. The others who have placed their trust in this country, in their own kinsmen, what can they do? They have literally no money, and they cannot get any very great credit.[19]

Portsea was supported by Cyril Garbett, Bishop of Winchester, a frequent visitor to the islands, which fell within his diocese. It was not only those with bonds and credits in various banks who had problems. 'The majority of those who have left the islands have no money in any bank . . . They find themselves suddenly uprooted and here, in what for them is a strange land, penniless.'[20]

Eventually a promise came from the Lord Chancellor that bank accounts would be unfrozen.

Portsea kept up his attack throughout the war, urging that newsletters should be dropped over the islands to keep those who had stayed informed on how their kin were making out on the mainland, and when conditions in the islands deteriorated sharply, that food should be sent in via the Red Cross to feed unnourished children. Time and again, ministers responded with soft words. Leaflet drops were dangerous because those caught picking them up would be shot; as to the risk of famine 'my noble friend is quite mistaken in thinking that people are dying as a result of lack of food or that their health is being impaired'.

Portsea, however, was not inclined to be slapped down by the likes of the Earl of Selborne, minister of economic welfare. He also knew more than Selborne could possibly have imagined. Portsea's successor as MP for Portsmouth North was Sir Roger Keyes, who combined his parliamentary duties with the job of chief of the Combined Operations Executive, the organisation responsible for assessing and, subsequently, dampening Churchill's ambition to recapture the islands. It is certain that the two men were acquainted. How much Portsea was able to gather from his colleague is speculative. But for an elderly peer without influence in the Churchill administration, he was remarkably well informed. Keyes must be the likeliest source.

One memorable exchange finished with Selborne assuring his noble friend that, 'I can assure my noble friend that I have very accurate information on these matters.'

Portsea replied: 'So have I.'[21]

3

UNWELCOME STRANGERS

Whatever the assumptions in London, after the fall of France there was never any doubt at German High Command that the capture of the Channel Islands was the next objective. Though the islands were of limited value as jumping-off points for the anticipated invasion of Britain, taking control of them would be a propaganda coup that would further reinforce the supposed invincibility of the Wehrmacht. But while the order from Berlin was clear enough, those directly responsible for mounting the operation, notably Admiral Karlgeorg Schuster, the senior German naval commander in France, and Vice Admiral Eugen Lindau, were inclined to plan cautiously.

Since there was no official word from London that the islands were undefended, the assumption had to be of a military presence ready to oppose a landing. There was the further risk of the Royal Navy getting involved. If the Führer was aware of the propaganda value of entering British territory, his lieutenants were equally conscious of the potential damage to morale. Surely Churchill would not allow the islands to be taken without putting up a fight? As Schuster and Lindau debated the odds, both were mindful that their reputations and career prospects were at stake. Reconnaissance flights reported activity at the main ports, but whether this signified an evacuation of civilians or the arrival of troops, or both, nobody was prepared to say. There was only one way to find out.

Late in the afternoon of 28 June, Sark, Guernsey and Jersey were visited by six Heinkel bombers. Sprays of machine-gun fire left Sark undamaged. The two main islands were less fortunate. One of those who took part in the raid was Hans Grah, who later recalled:

We took off at 18.35 hours. The flight-path was over Caen to Guernsey and Jersey. We looked at the northern French landscape, small fields, lined with hedges. From above the coast of the Cherbourg peninsula we already saw, lying in the haze, the islands. We flew on, the first raid against England. One aircraft attacked a small departing steamer [which] skilfully avoided the bombs through zig-zag manoeuvres. We then flew over the quays of St Peter Port. Everywhere on the island the glass roofs of the greenhouses were lit up in the sun . . . On the quay stood a mass of vehicles. Troops? Also a small ship lay there. We approached, the bombs aimed at vehicles, the first bomb, the second and so on, marvellous, none fell wide. Big pieces of debris flew about. Next run, the vehicles were burning fiercely. We descended to a lower altitude, circling the island, no defences! Again, bombs at the vehicles. I suggested that we should land and occupy the island. Lieutenant Knörringer had his doubts. We later found out, that on Guernsey, all the vehicles were loaded with tomatoes, which should have gone over to England, a fine mess that must have been. There were no troops on the island. It's a pity we did not land. It would have been a complete success.[1]

Ambrose Sherwill was on the telephone listening to the Home Office reassure him that an attack was most unlikely when the first bombs fell on St Peter Port. He held the instrument towards an open window to remove any doubts in London as to what was happening.

Among those caught up in the raid, the lucky ones took shelter behind a concrete jetty. The less fortunate sought refuge under parked lorries. Most of those who died were trapped by blazing vehicles. Malcolm Woodland and his parents were queuing for a bus when they heard the throb of aircraft engines.

> I looked up, and coming up from the south were specks of silver in the sky and they got closer and closer. Dad said, 'Look, there they are!' and I could see them! We could see by then that they were fairly large aircraft and they were in a formation. We were just getting on the bus when I said to Dad, 'Why are they putting ladders down from the aircraft?'[2]
>
> He looked up and said, 'Oh my Gawd!', and he called to my Mum, 'Quick, get off the bus, we've got to go!'

The family, along with many others, took shelter in the bus-station lavatories as the ground trembled with the explosions.

> Eventually the 'All Clear' sounded and we went out. One of the bombs we heard must have been very close because just across where the Albany is now, just across from the toilets, 20 yards at most, it had blown the tobacco factory there to bits and it was on fire.'[3]

So much for demilitarisation! There were other lucky escapes. Finding a procession of trucks at the quayside waiting to unload their tomatoes, Frank Herbert and his father decided to drive the short way home for a bite to eat while the backlog cleared.

> Never had we made such a life-saving decision as this, because no sooner had we arrived home, than we heard bombing and gun fire.... We pushed the dining room table against the wall and got under it, we did not know how close to our house they would come. It was a bit naïve of us perhaps, to imagine that a mere table would protect us, but we felt much safer under it, than above it and it was the only thing we could think of to do.
>
> Then the telephone rang. Bill Peel, one of dad's staff, just

happened to call from England, at that very moment, to ask if he had left the island too early and should he return to help my father with his business.[4]

Needless to say, he received a dusty answer.

Of the many tragic consequences of the bombing that gave Hans Grah and his aircrew such a thrill, was their apparent inability to identify an ambulance. Machine-gunned as it was driving away from the piers, it crashed into a tree. A nurse, the driver and all five casualties on board were killed.

An hour later it was Jersey's turn to be hit. Again it was a line-up of trucks on the quayside that attracted attention. Loads of potatoes went up in smoke while a store and a warehouse were set alight. Dr Guerill Darling was on duty at Jersey General Hospital.

I looked out of the window and saw three Heinkel bombers. As I watched I saw bombs beginning to fall. I left my patient and went through the hospital down to Casualty. And almost as I got there the first victim arrived. He had a great hole blown in the side of his chest and he died within a matter of moments. Fifty per cent of those who were admitted to the hospital and who died were killed by bombs. The other half died from machine gun bullets.[5]

Forty-four islanders were killed in the raids; the youngest was fourteen, the oldest seventy-one.

The near absence of retaliation – a light machine gun on the Isle of Sark mail steamer blazed away ineffectually – should have told German command all they needed to know. But Schuster and Lindau still feared a trap. And with some reason. That very morning a member of the House of Commons who sought information on the military status of the islands was silenced by the Home Secretary on grounds of security. Not even the civilian evacuation was to be publicised.

That evening, after the raids had taken place, the BBC nine o'clock news reported that the islands had been demilitarised, but there was still no formal announcement that the Germans could rely on. As a final test of British intentions another armed reconnaissance was planned as a preliminary to sending in assault troops. Senior officers of the Luftwaffe now began to fret at what they saw as the use of unnecessary delaying tactics by their naval colleagues. On Sunday 30 June, Captain Liebe-Pieteritz put himself in line for an Iron Cross second class by landing his Dornier at Guernsey airport. Finding the place deserted he flew off, only to return in the evening with transport planes carrying a small contingent of armed troops.

Realising all too uncomfortably that they had been upstaged, the German admirals in Cherbourg now gave orders for naval assault troops to take possession of the island.

When the people of Guernsey read their newspapers on the morning of 1 July, they had their first indication of what life would be like under German occupation. There was to be a curfew, all weapons had to be handed in, there was a ban on the sale of petrol, the airport was closed to all but military traffic and clocks were to be changed to Central European Time

The same day, ultimatums were dropped over Jersey calling upon the islanders to announce their readiness to surrender by putting out white flags and painting white crosses where they could easily be seen from the air. Since the order was in German a translator had to be found, by which time the Luftwaffe had again jumped the gun. Lieutenant Richard Kern landed at the airport to be assured that, while efforts were being made to find out what precisely the Germans wanted the island authorities to do, surrender was a mere formality. In the afternoon Alexander Coutanche with Charles Duret Aubin, his attorney-general, went to the airport to meet the first of the occupying troops led by Captain Obernitz. It was hard for Coutanche to take in what was happening. It was so unreal, more the stuff of a cheap thriller than of the quiet life of Jersey. He recalled later:

When we arrived at the airport in my car, flying my flag, we found about half a dozen German officers waiting for us. They had a civilian with them to act as interpreter. I imagine that he was a German waiter from one of the hotels.

The first thing which the officer in charge said to me was 'You realise that you are occupied?'

'Yes.'

He then read a proclamation which the interpreter translated to me. It was a purely military proclamation which dealt with such things as curfew, the control of spirits, the surrender of arms, the surrender of any British troops who might be in the island, restrictions on the sailings of ships and on the use of all forms of motor spirit and, what was perhaps most painful of all, an order that no wirelesses should be used except for the purpose of listening to German stations. He indicated to me that the reading of this proclamation concluded the formalities of occupation.[6]

John Blampied was outside the town hall when the Jersey flag was lowered to be replaced by the swastika.

A few hours after that we heard the sound of marching and there were the Germans. They congregated at the Cenotaph. . . . It was scary because we were looking at a modern army, we'd never seen this in our lives. . . . Even the older people, those who'd fought in the First World War, were a bit confused because our boys, the regiments that had been here, they all had First World War guns.[7]

The front page of the *Jersey Evening Post* was hurriedly reset to make readers aware of German demands. The Bailiff's appeal to 'keep calm and obey orders' ran alongside a report of the debate in the States on 'business of particular urgency and historic importance'. But it was a measure of the confusion, even disbelief that all this was happening, that such momentous news was juxtaposed with the incidentals that would normally have filled out the columns on a quiet day. So it was that a request for islanders to deliver 'every lethal weapon into the hands of the competent authority' was immediately followed by 'Uncle Harry' telling his young readers the story of the rose. ('In the days when the gods ruled the earth there was a very pretty lady called Rhodanthe . . .'), 'Birthday Greetings' and an item headed 'Smiles' consisting of weak jokes. ('Two Irishmen were on a tandem riding up a hill. 'Begorra Pat,' Mike said 'that was a stiff climb.' 'Sure Mike,' said Pat. 'If I hadn't kept the brake on all the way we should have gone backwards.'[8])

What the Germans made of all this beggars imagination. Maybe they were too busy extending their reach over the other Channel Islands. On 2 July Major Albrecht Lanz, designated the first commandant of Guernsey and Jersey, arrived in Guernsey with his interpreter, Major Maass:

> Now came a moment that I shall never in my life forget. Easily the proudest of this war. Maj Hessel and I entered the large richly furnished living room of the Bailiff. The old gentleman, in a dark suit, was standing in the background. In a few words the interpreter explained that Maj Hessel had handed over the command to me and that we had come, Maj Hessel to take his leave, and I to meet him in person. With his arms folded, the old gentleman bowed deeply before the representatives of the German Army. The first time in the history of England that a Governor and the direct representative of his Britannic Majesty has ever bowed to the German Army. He thanked us particularly and repeatedly for the correct behaviour of the German troops and promised to make all necessary arrangements for our wishes and regulations to be carried out in the smallest detail. Everything we needed was at our disposal.[9]

By then the United States ambassador in London, Joseph P. Kennedy, the representative of what was then a neutral country, had been asked by the Foreign Office to convey to Berlin that the islands were defenceless and thus 'cannot be considered in any way a legitimate target for bombardment'. For home consumption, news of the air attacks suggested that they had taken place *after* demilitarisation was common knowledge. In this way a small propaganda compensation was gained by portraying the Germans as ruthless killers of innocent civilians. In truth, lives would have been saved if London had come clean on demilitarisation at a much earlier date.

Landing on Alderney, the conquerors found it practically deserted. That left the Isle of Sark, a 'feudal paradise' according to its Dame. For sure, Sybil Hathaway was no pushover. Born with a physical disability (one leg was two and a half inches shorter than the other), she had compensated by leading an 'enterprising, boyish youth', learning to shoot, swim in tricky tides and to ride a donkey along the cliff tracks. She was not about to be overawed by a party of Germans. When she learned that Sark was to be visited by Major Lanz, she decided to stage-manage the event to her advantage. So it was that while the Major was bouncing over the waves in the old Guernsey lifeboat, the Dame and her American-born husband were rearranging the furniture.

> 'Let's take a leaf out of Mussolini's book,' I suggested. 'We'll put two chairs behind the desk at the far end of the drawing-room. It is a long room and they'll have to walk the whole length of it, which will give us a certain advantage,' adding, 'Besides, they'll have to walk up those few stairs from the hall and then turn right before they are announced, and that will also help us to look more impressive.[10]

After two hours on 'a rather rough sea which tossed us about violently', Lanz and Maass landed at 'the tiniest harbour in the world'. Reporting on his visit, Lanz went on:

> There was no sign of life, except that we were awaited by the Seneschal, a kind of steward who is also the chief of police. He conducted us through a long tunnel in the cliffs up the steep road to the Seigneurie, the seat of the ruler. We saw no one except for curious eyes peeping out from behind the curtains.[11]

The scrunch of military boots on the drive warned of the visitors' imminent arrival. As the Dame of Sark recalled:

> They both wore the drab green uniform of German officers,

service dress jacket, breeches, jackboots and forage caps. Both gave the Nazi salute as they entered the room . . .

Lanz was a tall, alert, quick-spoken officer, with dark hair and dark eyes. In civilian life he had been a Doctor of both Law and Philosophy, and I believe he came from a family of agricultural machinery manufacturers in Stuttgart. Maass was a Naval surgeon who spoke perfect English and had studied tropical diseases for eight years in Liverpool.[12]

The Dame's first impressions of Lanz were favourable ('a fair minded man who would never trick anyone by low cunning'). But she did not take to Maass.

His face was too smooth for my liking and I could well imagine that while in England he had sent back a lot of valuable information to Germany which had nothing to do with tropical diseases.

A large printed poster was produced, half in German and half in English, headed 'Orders of the Commandant of the German Forces in the Channel Islands'. Among the orders were a curfew from 11 p.m. to 6 a.m.; all forms of guns, rifles, etc., to be handed in at once; all sales of drinks forbidden and licensed premises to be closed; no assembly in the streets of more than five persons; no boats to leave the harbour without an order from the military authority.

Apart from her easy assumption of superiority, the Dame had one other advantage that paid dividends. She spoke good German.

When I had read the notice I turned to Lanz and said in German, 'Please sit down. I will see that these orders are obeyed.' Both men seemed astonished that I could speak their language.

Then Lanz gave me a wonderful opportunity by remarking, 'You do not appear to be in the least afraid.'

Looking as innocent as possible I asked in a surprised voice, 'Is there any reason why I should be afraid of German officers?'

This question had an immediate effect. They assured me that I was indeed right in my assumption. Their manners suddenly became almost affable and Lanz went so far as to say that if ever I found any difficulties I was to communicate directly with the Commandant of the Channel Islands in Guernsey.[13]

And so she did.

4

CHARM OFFENSIVE

One of the curiosities of Nazi Germany's compulsion to expand its frontiers in all directions was the apparent inability of the Reich to understand the enormity of the task it had undertaken. How could one country, whatever its military prowess, expect to exercise lasting dominion over the diverse nations of Europe? The answer lay in the malevolent character of Hitler, a combination of arrogance and inhumanity.

In the east, his diseased imagination rationalised the slaughter of millions of Poles, Russians, Ukrainians and Belarusians to create a vast open territory for German colonisation. In the west, the countries Germany walked over, then sought to control and manipulate – France, Norway, Denmark, the Netherlands and Belgium, with Austria as a semi-willing ally – were higher in the Nazi pecking order. In the upper reaches of the Hitler regime there was a genuine expectation that after the Jews, gypsies and other undesirables had been removed, these satellites – including Britain once it had accepted the inevitable – would follow the German vanguard, if only for self interest. A benevolent but firm rule was expected to bring benefits that would be hard to resist.

When the Channel Islands fell to the invader, the climax to a succession of easy victories, these ambitions for a German-led world power seemed within reach. Even France, the old and persistent enemy, was encouraged to believe that it could achieve a self-governing, dominion status within Hitler's Neuropa. But the Nazi charm offensive was strongest in the smaller occupied territories, the Channel Islands amongst them.

The German occupation of most of western Europe came as a surprise to everyone, not least the Germans, who had no idea it would be so easy. As they recovered from the shock of unprovoked attack and the realisation that the uninvited guests were in for a long stay, the leading island politicians had to decide on a response. For the most part they took a severely practical view of events. After the fall of France, resistance seemed hopeless. All they could do was to put their liberal principles on hold while trying to cushion German interference in internal affairs. They were heavily criticised at the time, and subsequently, for what was seen as a pacifist stance, but it is hard to see how the alternative, a sacrificial gesture, would have served the Allied war effort.

The accommodation reached with Germany by the smaller democracies (and also by Sweden, which avoided occupation by proclaiming a neutrality that, in reality, gave more comfort in Berlin than in London or Washington) was the only way of coping with a desperate situation. What was sold to the Reich from farms and factories would have been taken anyway. It made sense to try to keep up the appearance of sovereignty until there was a chance of regaining the real thing.

In the first phase of the Channel Islands occupation, from July 1940 through to the end of the year, relations were formal and correct, with both sides making a conscious effort to observe the basic courtesies. The Jersey and Guernsey governments were put on an occupation footing with, in each case, the States delegating responsibility to a smaller executive body. In August 1940, the Channel Islanders were told that they were now citizens of France, and as such part of the French department of Manche in Area A of the military government. In effect, relations with the Germans were centred on the bailiff's office. Although he was not to know it at the time, this put Alexander Coutanche, Bailiff of Jersey, in the unenviable position of being the most senior public figure in the British Isles to confront an occupying force.

Coutanche was forty-eight when the war started. A successful lawyer, he began his career in the Jersey administration in 1925 as solicitor-general, and was promoted to attorney-general in 1931. Four years later he was named bailiff, the last in the line of Jersey's Crown appointments for life. Not of robust health – as a teenager he had been diagnosed as having a heart murmur – Coutanche made up in personality what he lacked in physical energy. A portly man, he had a commanding, some thought forbidding, presence. He spoke eloquently, was a formidable adjudicator and kept calm in a crisis. Recovering quickly from the shock of a life turned upside down, he had no doubt where his duty lay. As he explained later, 'My instructions were that I would do my best for the people of the island whether I could get instructions from London or not. That I regarded as orders of my King . . . I hope I carried them out as intended.'[1]

He interpreted these orders as instructing him to reach an accommodation with the German military that, as far as possible, allowed daily life to resume its familiar pattern. This seemed to be the only sensible way to proceed, given that the islanders were outgunned and those of fighting age were outnumbered and outclassed. A policy of non-co-operation extending to hit-and-run tactics had a little more going for it than outright resistance, but the likely gains – minimal at best since there were no essential war industries to be disrupted – had to be set against inevitable repercussions causing widespread harm. Those who argued for a tougher stance were reminded that demilitarisation, i.e. no armed action, had been imposed by London. It was a bit late to argue that toss.

At the start of the occupation, the senior German officer in Jersey was Captain Gussek, 'a fighting soldier, short, neat and polite, who went briskly about the business in hand'.[2] His first encounter with Coutanche found the bailiff at home in his gardening clothes. Ushered into the drawing room, Gussek and his party were startled when, announced at the door by Duret Aubin, the attorney-general, as 'His Excellency, the Governor', Coutanche appeared with a large tear in his trousers.

His method of expressing some surprise at my appearance was to put a monocle into his right eye, the better to take me in. In those days I used on occasion to wear a monocle myself and it so happened that it was in the pocket of my jacket now. I was, therefore, able to repay the compliment and I did so. We took good stock of each other.[3]

This comic-book confrontation was brought to an end by one of Gussek's subordinates, who handed him a document which was then given to an interpreter to read out.

It was the same proclamation as that which had already been read to me at the airport. While this was taking place I could see through the window that Duret Aubin had retired to the dining-room and was fortifying himself with a glass of my port.[4]

Over the next two days an agreement was made on a form of government that would allow for German control without the inconvenience of actually having to run the administration. The existing civil and legal structure was to remain in place but new laws and regulations had to be approved by the German commandant before they could be enacted. Orders from the commandant, on the other hand, had to be accepted without argument, though offences against those orders, unless they came under German military law, could be dealt with by the civil courts.

Minor matters were open to discussion and compromise. The first of these was a decision on the opening hours for public houses. For the first two weeks of the occupation closing time had been set at 9 p.m. Coutanche suggested a one-hour extension. This was agreed by Gussek providing that only beer and wine were served; spirits were reckoned to be too provocative. He may have been right, though in the event he was to find that the likeliest offenders were among his own troops, an early example of a win for the home team.

Over in Guernsey it was the same but different. While the strategy for coping with the occupation was a near replica of the Jersey model, it was implemented not by the bailiff but by his attorney-general, Ambrose Sherwill.

As was said of another politician, Victor Carey, Bailiff of Guernsey, was a modest man with much to be modest about. Of no great shakes as a lawyer or administrator, he had risen to his present eminence on the strength of his name. By lineage and wealth, the Carey family held sway in Guernsey. In ordinary circumstances no one would have dared suggest that Victor Carey should stand aside. But July 1940 was, beyond question, extraordinary.

The delicate task of persuading the bailiff to surrender authority fell to the Reverend John Leale, a Methodist minister, businessman and, as holder of the ancient office of Jurat, a senior member of the States who could meet Carey on equal terms. But surrender to whom? There was one obvious candidate: Ambrose Sherwill himself. The only obstacle was social. As Sherwill noted, the Careys 'were out of the top drawer and not unaware of that fact while I came out of the bottom one'.[5] This distinction might not have mattered so much had not Sherwill married into the Carey family. The news of the engagement, he recalled, had not been well received.

> My wife's grandfather, a kindly old family doctor, told her that she would become a social leper. My future father-in-law, the then Dean of Guernsey . . . absented himself from the island to avoid officiating at our wedding.[6]

When the bailiffship of Guernsey fell vacant in the mid-1930s, but for the opposition of the House of Carey, Sherwill would have been well placed to succeed. Instead, he gave way with the excuse that, married with five children, he could not afford the social outlay that went with the job.[7] Come the occupation there were no such qualms. It was of credit to Carey that, recognising his limitations, he withdrew into the shadows. According to Sherwill:

> It came to me as a complete surprise when, late one morning, John Leale came to see me and told me that he had called together the other Presidents of States Committees and, with their assent, had already asked the Bailiff to summon an emergency Meeting of the States for that very afternoon and that it was the intention of those he had consulted that, at that Meeting, my name would be put forward as President of a Controlling Committee with power to appoint the members of that Committee. I was reluctant that this should be but John Leale put the matter so forcefully that before he left he had obtained my assent.[8]

Like Coutanche, Sherwill was a lawyer educated in France. But while Coutanche had held a desk job in the Great War, Sherwill had been a front-line soldier, awarded a Military Cross for conspicuous bravery. Not surprisingly, his military experience made a lasting impression on him. With his neat moustache, erect bearing and clipped speech, Sherwill was every inch an officer and a gentleman. Lacking Coutanche's subtlety in negotiations he was quick, sometimes too quick, to make decisions.

Sherwill's life was bounded by a sense of honour, his own and other people's, which in the case of German officers he took for granted. In his dealings with the occupying force, he behaved like a character from *La Grande Illusion*, the 1937 movie in which opposite sides on the Western Front find that mutual respect and common values can override enmity, until reality sets in.

Having decided that his job was to act as a buffer between the occupying forces and the civilian population, Sherwill made it his priority to get onside with the senior German officers on the island. Almost without exception he found them to be 'honourable, humane men', a view he continued to hold even after events turned against him, though he came to recognise that his attempt 'so far as I could, to run the German occupation for them . . . was a fatuous thing to do'.[9]

Sherwill's chief contact in Guernsey was Major Albrecht Lanz, 'every inch a soldier and not very easy to get to know but absolutely straight and kindly'.[10] In contrast to the Dame of Sark, Sherwill took an immediate liking to Major Maass, the English-educated interpreter: 'His presence was a godsend, his cheery face was a tonic and there can be no question that his friendly activities helped the situation enormously'.[11] With Lanz's adjutant, Lieutenant Mittelmüller, he recalled, 'I got on well and became friendly. He spoke no English and I knew no German but we both spoke French so French became the language of our communications.'[12]

Sherwill was soon to discover the perils of trying to do the decent thing. One of the greatest concerns for islanders was the absence of news from family and friends on the mainland. How were those classed as refugees faring among strangers? What if anything did they know of circumstances at home except by rumours fed by ignorance or propaganda? After two months of near-total isolation, Coutanche struck a deal which allowed for a limited dispatch of controlled correspondence. Messages were to consist of just a few words of comfort or inquiry. They had to pass two lines of censorship, one administered by the island authorities, the other by the Feldkommandantur, the bureaucratic wing of the Germans military. Even when approved, there was no guarantee that they would be selected for transmission. A first batch from Jersey was limited to 220 messages.[13] Among the excluded were all communications addressed to those who had left the island as part of the evacuation, since a twisted logic ruled that anyone who had felt compelled to escape had insulted the Wehrmacht; if they had stayed put to enjoy the blessings of German occupation there would have been no need for the Red Cross to act as postman.

On Guernsey, the Germans had their own ideas on solving the communication problem. Knowing Sherwill to be more pliant and certainly more of an innocent than Coutanche, Lanz put to him a simple and effective way for reaching out to all who were seeking to know what was happening on the island. As Sherwill explained later:

He told me that arrangements had been made for me to speak a message of about 100 words into a recording machine and that the record would be played and transmitted over the German Radio. I asked for and obtained an assurance that it would not be doctored and went away to compose my message. It ran to many more than the allotted number of words but this was not objected to.[14]

So, announcing himself as 'His Britannic Majesty's Procureur in Guernsey', Sherwill addressed himself to 'the people of the United Kingdom and, in particular, to those who left Guernsey and Alderney during the evacuation'. He went on:

> I imagine that many of you must be greatly worried as to how we are getting on. Well, let me tell you. Some will fear, I imagine, that I am making this record with a revolver pointed at my head and speaking from a transcript thrust into my hand by a German officer.
> The actual case is very different. The Lieutenant-Governor and Bailiff, Mr. Victor Carey, and every other island official has been and is being treated with every consideration and with the greatest courtesy by the German Military Authorities. The Island Government is functioning. Churches and Chapels are open for public worship. Banks, shops and places of entertainment are open as usual.

These assurances were a hostage to fortune; conditions were to get a lot worse before long, something Sherwill might reasonably have anticipated. His optimism might have been forgiven, but his listeners found his over-eager endorsement of the occupying force harder to understand.

> The conduct of the German troops is exemplary. We have been in German occupation for four and a half weeks and I am proud of the way my fellow-islanders have behaved, and grateful for the correct and kindly attitude towards them of the German soldiers.

We have always been and we remain intensely loyal subjects of His Majesty, and this has been made clear to and is respected by the German Commandant and his staff. On that staff is an officer speaking perfect English – a man of wide experience, with whom I am in daily contact. To him I express my grateful thanks for his courtesy and patience.

Sherwill ended with a few personal messages and a general blessing.

To all men of military age who left here to join His Majesty's Forces, God speed. To all wives and mothers and sweethearts, God bless you. To all Guernsey children in England, God keep you safe.

Notices in the press urged islanders to tune into Radio Bremen to hear Sherwill's message. That it was three weeks before it was played may have been motivated by the hope of attracting listeners to the nasal tones of the traitorous William Joyce, better known as Lord Haw-Haw, the fascist sympathiser who took to the airwaves in Berlin. When Sherwill eventually came on air, the implied link was hard to ignore.

Looking back, it seems incredible that Sherwill did not recognise the valuable free gift he was handing German propaganda. 'I set out to be as informative and reassuring as possible,' he wrote later. 'Not one word or one figure was other than the absolute truth.'[15]

Maybe so. But interpretation was all. For those who sought reassurance, Sherwill provided that and no more. For others, who had no personal stake in the Channel Islands, his honeyed words smacked of traitorous intent. That Sherwill meant no harm is beyond dispute. His courage later in the face of Nazi persecution speaks of a man whose heart and loyalties were in the right place. But he was naïve in the same way that P.G. Wodehouse was naïve in thinking that he could use German radio to make fun of his captors. Neither had any concept of the propaganda value of misplaced sentiment.

Official reaction on Guernsey was favourable, with the *Guernsey Evening Press* praising 'one voice speaking for all'.[16] But since the paper was under German control that is hardly surprising. No mention was made of the clever way in which the broadcast implied that here was clear evidence of German good intentions, that British allegations of suffering in occupied countries was all lies and that the Channel Islanders, now that they knew what the Germans were really like, were happy to welcome them into their midst.

At the first meeting of the Guernsey States since the invasion, Sherwill compounded his error of judgement with a speech on mutual tolerance and respect that gave altogether too much credit to the occupiers' good faith.

> So long as we continue to comport ourselves as we have during the past five weeks, refraining from provocative behaviour and going quietly about our tasks, there is no reason to fear harm to anyone.
>
> May this occupation be a model to the world – on the one hand, tolerance on the part of the military authority and courtesy and correctness on the part of the occupying forces, and, on the part of the civilian population; perfect obedience to law and order, conformity – the strictest conformity – with black-out regulations and with orders and regulations issued by the German Commandant and the civil authorities.

Sherwill's error of judgement was compounded by John Leale, who suggested that by remaining on the island, the Guernsey people had accepted an obligation to submit to German rule.

> In June of last year, any of us who wished to do so could have left the island. Two very large vessels left on the Saturday evening of evacuation week; one of them practically empty, the other entirely so. We stayed here knowing full well that German troops could, without any resistance, occupy the island whenever their Command ordered them to do so. Our staying here meant that we accepted that position and were prepared in the event of occupation to act as good citizens.

Many who had been caught up in the panic of the evacuation could only laugh at the idea that they had exercised a free choice.

As part of the move to put the occupation on a permanent footing, the Feldkommandantur had taken over responsibility for civil administration. The stage was thus set for political wrangling ('Your troubles are about to begin,' Sherwill was warned) though at this stage the German infighting was kept under control. This was partly because, as Feldkommandant, the elderly Major Friedrich Schumacher favoured the quiet life but also because, with the appointment of Colonel, soon to be Lieutenant General Graf von Schmettow as commander-in-chief, in October 1940, there was a clear chain of command with the Wehrmacht at the head of the pecking order. Coutanche described von Schmettow as 'a typical soldier':

> He reminded me very much of the British Generals with whom I had had so long to deal in the persons of Lieutenant-Governors of Jersey. He was smart, well dressed and dignified, and the kind of man with whom one would be instinctively careful not to try to take any liberties.[17]

He was also an aristocrat, head of an old-established Silesian family with a long military tradition. More to the point, he was a nephew of Field Marshal Gert von Rundstedt, who had led the invasion of France. Coutanche was convinced that here was someone with whom he could do business.

> We agreed mutually that we were enemies and that there must be no sort of social intercourse between us of any kind whatsoever. Within those limits, however, we could still both behave like gentlemen and that was what we tried to do. Another thing which underlined our relationship was that we only interfered personally, and tried to see each other, in cases of major difficulty. Normally we left the ordinary day-to-day running of affairs to those who were working with us.[18]

Sherwill was also impressed. Von Schmettow, he wrote, was 'a man of great charm and humanity'. Not that Sherwill had much direct contact with him. His chief business was with the Feldkommandantur in Guernsey, headed by the 'small and dapper' Prince Eugen Oettingen-Wallerstein.

As the new arrivals settled in, the old guard of the occupation moved on. They included Captain Gussek from Jersey, and, from Guernsey, Major Lanz, who was succeeded by Major Bandelow, 'a completely different type of man'; more approachable, according to Sherwill.

He asked me to meet him at the Kommandantur and he had laid on a very young German soldier who had apparently expressed himself as competent to act as interpreter. The boy was hopeless at the job and the usual German officer would almost certainly have torn a strip off him and sent him away humiliated. Not so Bandelow; he was kindness itself to the lad and eased him out of the situation with great understanding. I was most impressed and reassured as to future relations with the military.[19]

Lanz, who was soon to be counted among the dead on the Eastern Front, was given the credit due to him with the award of an Iron Cross and a promotion from major to lieutenant-colonel. In September 1940 he called on Sherwill to say goodbye. As the latter recalled:

He was extremely well turned out (usually he wore the shabbiest of uniforms) and was wearing his new decoration, on which I remember congratulating him. He was in a much more cheerful frame of mind than was usual. After some general conversation, I told him that I had done all in my power to avoid difficulties between the occupying forces and the civilian population during the period of his command. 'Did he appreciate that it was not because of lack of loyalty to my own country but because I was convinced that, during an enemy occupation, this was the only way of securing the greatest possible measure of liberty and normality for the people of the island?' He replied – through an interpreter – that he had never had any doubt as to where my loyalty lay or that I was doing what was in the interests of my own people.[20]

*

The changes in command and the imposition of a more convoluted administration signified a military upgrade for the Channel Islands. With the prospects of an easy victory over Britain fast receding, Hitler had every reason to expect a counter-attack on the only part of that country under his control. It was fixed in his mind that the islands had to be made invulnerable. Along with the new raft of senior officers came a strengthening of the garrison.

For the most part the young soldiers assigned to the islands could not believe their luck. Like all ordinary servicemen in a foreign land, they were not quite sure why they were there or what they were supposed to be doing. But they soon discovered that they could walk the streets without someone taking a shot at them. And there was a romance attached to the islands that was clearly infectious. Werner Grosskopf, who crossed from Granville with his platoon, recalls his first sight of the Jersey coast:

> It was a wonderful, bright day when we sailed. There was enthusiasm on the ship when we saw the harbour front of St Helier, the white villas and houses, the blue and clear sea. I was thinking back to my exchange as a pupil to England in 1929 when I had learned all about the British way of life. So from the first day I said to my soldiers, 'Now we are in a country of milk and honey.' We all felt on the top of the world.[21]

Or, as another early arrival put it, it was 'like being sent to a little paradise'.[22] The main attractions were all those that had for generations appealed to holidaymakers: a warm, sunny climate, long sandy beaches, fabulous cliff-top views and fresh air. 'Everything was very, very clean,' recalls Hans Constable, then a naval ensign, 'much cleaner and nicer than in France. I liked the British people too; there was no hate between us. And there was a big market where we could buy tomatoes, potatoes and melons.'[23]

It was only on Alderney that the euphoria died.

> There was no civilian population. The battery itself was installed in an old fort, and the people, the crew, were housed in the old casements, which were very wet, damp, not much protective soil. As the fort had not been used for years, there were hardly any doors in it. There was a large number of rats which were running around when we came.[24]

But even the derelict Alderney shared one great advantage with the other islands. Whenever they were feeling depressed, soldiers comforted each other with the popular truism that they were all together in the 'safest air raid shelter in Europe'.

Among the senior ranks, well-connected families were generously represented. Whether this was by virtue of the social network favouring safe jobs for the upper classes, or of the Wehrmacht seeking out useful employment for those whose promotion had outpaced their military capabilities, it is hard to say. Maybe a bit of both.

Von Schmettow was a case in point. Having followed the family footsteps into the army, his career was put on hold when he lost a lung in a gas attack on the Western Front. He was forty-seven before he reached the rank of major. Two years later, at the beginning of the war, he was sent on active service in Poland and France. He performed creditably, indeed was decorated for his contribution, but by now it must have been clear to Field Marshal von Runstedt that his nephew would not rival him as a commander or strategist. What better, therefore, than to shuffle him off to the Channel Islands to fill a none-too onerous job that just about justified his exalted rank?

Von Schmettow was only too happy to oblige. The islands appealed to him as self-contained pockets of civilisation, a welcome release from front-line duties. Though proud and erect, he tried hard to be liked, appearing in public without an escort and carrying sweets in his pocket to hand out to children. By his own admission, his proudest achievement while commandant was the commissioning of *Festung Guernsey*, a lavishly illustrated account of the history of the island up to and including the occupation, with detailed studies of the fortifications, ancient and modern. Described as 'the single most important document to come out of the occupation', it was compiled by fourteen army photographers, artists and cartographers who spent nearly three years on the project.

Soon to join the aristocratic roll call was Baron Max von Aufsess, 'dark and broad shouldered, a charming type of German who had travelled widely and in peacetime had been a successful lawyer'. This was the verdict of the Dame of Sark, who was indirectly connected to von Aufsess by a marriage of cousins.[25] Like Oettingen-Wallerstein, the Baron was of Bavarian ancestry, the owner of a fabulous castle dating from the ninth century. These dilettante soldiers have been treated with scorn by some historians, who have dismissed them as the equivalent of draft dodgers.

> Von Aufsess himself provides an excellent illustration of an aristocrat who believed that inherited position still equalled influence and that this followed him wherever he went . . . Aufsess had far too much time to spend on books, intellectual dribbling with like-minded compatriots and a select crowd of self-important islanders and the pursuits of the country gentleman.[26]

There is some justice in this. While it was praiseworthy that von Schmettow, Oettingen-Wallerstein, von Aufsess and others rejected the excesses of Nazism, they did little actively to oppose the regime (although back in Germany von Aufsess's wife was imprisoned for expressing unguarded regrets when Hitler survived the 1944 assassination plot). And when Sherwill fell from grace and was imprisoned in France and later interned in Germany, 'it was Schmettow he thanked for saving his life'.[27] However, such endorsements are rare. The commanders made little effort to intervene on behalf of those who suffered most from German rule. As Coutanche reveals in his memoirs, the shrug of the shoulders was the usual reaction to reports of maltreatment. But for the first months of the occupation the 'mutual tolerance and respect' promoted by the senior officers of state looked set to achieve a trouble-free co-existence.

5

LIVING WITH THE ENEMY

It came as a relief to the islanders to find that German soldiers were not the brutal Huns of comic-book caricature. The first Germans to arrive – young, fit, confident – made an impressive sight, a contrast to the recently departed tommies, often undernourished children of the depression kitted out in baggy, hirsute uniforms resembling leftovers from a jumble sale.

Except at command level, the two sides kept their distance. For the young Michael Ginns, his first sight of Germans was when an army truck passed him on the road. 'They looked at me; I looked at them and that was it. They didn't have horns on their heads, or cloven hooves or anything. They didn't go round cutting off index fingers so we couldn't fire a rifle, as had been rumoured. They were well behaved and polite.'[1]

Others recall how German soldiers were courteous when asking directions, how they saluted their elders and were particularly kind to children. Leslie Ricou, then aged seven, was given a tour of the military stables where he was shown how they groomed the horses. Later he was to be found with his new friends kicking a ball around on the beach. 'You could have a laugh with them, they were very good to us.'[2]

John Boucheré remembers:

The first German that I saw in the island, oddly enough with all their power, was on a bicycle and he came past the village where I lived. As he passed near our house his chain broke and he asked me to provide a hammer for him, which I did. I suppose you could call that Jersey's first bit of collaboration.[3]

Playing in the fields one day, Reg Langlois came across a German soldier who was carrying a spade.

He gave me a grin and offered me the spade and when I shook my head, he grinned again. I thought that I had made a friend. He started walking towards the farmhouse. I followed my new friend and stayed nearby when he started digging on high ground near a pathway close to the house. He must have been there a long time because he had dug a hole as big as a table. It was so deep that, from where I was standing, I couldn't see the bottom.

As my new friend could not speak my language, when I asked him why he had dug the hole he just grinned again and, when he had finished, he shook my hand and went. I never saw him again although I sat near the hole for several days waiting for him to come back.[4]

There were many examples of attempts at friendship. Jean Badden recalls walking up Brock Road in St Helier:

I had a sack of twigs, kindling, sort of small bits and pieces . . . and this little German approached me and said – 'Your *Mutter*?' – so I said – 'Down the road' – 'Too heavy for little girl, I carry'. Well I was worried that he was going to pinch it! Well he took the sack and it must have been awful because I was hanging onto the back of it – he's not going to get my sack of twigs! My poor father's face! He was standing at the gate in Victoria Road – 'What the . . .?' 'He's only helping me carry it!' I said. I suppose I must have been about 9 or 10 then. He was genuinely concerned that I was carrying a heavy sack, they were like that.[5]

Children were a great unifying factor, as soldiers naturally missed their own children or their younger siblings. 'Where we lived, opposite the cookhouse,' writes Margaret Le Cras,

the Germans used to pass across our yard twice a day, so we were quite used to them. Although they couldn't speak to us because we only spoke the patois, which they didn't understand, they smiled, they showed us photographs of their children, and many were the tears in their eyes when they watched us play.[6]

A strong memory for Ruth Walsh related to the vital task of gathering in food.

I used to go with my two brothers who were 18 months and 3 years older than me, picking up potatoes dropped from the lorries being loaded . . . I had picked up 3 or 4 that were quite a reasonable size and quite nice and I thought, 'Oh mum's going to be very pleased with me', you know then all of a sudden – it was quite a young soldier who was up on the tailboard, handing these sacks of potatoes down. He started calling and beckoning . . . he wanted my bag, and I thought 'He's going to take my potatoes away!' I was really very angry. I wasn't going to let it go. My brothers said 'Go on, you better give it to him', and do you know what he did, he opened up a sack of potatoes, he filled up my carrier bag, handed it down to me, saying 'Go, – off!'
I've often wondered what happened to that soldier and I hope he survived. I hope he's had a good life.[7]

The politest nickname for a German soldier was Greenfly, after the colour of the uniform. 'No, they didn't have thick square necks as all the cartoons showed them,' recalls Bob Le Sueur. 'They looked just like us.' This realisation that propaganda impressions could be misleading encouraged optimism. 'I thought, maybe it won't be so bad. And, it wasn't, in the early days.'

Of course, much depended on whether you were on the receiving end of military necessity. A lot could be forgiven, if it happened to other people. Living on the seafront outside St Helier, Bob Le Sueur's family were naturally worried when a concrete bunker was built just across the road.

> ... there were five houses in a row, ours was the middle one, and quite obviously when the bunker was ready they would need one of these houses for the crew. Which one would it be? And it was the one on the end. And we were all terribly, terribly sorry for the couple who had only 48 hours to get out and find somewhere else to live. But of course the human reaction was 'Oh thank heavens it wasn't us'.

A few weeks later the Greenflies were back. Bob's mother did not know what to make of the German who walked into her kitchen to take the largest saucepan.

> Three days later the saucepan came back. Burnished because they had cleaning materials and we didn't, but containing tripe. This was like the nectar of the gods. This was how fraternisation, which some people would call collaboration, could start.[8]

The small community philosophy of minding your own business, keeping yourself to yourself, not interfering in matters beyond the immediate family, was strong enough to overcome the bitterness of knowing that what was being handed out so generously by the occupiers was not theirs to give, that it had been purloined by force. But for some, like Fred Hockey, the effort made by the Germans to appear as the good guys was cloying in its intensity.

> They were so damned polite. They soft-soaped us all the time. They saluted us, they stepped off the pavement to let us go by. It

just made everybody sick, and there was nothing we could do about it. A couple of days after the occupation, for instance, I was told that I should no longer be allowed to go to my signal station at the end of White Rock, but I should have a new office in the harbour building at St. Peter Port, nearer the shore. When I arrived, I found two German officers sitting there. They stood to attention and saluted me, and then shook hands, saying they hoped that, as colleagues, we would be the best of friends. It went against the grain, but what could I say except that I hoped so too?

Fred was happy enough to be allowed to get on with his work but had no wish for a closer relationship.

They always treated me well – too well really, that was the trouble. . . .They were always giving us things, and would not permit us to refuse them. They offered us cigarettes, drinks, even packets of coffee. They were always mixing with us in the pubs. . . . All we Guernseymen would turn our backs, but the Germans would force their way up and offer us drinks. We would say we had had enough, or make any sort of excuse, but it was no good. They would buy the drinks, put them down in front of us, and we had to drink them. Then they would bring out cigarettes and cigars, and compel us to accept them. . . . If you refused there was trouble.[9]

A popular game for boys was playing German soldiers. When troops were marching in town, the children would march alongside, attempting the goosestep causing laughter all round. 'Boys play soldiers,' says Malcolm Woodland. 'We played German soldiers. They were the only soldiers we knew.'

We played dugouts, we played manoeuvres, we played with our toy rifles. I had a grey coat and my mother went spare about me wanting to put German insignia on my shoulders but all the other boys were getting their mothers to stitch on shoulder tabs. We used to march along in platoons and everyone wanted to be the corporal or sergeant and march alongside them, and usually the biggest boy would get to do this.[10]

Many individual acts of kindness are on record. Leo Harris remembers a surprise visit by a German soldier, ostensibly on the lookout for illegal possessions, who 'did his best to help by telling me to hide some incriminating pieces of evidence'. Soldiers going on leave or posted back to the continent were often willing carriers of letters from islanders to friends and relatives in France.

There were even occasional touches of humour. The first encounter with German soldiers for Michael Ginns' mother was when she and a friend were taking the dog for a walk.

They came across these men laying a barbed wire fence round the edge of the common. My mother's friend always wanted to know what was going on so she asked, 'What are you men doing?' And one of them looked up, spoke English and said, 'We're building a secret line for you to hang your washing on.'[11]

All this accorded with instructions to German troops on how they should conduct themselves when the big prize fell to them. Once Britain had surrendered there was to be no looting and 'acts of violence against orderly members of the population will incur the severest penalties under military law'. Within the inevitable restraints imposed by occupation, civil life was to continue without 'unnecessary interference'.

Even over-enthusiastic shopping was discouraged, though experience in St Helier and St Peter Port suggested that this was one rule not taken too seriously. It was asking too much of young servicemen, with nothing else to spend their money on, to ignore the shops crowded with souvenirs for the tourist season that never was. One Jerseyman recorded how 'new arrivals are to be seen standing in front of shop windows with their mouths open'. It wasn't long before they were inside, eager to clear the shelves of items not otherwise available to servicemen. Tradesmen were relieved to be paid, though they were not too happy to accept reichmarks instead of sterling. A rapid recalculation of prices allowed for a fixed exchange rate of seven marks to the pound.

Complaints from civilian shoppers that supplies of basic goods were running down at an alarming rate were met by a military order forbidding the purchase at any one time of more than '50 cigarettes or 25 cigars, 1 bottle of wine or two bottles of beer, three shirts, collars and ties and one suit length of cloth'. This last item was a favourite among the fashion conscious who wanted Scottish tweeds to take to London to be made up by Savile Row tailors. There were fewer complaints from retailers, who took advantage of the unexpected boom in sales to shift unwanted stock including, in one case, twenty thousand cigars which had been in store since before the Great War.

> The cigars were brushed and cleaned up and were reported to have given particular satisfaction. Bales of shoddy and unreliable suiting which had been in the island for at least thirty years and thousands of yards of perished elastic which must have let down many a careful German hausfrau were sold by some of the more patriotic shopkeepers who had the good sense to keep back their sound goods, which proved invaluable to their own people later on.[12]

*

There was another side to the story, with frequent reminders that the Germans had guns on their side and might be prepared to use them.

> Last night the wife and I were standing in the porch, admiring the beautiful moonlight view. Two of our visitors entered the grounds, placed a revolver in my side and ordered me indoors – they then entered the house, kicked the table and extinguished the light and, retiring with revolvers pointed at us, ordered us

to bed. It was not an enviable experience but it is no use complaining. Our visitors can do no wrong, Jerseymen are always the culprits.[13]

For Joe Mière, a church service turned into a disturbing experience.

We were at the altar having Holy Communion and I happened to look at this priest with the cropped hair; [he was wearing] green trousers with dress boots with laces, army boots. . . . I nudged my father and said [the priest was] German, and we all got up from the rail and sat down. Our priest, Father Mare, a family friend, came up to us at the end and said to my father 'that wasn't a very nice thing to do after all he's a man of God'. My father said 'your boss died on the cross; this one wears a crooked cross'. After we'd left this German chaplain came out and went through the side gate, and I noticed he was carrying a side arm. . . . It was funny to see a priest with a revolver.[14]

That such guns were not simply ornamental was underlined only too clearly by the execution of François Scornet, a young Frenchman who, escaping from France, had landed in Guernsey. In his interrogation he made no secret of his intention of reaching England, a 'hostile country'. 'On the morning of his execution,' recorded Arthur Kent in his diary,

the boy was taken from Fort Regent and driven in a lorry five miles to the grounds of St Ouen's Manor, his seat in the lorry was the coffin in which an hour later his mutilated body would lie. A poignant sequel to this brutal murder is told. The boy had been tied to a big tree in the Manor grounds, the tree having two large forks which abutted some few feet from the ground, and the firing party put a score of bullets into his body. The next morning workmen were amazed to see that one fork of the tree had partially snapped and the end lay resting on the ground dipped as though in salute. No doubt this phenomenon was in some way caused by the impact of so many bullets, but nevertheless it makes strange reading.[15]

For most islanders there remained an unbridgeable gulf between 'them' and 'us', a division made wider by the failure of the occupiers to take proper account of domestic sensitivities. Apart from a tendency to buy up everything in sight, the arrogant assumption that the war was all but over ('just a manoeuvre'), though not entirely irrational, was a frequent irritant compounded by an ignorance of British geography.

Like London, St Helier has a Charing Cross. Leo Harris was stopped there by a German soldier.

Was this London? He was looking at the sign saying Charing Cross and must have heard of the name and he wanted to know where he was more or less; I wasn't too helpful as you can imagine.[16]

Another fresh-faced innocent thought Jersey was the Isle of Wight and that it would not be long before he and his comrades were wading over to England.

Stories such as this are not to be found in German accounts of the occupation, which invariably stress the formal but friendly relations between themselves and the islanders. As in Holland, Denmark and Norway, German recollections are full of efforts to show that the occupied and the occupiers were all the same people, with shared historical and linguistic roots. But, as with Orwell's farmyard animals, some were more equal than others.

We saw this German officer who had his revolver in his hand. There were several soldiers around, also with their rifles at the ready, and he was asking our neighbour if he knew where the telecommunications centre was between here and the UK. Someone says, 'Oh, it's a few miles down the road.'

So, without 'by your leave', or 'do you mind?' this officer sent one of his soldiers into our yard, which was alongside, and picked up our brand new Hillman Minx that had hardly been run in, and the last we saw of this car for five years was these Germans driving down the hill![17]

And this was only the start.

Not long after, there was a knock on our door, and German soldiers were there, with rifles in hand again, saying 'We want your house now. You have two days to leave. Collect all your furniture, and away you go.' So that was that. So, my early introduction to the German occupation wasn't a very happy one, to say the least.[18]

The finest hotels were requisitioned for officer accommodation while, at short notice, hundreds of private houses, along with their contents, were taken over as billets. The swastika was everywhere. Even when payment was made for impounded vehicles and other items that happened to take the fancy of the military, valuation was the prerogative of the purchaser, who naturally pitched for the lowest figure he could think of. It was not unusual for a car worth £300 to change hands for less than the price of a modest dinner. The Germans often issued promissory notes, supposedly for payment at some future date but actually with no greater worth than the paper they were written on. One Guernseyman recalls the requisition of photographic equipment, ostensibly for speeding up the issue of identity cards, and a house-to-house collection of mattresses for which chits were handed over. Leslie Sinel, who kept a diary of happenings on Jersey, reported that yachts and high-powered cars were invariably shipped off to France.

Purloining property, with or without menaces, raised the question of what, if anything, the civil authorities could do to support citizens' rights. The answer was not much. 'It seemed to me that we were always handing something over,' writes a Guernseyman.

How was this permitted given the German directive that forbade looting and 'unnecessary interference' in civil life? Simple. There was another ordinance drawn up by the German general staff in mid-1940 which gave pretty well total freedom to the military government 'to make full use of the country's resources for the needs of the fighting troops and the requirements of the German war economy'. When circumstances demanded, the velvet glove could be quickly discarded.

Though German orders were channelled through the civil authorities there was rarely any chance to amend the rules in favour of the islanders. The best that could be expected was that the edicts could be applied impartially and the burden fairly distributed. One example was cited by W.H. Marshall, later town clerk of St Helier but then a junior official.

They wanted fifty bicycles. We had therefore to work out some means of taking them away from the local people as fairly as possible. We tried to do this on the basis of whether a bicycle was necessary for one's job. . . . We never had a case where somebody resented it . . . I think the local people understood that it was better to deal with us than to deal with the Germans.[19]

The military was keen to involve the islanders in communal entertainments. The most popular were the band concerts, which attracted large crowds. But close encounters between soldiers and locals were discouraged, for fear that soldiers would give away too much information. Cinemas were segregated and dances initially banned though the rules were relaxed in 1942, when it was clear that fraternisation was a prerogative that young people refused to surrender. Most local girls were restrained either by their own moral values or by parental diktat. But inevitably, one anonymous German soldier remembers, there were temptations in the way of lonely teenagers who sought male company.

In the summer, naturally it was very easy to come into contact with girls on the coast, and while swimming and bathing. In winter it was worse. But in the houses where we lived, there were Swiss girls who were already here as *au pair* girls in the summer, and who now had these houses in their care and kept them clean and tidy. And sometimes they had friends round.[20]

It helped that chocolate, cigarettes and other scarce items were on offer. However, it was soon clear that the shortage of female company was causing problems for the German command. Their solution was to set up brothels in St Helier and St Peter Port with prostitutes brought in from France. When this became common knowledge there was much consternation among the more puritanical islanders, though their wails were drowned out by laughter when it was learned that for the issue of ration books the girls were to be classed as 'heavy workers'.

Not every German conscript was devoted to the Führer. The experience of the occupation years in the Channel Islands suggests that many young Germans were caught up in something they did not quite understand.

We knew two quite well, and neither of them wanted to be in the war. One was Austrian. He'd been the village postman, his rifle was practically as big as him, and he didn't want to be in the war. The other one was a farmer, he had children, and I remember him coming back from leave, I didn't know why at the time, but my mother told me later. He came to us and he was crying his eyes out, and my mother asked what was wrong, you know, as much as she could understand what was wrong. His boy was in the Hitler Youth, and he had been saying that the war was over, and things against the war, and his son turned up and said he would report him if he didn't stop talking like that, and it broke his heart.[21]

Leo Harris tells an evocative story about a Bavarian sergeant.

One autumn morning in 1942, Ken Richardson, our farmer friend and my father were standing talking when they heard the sound of a heavily laden bicycle approaching. . . . Bouncing to a halt, a jackbooted sergeant swung a heavy leg over his saddle, pushed his machine to a nearby granite wall, pulled at his uniform and walked heavily over to the waiting pair. 'Gut morning,' he said, in heavily accented English and pushed out a gloved paw to Ken who took it. The sergeant then turned to my father with his hand still on offer, 'Who is your friend, Mr Richardson?' he asked looking straight at my father. Ken muttered some introduction, but my father kept his hand pointedly by his side. . . . Slowly the big hand dropped and the sergeant scuffed his jackboots back a pace.

'You do not like me because I am a German?' he growled. My father agreed. 'You were in the first one?' My father nodded knowing that this referred to the First World War. 'You would like to shoot me?' The German did not expect a reply, but took my father's look for agreement. In a sudden movement he undid his holster over his left hip and drew out an automatic pistol, operated the action to slide a bullet into the chamber and to Ken's surprise grabbed my father's hand and slapped the heavy gun into his open palm. 'There,' he yelled, stepping back a pace and extending his arms out sideways from his body, 'so shoot!'

Of course my father could not. 'You see,' said the sergeant slowly recovering his weapon, 'you could not shoot me and I do not want to shoot you.' He restored the gun to his holster and pushed out his hand again to my father who laughed and took it. . . . A big man in every way.[22]

But this island version of the phoney war with its occasional heart-warming anecdotes had to be seen in the wider context of a battle for survival.

On a bitterly cold night a local family was sitting at home enjoying a drink of hot coffee – or what passed for it. At the bottom of their garden a German anti-aircraft gunner stood on duty beside his gun. One member of the family – a most loyal and Christian man – took a cup of coffee to the man who was duly grateful for the warmth and comfort which it gave him. 'I could not do less for any human being on such a night, enemy or no enemy,' said this kind-hearted man. A few moments later Allied airmen flew over the island – it was at a time when a series of raids were being made on St Nazaire. The anti-aircraft gun at the bottom of the garden opened up with an ear-splitting roar. A younger member of the family remarked: 'Your warmed and comforted young gunner may be all the more capable a marksman for his hot cup of coffee'.[23]

6

MAKING DO

After a month of occupation, life on the islands was said to be more or less normal. But on Jersey, as Leslie Sinel noted in his diary: 'Stocks of certain commodities are diminishing and purchases of some goods are restricted. . . . Rabbit-keeping is now an island-wide proposition.'[1] A few days later he commented on the two meatless days a week recently decreed, adding, 'this order, like many others, was observed for a time and then gradually forgotten'.

Some rules could not be ignored.

The most difficult thing at first was to get used to obeying the new regulations – and most of the time you had to obey them strictly, no mistake about that. The curfew, for instance. Nobody was to be out of doors after 10 p.m. . . . In the first week two of the islanders were caught outside the Channel Islands Hotel, where some of the Germans were quartered, at 10.02 p.m. They were arrested, and taken into the hotel for the night. Next morning they came up before the Kommandant. They were fined £1 each, and then they had to pay 5s. for their hotel accommodation! For the privilege of spending the night with the Germans![2]

The chief irritant was the German tendency to produce a new rule at the drop of a military hat. Concerns that fishermen might take off for England or France led to restrictions that were as amusing as they were frustrating. The Dame of Sark, expressing her views in characteristically forthright terms, protested against the armed soldiers placed in each boat in spite of the fact that no boat had enough petrol to get to the mainland. The military mindset also fixed the time of day for fishing.

> For instance, a notice would be affixed saying, 'Fishing tomorrow will be allowed between 10 a.m. and 3 p.m.' The guards would be waiting at the harbour but the fishermen would not, knowing that at 10 a.m. it would be useless to fish, and being unwilling to waste their precious rationed petrol. The guards reported their absence to the local Commandant, who came to me to complain. I explained over and over again that the success of fishing depended entirely upon the tide. . . . In the end comprehension dawned.[3]

The point had to be conceded because the Germans needed the catch as much as anyone. Fun was had by the Sark fishermen who steered their boats head on into the waves. Their German passengers were soaked and sea-sick.

By the end of the year there were shortages of every kind, an inevitability given that the islands' traditional economy was dependent on exports to Britain. When that trade was cut off the repercussions were widespread. On Guernsey at the time of the occupation, tomatoes were ripening at a rate of 2,000 tons a week with no prospect of finding a market. Housewives were used to preserving the fruit but there were no facilities for turning a domestic activity into a commercial operation.

Moreover, most tomato growers were dependent on bank overdrafts to carry them over the cultivation season. With no income, the debts mounted. To soften the blow, the Controlling Committee came up with a plan for voluntary nationalisation. Growers who were in financial trouble had the option of becoming employees of the States of Guernsey, with the guarantee of regular wages for their labour force.

On Jersey, with its more varied output and a better supply of basic foodstuffs, circumstances were not quite so desperate. Even so, hardship was soon manifest.

The town is, of course, very dull. The shops, which in any case are nearly empty, are only allowed to open from 10 to 12.30 and from 2 to 4.30, and many are closed altogether for two or three days in the week. Many shop windows are boarded up. As to the shops' contents, most things that we used to take for granted are unobtainable. Imagine a life steadily becoming devoid of such things as needles, pins, tape, elastic, wool and cotton; kitchen utensils of every kind; all facilities for cleaning anything; tinned foods; beer and spirits; tapioca, rice sago, pearl barley and the like; pepper, salt, mustard and all other condiments and sauces; coffee, cocoa, chocolate and sweets of all kinds.

By January 1941:

The weekly butter ration is down to two ounces and tea to one ounce. There are no cooking fats to be had. The meat ration, including offal, is 12 oz a week; bacon is unobtainable; eggs pure gold; while chickens and rabbits still exist in small numbers for millionaires only. There is no jam or marmalade. Baking powder is almost finished. As yet there is no rationing of bread, but the quality is very poor and white flour is a thing of the past.[4]

Fred Hockey an escapee from Guernsey, told a reporter from the *Daily Herald* that coal stocks were low and that no coal was being sent in. 'My mother used to go to the gasworks,' recalls Doreen Hills. 'She would get a bucket of tar for sixpence and bring it home to pour over the wood or sawdust or whatever we had. Of course, that made a terrible mess of the grate.'[5] In the months leading up to winter, trees were felled at an alarming rate.

For ordinary families such as Daphne Breton's, adaptation to a more modest lifestyle took curious turns.

I remember eating all sorts of funny things, carrot pudding, drinking blackberry leaf tea. I used to go and get it in St Peter Port on the horse bus. It ran from the Vale to town and it used to be one step at a time, and you would get there eventually, but the poor horse was hungry as well, and he used to cart a lot of people.[6]

Sark's inhabitants made their own tobacco using 'vine leaves, dried clover heads, rose leaves and blackberry leaves . . . Some of us used green pea pods for tea. Coffee was made of a mixture of barley, dried with sugar beet and parsnip, all grated or ground up together.'[7]

Home-produced tobacco could be the equal of any commercial brand, claims Reg Langlois.

When Grandpa cultivated the tobacco crop, he bundled the giant leaves together and hung them up in the rafters around the farm buildings to dry. He then placed them in a homemade press which was only about eighteen inches long and five inches wide. It had a lump of wood on the top of it to squeeze the juice out of the leaves. I can just see grandpa now tightening the screw-down bolts every day with loving care. Lighter fuel was non-existent and matches were hard to find so you either had to do without or think up means of igniting your home-grown cigarettes or pipes. Grandpa had a friend in the motor trade who came up with the idea of using a four-cylinder impulse magneto which, by joining all the leads, produced a longer spark that worked well. Grandpa used a tin with a hole in the lid with a piece of window sash cord through it as a wick. The oil in the tin came from engine oil, fish oil and chicken fat and sometimes all three. I shall never forget the horrible smells of the burning oil and of grandpa's pipe.[8]

'The thing we missed most was bread,' recalls Grace Buttery, 'we simply didn't have enough of it.' Farm workers in Jersey got a little bit extra along with the ultimate luxury, a pint of full-cream milk a day. There was a great shortage of salt.

We used to get sea water and used half sea water and half plain. In the months of April and May we could get crabs, if you were fairly active you could go and catch crabs at low tide. . . . A Jersey crab is a spider crab, it's much bigger than the English one. And you could get a sack full if you were clever. I sometimes had half a dozen walking around my kitchen floor while I was sitting outside boiling a large can of water to cook them in. Little did they know what was coming to them![9]

Culinary ingenuity was suddenly all the rage. Louise Board remembers her carrageen moss pudding, made from a seaweed which had to be dried and then crumbled into a powder.

You put this into a saucepan with milk and it makes something like blancmange. Very nourishing – it has a wide range of nutrients but I started taking it because I had lost the lining of my stomach and this carrageen moss with milk restored it for me.[10]

Produce that would have been discarded before the war acquired a value, even if it was an effort to eat the resulting dishes. A few kitchen creations became quite popular. Margaret Le Cras enjoyed her grandmother's potato-peel cake so much that she continued to eat it even after the war.

In Guernsey, there was even a restaurant, the Home From Home, that was famous for its ersatz dishes. The proprietor, Frank Stroobant, created a varied menu.

His fish cakes made from minced limpets and parsnips were much in demand as were his swede rissoles. Raspberries later came on the menu, doused with a so-called 'cream' which was at first made with a combination of ice-cream powder, powdered milk and soya bean flour. The taste of the 'cream' improved later when it had only one ingredient – powdered milk in a thick consistency.

Chips were fried in linseed oil but the fumes were so unpleasant in the kitchen and even penetrated the café that some absorbent was essential. At first onions served quite well and also improved the flavour. But as he had soon to economise on the onions he floated small pieces of wood in the oil as smell absorbers.[11]

In the early days of the occupation there were abundant supplies of fish.

Mackerel used to come in shoals and shoals. The Germans used to be on the beaches alongside the civilians catching fish; and then every so often, the Germans would get carried away and throw a hand grenade into the water, and then it became white with fish and you were all in there, baskets full of the stuff which was rather lovely.[12]

But it was not long before even the fish became scarce. Most of the beaches were mined (which cut back on the collection of crabs and other shellfish) while the haul from the professional fishermen was intercepted by the military.

With daily gas and electricity cuts, often of several hours' duration, the old practice of using a haybox to generate heat for cooking came back into fashion. Lighting was more of a problem, remembers Bob Le Sueur.

We had a medicine bottle containing diesel oil . . . with a bootlace for a wick and of course if you walked too quickly across the room it went out and my father would go berserk because we were down to our last box of matches.[13]

Substitute became the commonest word in the English language.

Coffee made from acorns, tea made from carrots and sugar-beet; milk puddings from potato-flour, vegetable marrow and carrageen moss . . . French cycle tyres made of some compound which cracked after a month's usage. Boots and shoes made with wooden soles; combs were wooden too. Toothpaste and soap were made from substitute chemicals. Oh! that French soap! We had one tablet each, about every three months.[14]

The shortage of petrol kept any cars still in private hands off the roads. Horse and hand-drawn carts reappeared, but for simply getting about the bicycle became the chief means of transport, if not always the most comfortable. It took a particular engineering talent to solve the problem of threadbare tyres.

I can remember my father putting new tyres on my bicycle. They were made of rubber hosepipe which he wrapped around the wheels, threading a length of thick wire through the hose and tightening it with a pair of pliers to keep the tyres on. When I was on my bicycle I could count the number of times the wheel turned because, each time, there was a small bump where there was a join in the hose.[15]

The scarcity of new clothes hit hardest at families with fast-growing young children, such as Kate Le Cheminant. Driven by necessity, their mothers found ingenious ways of making do.

There was no rubber for soles and heels on shoes so they had wooden soles and heels with steel tips and 'horseshoes' on the heels. I liked these because you could pretend to be a German soldier, they made such a noise, but they made walking very tiring. A pair of sandals I grew out of; my mother cut off the toe-piece to let my toes stick out and sewed small pieces of coloured wool in the holes. She did the same for sandals of my friends so we went into our 'Red Indian' phase then and all padded about in our 'deer-hide' moccasins pretending to be Hiawatha and so on.

When my skirts could no longer be lengthened my mother attached them to a broad band of green baize cut from the card table. With a pullover pulled well down, the baize did not show. It was nice and warm in winter too.[16]

In Jersey, Sidney Farnworth, a retired clogger, was re-employed by a shoe factory. Fortunately he had kept his tools and had lost none of his old skills. The same business offered a 'cannibalising' service whereby soles from old pairs of shoes were fitted to still waterproof uppers.

Deprivation had an inevitable impact on public health. With fuel shortages hot water was a precious commodity.

Most of the housewives devoted what fuel they had to cooking, rather than to bathing their kids, which would have been a luxury. So the children by and large were pretty dirty . . . and that led to all sorts of outbreaks of minor ailments like threadworms and scabies, this sort of thing that you wouldn't normally get in a modern society.[17]

A widespread outbreak of diphtheria in Jersey was a death threat to the very young.

The only treatment in those days was an anti-serum, something that you discovered if you bled healthy young people who had recovered from diphtheria. Their blood would then contain a powerful anti-toxin which you could then inject into a new patient, and if you were lucky it could kill it. That was the only cure that was available. Much more important than that was preventative treatment; this is where Overdale came in. Overdale was established by the Medical Officer of Health, Dr McKinstry, as an isolation unit, so the moment he diagnosed the patient with diphtheria or scarlet fever, they'd be shipped up to Overdale. Then with very strict barrier nursing, you could at least prevent it from spreading around the population. That was much more important than any treatment that we could offer.[18]

By all accounts, McKinstry was a remarkable character. Soon to take a leading role in helping fugitives from German summary justice, he was also a doughty fighter for good health. His one-man campaign against the slaughter of dairy cows to maintain the meat ration ensured that children up to the age of sixteen had a daily milk allocation.

Even with strict rationing, it was soon clear that there was simply not enough in the way of basic products to support the islanders and the ever-expanding occupying force. The only other possible source of supplies was German-controlled France. A joint purchasing commission, known as the Essential Commodities Committee and based in Granville, was run by Raymond Falla for Guernsey and Jean Jouault for Jersey. The initial finance for the operation was raised from the sale of cars. The owners were credited with the purchase price, which was then handed over to the purchasing commission in Occupation Reichsmarks.

Because Germany would not allow the Island Treasury to have a banking account in France, occupation marks had to be moved in tea chests, then carried by barge between Jersey and Granville, where they were stored in large cupboards.

Most of the buying was in Normandy, but on occasion the commission, escorted by two German officers, ventured as far as Nantes and Paris. The results were modest but the scheme did at least ensure regular, if small, supplies of coal, coke and diesel oil and other essentials such as medical goods and sulphate of aluminium to ensure clean water.

Bartering took over from the usual commercial transactions. 'Which of us will ever forget it,' asked Arthur Kent rhetorically.

Dealings in kind were as common as monetary transactions. To obtain some wheat you would exchange some soap, a baby-carriage or perhaps a gramophone. A goat for a bicycle; a dozen eggs for a pair of shoes; salt for a tennis-racket or perhaps a fowl for a couple of packets of razor-blades! Of course there were hundreds of 'swops' of shoes, boots and clothing for similar articles of a different size. Each evening the local newspaper ran an 'exchange column' which, besides being the medium for innumerable exchanges, was always a source of fun owing to the fantastic array of barter goods on offer.[19]

For those with money in the bank or under the bed – there were quite a few – the black market could provide just about anything, at a price. Troops returning from leave rarely passed up the chance to collect a few extras that could be sold on. Bending the rules provided other entrepreneurial opportunities.

A lance-corporal who drove a lorry with newly arriving rations was befriended by a young Guernsey constable. As the lorry was very old and not well suited to the transportation of delicate goods, there were many 'damaged in transit' goods, which were just the ones we needed for cooking![20]

Rumours of the idle rich living off what fat there was became ever more grotesque. Even the Bailiff was not immune. One popular story was of the turkey or goose sent over from France for his family Christmas dinner.

Somebody knew a man who had actually seen the bird being put on to a boat in St Malo (or was it in Granville?). Clearly labelled, of course. Somebody else had spoken to another man who had seen the bird during the voyage and yet another had watched it being brought ashore in St Helier. The tale came to its climax, with dramatic accounts of the bird's progress across the island, all the way to the Bailiff's residence.[21]

More reliable were the tales of families who were skilled at playing the system to augment their home comforts. Bob Grant's father 'never knew when the milk inspectors would come to the farm to see the cows milked'.

They were checking to know if all the milk was being sent to the dairy. A very well known farmer from Torteval asked dad if he could buy a cow for slaughter but the day the animal went the milk inspectors arrived and wanted to know where the missing animal had gone. So we phoned Mr Sarre. He said don't worry, just tell them that I bought it and you won't hear another word. He said 'I supply some States members and others in the Police with meat'. We never heard another word about it. I must be honest, we did have a nice joint out of it ourselves.[22]

Under-reporting by the farmers was standard practice. After potatoes were gathered or corn harvested there was always a quantity set aside for sale or for family consumption, though keeping valuable produce away from prying eyes was a challenge to ingenuity. Jeanne Michel had a neat way of hiding corn.

So I had a mattress and a feather bed on top, so I took the cover from the mattress – it was white cotton, nice and strong as well, and then we put the corn in it and spread it all along the under-mattress, you know, and we put the feather bed on top again, so we were sleeping on the corn all the time.[23]

With deprivation went boredom. In the 'winter of our discontent' when, unusually, Jersey was snow-covered, Horace Wyatt suffered a severe bout of depression.

The discomforts of our position are steadily piling up. All gas fires in sitting rooms, bedrooms and passages have been disconnected. Also all gas-fed water heating and circulating apparatus. Thus gas can only be used for cooking and the hours at which any supply, even for this purpose, is available are strictly limited; one result being that those who have depended on gas for lighting are left in darkness early in the evening. Candles are at a premium and only a few people have any left.[24]

In the absence of commercial entertainment, amateur drama and music societies came into their own, although anything scripted had to be approved by the censor. Surprisingly, the lyrics of an operetta, *The Paladins*, written by Horace Wyatt and presented at the Jersey Opera House, escaped the blue pencil. The Ruritanian setting was but a thin disguise for numbers like 'Faithful and Free', which extolled the virtues of a friendlier land just across the water.

Myrtle Tabel has happy memories of a choir which toured the country churches by horse and cart.

My parents, being Salvationists, joined in these outings with enthusiasm and they were certainly enjoyed by the children. I remember we always had a 'picnic' after the service.[25]

When all else failed:

We had half a church candle, a nice thick one, and for an hour each evening we burned this to do whatever needed light. After that we sat in the dark, wrapped in eiderdowns and blankets playing word games – the blankets were the warm to wrap ourselves in for bed-time.[26]

The one form of intellectual stimulation favoured by the occupiers was almost entirely rejected. Nobody wanted to learn German. Pity those islanders who could already speak German and who were charged with passing on their knowledge to the younger generation.

I'm afraid the poor man who was teaching us was given a pretty rough time, and I really felt sorry for him afterwards. Eventually he gave up, so that was that, although a German officer gave me a little German-English dictionary with my name on it. But I didn't learn much German.[27]

It was the same for Brian Le Conte, though he did manage to count up to twenty in German and there was one phrase he learned by rote: '*Nicht furst stein*', We don't understand.[28]

It was a tiny act of defiance, barely worthy of the name. But it signified an underlying determination to remain a community apart. Before long there was further evidence, for those who cared to see it, that any expectations of the Channel Islands becoming a little Germany were liable to be disappointed.

7

CHURCHILL'S FIASCO

Churchill's pledge on behalf of the British people never to surrender was thankfully not put to the supreme test. But there can be no doubt that he meant what he said. Seventy years on, we may be permitted to question unanimous enthusiasm for the ultimate sacrifice. But at the time, with the patriotic fanfare drowning out the whispers of fear and despair, it was all too easy to assume a country united as one in its resolve to defy the usurper.

Which is why Churchill found it hard to understand what the Channel Islanders were up to. Where was their determination to resist? Why were there no reports of Germans dead in the streets? The effect of demilitarisation – the islands were denuded of effective weaponry – was conveniently forgotten. In Churchill's opinion, the only one that really counted in London, the fighting spirit in Jersey and Guernsey required a kick start.

Two days after the surrender, on 2 July 1940, the War Cabinet approved what the prime minister described as a 'cutting-out expedition' to the Channel Islands, to be carried out by one of the newly formed Commando groups of the Combined Operation Executive (COE).[1] Later that day, Churchill gave his chief of staff, General 'Pug'

Ismay, a firmer idea of what he had in mind. Intelligence was needed on the strength of the occupying force, after which troops would be sent in at night to 'kill or capture the invaders'. What if the Germans counter-attacked from their bases on the French coast? No problem. 'The only possible reinforcements which could reach the enemy during the fighting would be by aircraft carriers, [a sitting target] for the Air Force fighting machines.'

In nominating the Commandos as liberators, Churchill was making the false assumption, common to less successful military and political leaders, that he had only to say what he wanted to be done for it to be done. Along with the Special Operations Executive (SOE), the Commandos were a recent creation, barely a fortnight into recruitment. Whereas the SOE was to engage in espionage and sabotage behind enemy lines, the Commandos were to be trained for direct action, starting with raids on the enemy-held French coast.

They were supposed to be ready for anything. But in July 1940, as John Durnford-Slater of No. 3 Group prepared for the first Commando operation against the enemy, they were ready for nothing. 'Later,' wrote Durnford-Slater, 'the very word Commando was to become synonymous with perfectly trained, tough, hard-fighting and skilled specialists. You don't achieve that overnight.'[2]

That much was soon to become clear. Three days after Churchill's minute to Ismay, twenty-year-old Second Lieutenant Hubert Nicolle, a Guernseyman serving with the Hampshire Regiment, was summoned to London for a meeting at the Admiralty. There he was greeted by Major Warren of the Royal Marines and Colonel Cantau, a fellow Guernseyman and the son-in-law of the Dame of Sark. Nicolle was asked if he would undertake a dangerous mission. He was to be taken inshore by submarine close to a landing spot of his own choosing. For the last stretch he would, literally, be paddling his own canoe. Two days were allotted to his assignment – to gather information on the strength of the German forces and defences in Guernsey – after which the submarine would return at night to pick him up. If caught there was nothing anyone could do to help him. He would almost certainly be put on trial as a spy and shot.

Though unprepared for such a mission, apart from ordinary military training, Nicolle readily volunteered. But he must have had a few doubts when he found that such was the efficiency of his back-up that no one had thought to have a canoe ready and waiting for him. A messenger was sent off to buy one at Gamages, a well-known department store, which was evidently better equipped than the Navy. He came back with a long brown-paper parcel for Nicolle to take with him on the train to Plymouth. It was not until he was on board the submarine that the canoe was unwrapped and he discovered the first flaw in an ill-conceived plan: the assembled canoe was too big to go through the submarine hatch. At this late stage in the game, hinges had to be fitted to the struts so that the canoe could be partly folded.[3] And so was fixed the pattern of events for the next ten days, a succession of on-the-spot improvisations leading inevitably to humiliating failure.

It was a moonlit, cloudless night when Guernsey was sighted, perfect weather for paddling ashore but less good for a submarine commander trying to keep his surfaced vessel out of sight. There was another problem. Nicolle was supposed to paddle in alone, then hide the canoe so that it was easily recoverable for the return trip. But where could he hide what was, after all, a bulky craft, and at what risk of it being discovered by the Germans? For the submarine to stay at a safe distance and for the canoe to be protected it made sense for Nicolle to be accompanied by the submarine's navigational officer, who would act as ferryman.

It was close to midnight when they set off. With two miles to paddle the weather, so good up to now, turned nasty, so that it was a wet and exhausted spy who waded ashore at Le Jaonnet, a tiny bay on the south coast, and scrambled up the cliffs by a route he had known as a boy. He spent the rest of the night hiding in the bushes.

At daylight he set off on his mission by making contact with friends and family, presumably unaware of the danger he was putting them in. His first call was a dairy farm belonging to his friend Tom Mansell, who was out delivering milk. Borrowing Mansell's bicycle, Nicolle rode off to his parents' home in St Peter Port. That was where Mansell found him when he called by with the milk.

I had a bit of a shock when I saw him. Anyway, he came and helped me put the cattle near the airport and took note of what was happening there. At that time there were a few German gun emplacements and a few Messerschmitt fighter planes and he took note of all that.[4]

Other information came via Nicolle's father Emile, who was Secretary to Guernsey's Controlling Committee, and from a neighbour who, as a supplier to the German troops, knew their strength and location. As a bonus, young Nicolle's uncle, an assistant harbour-master, provided shipping movements. Well satisfied with his haul of information, Nicolle returned to Le Jaonnet for the pick up. It was his third night on the island.

The canoe arrived more or less on time but, much to Nicolle's surprise, it had three occupants. Along with the submarine's navigation officer came second lieutenants Philip Martel and Desmond Mulholland, the advance party for the Commando raid planned for two days ahead. Nicolle might reasonably have questioned a plan that allowed him just a few minutes to hand on essential knowledge. But it was characteristic of the way the entire operation was mounted. The two latest arrivals were told that the 469 Germans on the island were mostly in or around St Peter Port and that there were machine-gun posts all along the coast.

Once Nicolle was back on the mainland, his father went to tell Sherwill about his son's unexpected appearance on the island. Sherwill was left to put his own, as it happened naïve, interpretation on the visit. As he later recorded:

The British Government, no doubt anxious to learn how we in Guernsey were getting on, sent in a young officer in plain clothes to find out. He came and stayed with his parents and left again . . . The news worried me greatly. . . . Was this the first of a series of such visits and, if it was, how would the matter end. To say that I was distressed as to the possibilities is to put it mildly. I hoped, however, that the matter was at an end.[5]

He was to be disappointed. Operation Ambassador was already underway.

The plan was for a Commando raiding force, 140 strong, to land on Guernsey on the night of 12/13 July, having transferred from two destroyers to air-sea rescue launches for the last leg to the beaches. There were to be three landings, with one group making for the airport, another to attack a machine-gun post and German billets at Telegraph Bay while the third, led by Durnford-Slater, created a diversion for the assault on the airfield. Less than two hours were allocated to the entire job including the pick-up, timed for 2.30 a.m.

The task for Martel and Mulholland was to signal the approaching launches if it was safe to come in. As it happened, they were wasting their time. Martel explained:

The night of the landing came and Desmond Mulholland and I took up positions on two of the beaches. I was sitting on a large rock and shining my torch out to sea. But they didn't come. At one point an aircraft flew overhead. I have since learned that it was an RAF plane which was supposed to drown the noise of the landings. The Germans fired at it and this seemed to come from somewhere quite close at the top of the cliff. It certainly put the wind up us.[6]

What the two officers had no way of knowing was that bad weather had forced a forty-eight-hour postponement. When the operation did get under way, one disaster followed another. One group missed Guernsey altogether, landing instead on Sark. Faulty compasses were blamed. The second party almost foundered, then recovered only to miss the landing beach. There was nothing for it but to return to the destroyer.

The only landing was made by Durnford-Slater and his men, and it was touch and go. About a hundred yards from the beach 'the launches, simultaneously and side by side, hit bottom'. As they had not been designed as landing craft, they drew several feet of water. Moreover, it was still high tide. Instead of smooth sand, the drop-off was onto jagged boulders. 'I jumped in, armpit-deep. A wave hit me on the back of the neck and caused me to trip over a rock. All around me officers and men were scrambling for balance, falling, coming up and coughing salt water.'[7]

Weighed down by sodden battledress the bedraggled warriors made for the long flight of steps leading to the cliff top, a 250-foot climb.

In my eagerness I went up too fast. By the time I reached the top I was absolutely done, but Knight was even worse, gasping for breath like an untrained miler at the tape. I was exhausted myself, and my sodden battledress seemed to weigh a ton. My legs were leaden, my lungs bursting. I could hear the squeak and squelch of wet boots as the rest of the troop followed us up from the beach. Fortunately the night was warm.[8]

As they moved forward, the dogs in nearby houses set up a chorus of barking. It seemed incredible that the Germans were ignoring the warning signal, incredible that is until Durnford-Slater led the assault on a barracks and machine-gun post and found them bereft of the enemy. There was, as he put it ruefully, 'no one at home'.

Exhausted and frustrated, the Commandos made their way back to the beach, where further calamities were in store for them. Durnford-Slater was last down from the cliff top.

Near the bottom I accelerated and suddenly realised that my feet had lost the rhythm of the steps. I tripped and tumbled the rest of the way, head over heels. I had been carrying my cocked revolver at the ready. During the fall it went off, seeming tremendously loud and echoing against the cliffs. This, at last, brought the Germans to life. Almost at once there was a line of tracer machine-gun fire from the top of the cliff on the other side of our cove. The tracers were going out to sea, towards the spot where I thought our launches must be awaiting us.[9]

They were, but the sea was too rough for them to get in close. Instead a single dinghy, able to carry only two or three men with their weapons, began a protracted shuttle which ended when the fragile craft smashed against the rocks and one trooper was lost, presumed drowned.

Those still on the beach were told to swim for it, at which point Durnford-Slater found that three of his group were non-swimmers. They were left behind with a promise of an attempted rescue the following night. It was not to be. The senior officers who had bungled the operation decided not to risk any further embarrassments. As Durnford-Slater concluded:

> The raid was, of course, a ridiculous, almost a comic failure. We had captured no prisoners. We had done no serious damage. We had caused no casualties to the enemy. Even the roll of barbed wire for [a] road block had proved too heavy to lift up the steep steps. There had been no machine-gun nest and, to all practical purposes, no barracks. We had cut through three telegraph cables. A youth in his teens could have done the same.[10]

Churchill, forgetting his own part in the drama, called it a 'silly fiasco'.

There were now six British soldiers stranded on Guernsey – Martel and Mulholland, the three Commando non-swimmers and the trooper thrown out of the launch, who had managed to scramble ashore. For the moment they were reasonably safe because the Germans had no idea what had happened beyond a certain amount of night-time disturbance. When on the morning of 15 July a stone barricade was discovered on the Jerbourg peninsula, the first assumption was of local subversion. Sherwill was told to investigate.

> I got into touch with the Police Inspector who went to the spot. Down in Petit Port Bay there were found rifles, machine guns, steel helmets, uniforms and equipment and it became clear that a British landing party had been at work. It was ascertained later that some of them had been seen and, for some obscure reason, they had cut the telephone wires of, I think it was, nineteen subscribers. The whole of the facts were reported to the German

Commandant who directed that the Police and Special Constables should commence a search the following morning at dawn for members remaining ashore of the raiding party.[11]

It was not long before the four Commandos were found and taken prisoner. With better knowledge of the lie of the land, Martel and Mulholland remained at large.

> We found an empty house in St. Martins which my father owned and after that we slept in a barn. Then we went on to St. Sampsons to the Calderol, another unoccupied house. But we knew that this couldn't go on.[12]

Their second hideaway happened to belong to the Dame of Sark's daughter, who was with her soldier husband in England. News of the squatters soon reached the Dame, who recalled:

> I took some tinned supplies and went across to Guernsey on the pretext of being in charge of my daughter's property. The young men were in a desperate plight. Their last remaining hope was that I might be able to arrange for a fishing boat to come from Sark and get them back to England. It was a miserable business having to explain that this proposition had no chance of success because our fishing boats were strictly guarded by the Germans and, apart from that, there was no possibility of getting sufficient petrol for such a venture.[13]

The two fugitives were urged to give themselves up, but were naturally reluctant to risk the firing squad. With no chance of getting food without exposing themselves to unfriendly attention, they turned to their families. Martel went to his sister, Mulholland to his mother.

Their move was no more than a postponement of the inevitable. With no means of escape they were simply putting those closest to them in mortal danger. Somehow word got to Sherwill (his own account of his involvement has been lost but another version has Martel and

Mulholland turning up at his back door[14]) who saw only one solution. The young officers were kitted out with uniforms of the Guernsey Militia doctored to pass as British battle dress. So it was that when they surrendered it was as soldiers entitled to be treated as prisoners of war, not as spies asking to be shot. Incredibly, their story was accepted. They and those who had harboured them were sent off to France, the two women being allowed to return to Guernsey in January 1941.

Sherwill was relieved but angry. He was only too well aware that 'the possible discovery by the Germans that, whilst appearing to be cooperating with them, I was aiding espionage was likely to be followed by the Controlling Committee and me being swept away and by the full rigour of direct military government being imposed'.[15]

And for what? Operation Ambassador had achieved absolutely nothing of any benefit to Guernsey or to the British war effort. Quite the opposite, in fact. The Germans had been made aware of the weaknesses in their defences and were determined not to be caught out a second time. As for the islanders, what little they knew of the Commando raid suggested that liberation was a long way off. It was a depressing thought.

In an effort to restore German confidence in his good intentions, Sherwill proposed writing to the Home Office, pleading on behalf of 'many prominent people here' for attacks on the demilitarised island to cease. A draft of the letter was handed to the Kommandant for forwarding to London but, as Sherwill might have anticipated, the Germans were not inclined to request British clemency. Sherwill's offer was rejected.

Even if the letter had been sent, it is unlikely that it would have made an impact. Churchill was disinclined to take note of special pleading, not while there was a war to win. While recognising that sending in the Commandos may have been an over-hasty step, he was keen 'to obtain secretly the best possible information about the German forces . . . to establish intimate contacts with local people and to plant agents'.[16] In the back of his mind was the early prospect of another military adventure.

The challenge was taken up by the Combined Operations Executive, now responsible for amphibious operations against the enemy coast.

Unaware that Martel and Mulholland had surrendered, the director of COE, Sir Roger Keyes, reasonably concluded that the quickest way of gaining intelligence was to rescue the two officers. With this objective, on 3 August Sergeant Stanley Ferbrache was landed at Le Jaonnet Bay. Soon finding that he was too late to help Martel and Mulholland, he gathered what intelligence he could and, after one failed pick-up, returned safely to Plymouth.

The next move was not so smart. Hubert Nicolle was asked if he was prepared once more to risk his own life and the lives of his family. He agreed. On 4 September, he was landed by motor torpedo boat at Petit Port along with James Symes, a fellow officer and Guernseyman with the Hampshire Regiment. A third member of their party who was supposed to go on to Jersey instead returned to Portland when it was realised that a dawn approach would make a landing too hazardous.

Having found refuge, Nicolle with his uncle Frank Nicolle, the assistant harbour-master and Symes with the father of his girlfriend, Mary Bird, they spent three days gathering what knowledge they could of the occupation and its impact on the islanders. Then it was back to Petit Port for a night-time rendezvous with their motor torpedo-boat. It wasn't there. Bad weather had held it back. It was the same the next night and the one after that. They were stuck. The only option likely to serve the purpose of COE was to send in yet another agent. This time it was Captain John Parker, a regular soldier who spent his childhood in Guernsey. The mission was for him to get ashore under cover of darkness, contact Symes and Nicolle the following day and then, on the third night, for the three of them to escape the island. If only.

He arrived in an MTB, which came in for the last five miles on electric motors to cut out noise. It was a black night, with a new moon, when he landed near Corbière. He proceeded to try and work his way up the cliff by crawling forward on his elbows in the approved manner; but unfortunately the people who write training manuals had not reckoned on gorse. His arms bleeding, Parker had to proceed on foot, to the alarming sound of the popping gorse pods. He trod as lightly as he could – 'like a ballet dancer' as he put it afterwards – and managed to reach the top of the cliff before, in the groping darkness, he plunged with an appalling clatter into a trench which had an ammunition box at the bottom of it. He had tip-toed into a German A.A. gun battery.[17]

Parker was detained and sent off to Cherbourg for a lengthy interrogation. His only luck was to have arrived in uniform. He could thus argue convincingly that he was not a spy, though it was hard for his captors to imagine what else he could have been. The only other possibility was that he had come to join other servicemen already on the island. The occupiers had yet to find out about Nicolle and Symes, and Parker did not enlighten them, but it was only a matter of time before an attentive German picked up on the gossip. Too many people were in on the secret. Nicolle's dairyman friend, Tom Mansell, blamed Nicolle's fiancée ('That's how it all got around and she was interned as well. But it was her that gave us all away'[18]). Perhaps. It is equally likely that others close to the two men found a need to share their worries and seek moral support.

Having failed to shake Parker, there was talk in the German command of mounting a house-to-house search of the island for invaders assumed to be still at large. But this costly and time-consuming strategy offered no guarantee of success and could merely serve to strengthen civilian resistance. Von Schmettow favoured a more subtle approach. The strategy proposed by the commander in chief was for an amnesty: any British soldiers who gave themselves up would be treated as prisoners of war. Major Bandelow, the Guernsey commandant, was told to try out the idea on Sherwill, whose active co-operation was essential to the plan. Bandelow, in turn, handed on responsibility to his adjutant who, as Sherwill recorded, was not the most tactful of negotiators.

On the Sunday I attended at the appointed time to be told by the adjutant that the Kommandant had been out all night visiting picquets [guard posts] and was then asleep. He apologised and said the Kommandant would make another appointment. He explained what the Kommandant had in mind and said that if members of the British Armed Forces gave themselves up by the day to be appointed, they would be treated as prisoners of war and nobody who had harboured them would be punished. He went on to say that if, however, members of the Armed Forces were discovered later, the Germans would select twenty prominent citizens and shoot them.

I said: 'And one of those will be me.' He replied: 'Oh no, Mr Sherwill.' I said: 'If not, why not. I tell you that if you do this awful thing, the British will never forgive you.' He then said: 'Let us talk of more pleasant things. Have a cigarette.' I had a cigarette and we talked for a few moments of more pleasant things.[19]

It must have been a heart-stopping moment for Sherwill. He was well informed on Nicolle and Symes, though he had made clear to Nicolle's father that he could not be involved.

I told him – he already realised it – that aiding espionage in wartime was a highly dangerous occupation, that by reason of extraordinary luck, I had got away with it in the case of Mulholland and Martel but that I had to remember that, as head of the Controlling Committee, my first duty lay to that Committee and to the people of Guernsey. The possible discovery by the Germans that, whilst appearing to be cooperating with them, I was aiding espionage was likely to be followed by the Committee and me being swept away and by the full rigour of direct military government being imposed. In the circumstances, whilst I fully understood that he felt compelled to shelter his son, I must refrain from any part of it.[20]

But after the meeting with Bandelow's deputy it dawned on Sherwill that the mere fact of his knowing about Nicolle and Symes would make him culpable in German eyes. Two days later he was summoned to Bandelow's office.

He was his usual cheery self and uttered not one word about shooting anyone. He told me that he felt pretty sure that some soldiers had remained behind when the German occupation began or had entered the island since. We must clear the matter up. He wished to arrange a date with me by which all such personnel must surrender. If they did, they would be treated as prisoners of war and no one who had harboured or helped them would be punished. If any did not and were subsequently discovered, they and those who had helped them would have to take the consequences. After all, there was a war going on.[21]

The offer was good enough for Sherwill, who recognised the vital significance of the promise not to bring any spying charges. Yet the Germans must have known that anyone caught in the amnesty net had been engaged in spying. Why then were the commander-in-chief and his opposite number, Colonel Schumacher, the Feldkommandant, so generously inclined? Probably because they wanted the whole operation to be low key. The detention of a few British servicemen who happened to be stranded on the island could be passed off as a routine matter, barely worthy of the attention of higher authority. To admit to finding spies active on German-controlled territory was altogether a more serious affair, inviting the attention of the men in leather coats whose none-too-gentle methods of investigation could lead to unfortunate repercussions for senior officers who were seen to be neglectful.

Sherwill can be forgiven for not thinking this through. His only immediate concern was for the amnesty offer to be taken up by both sides without delay. Having relayed an assurance to Nicolle and Symes that the German word of honour could be trusted, he drafted an exchange of letters with Bandelow for publication in the *Guernsey Evening Press* for 12 October. Recognising his own vulnerability, he was keen to emphasise his role as a supposedly independent arbitrator.

Having noted the 'pleasant relations which have hitherto existed between the Army of occupation and the population' and the agreement to set a time limit for the surrender of 'any personnel of the British Armed Forces in hiding in this island' adding cautiously 'if such there be', Sherwill continued:

> This, Herr Commandant, is a generous gesture on your part. . . .
> It gives me ground for confidence that, at a period when the
> nations to which we respectively belong are locked in a combat,
> the consequences of which will be momentous to Europe and the
> whole world, it is possible – though only in the Channel Islands
> – for a German officer and a British official to enter into friendly
> correspondence, to engage in full and frank discussions and to
> exchange courtesies.

His sentiments were, as he later admitted, 'a bit too smarmy'. They certainly caused consternation at home and in London but Sherwill felt that the end justified the overkill, the more so when he managed to have the surrender date delayed from 19 to 21 October, allowing time for two uniforms to be rifled from a store of Alderney battledress in one of the harbour sheds. On the evening of the twenty-first Nicolle and Symes presented themselves at their nearest police station and were taken into custody.

And there it might have ended had not von Schmettow and Schumacher felt duty bound to report on events to their superiors in France. The bureaucratic wing of the Wehrmacht was unhappy with an arrangement that seemed to condone spying, and an investigation was mounted, with counter-intelligence officers arriving from France to lead the hunt. While Nicolle and Symes were put under interrogation, thirteen of their friends and family were rounded up and questioned and their stories examined for inconsistencies, of which there were many. Most damaging of all, for everyone concerned, was the revelation that Nicolle was on his second visit to a hostile shore.

It was not long before Sherwill was under investigation. He tried to brave it out but it did not take a skilled detective to conclude that he must have had prior knowledge of the Nicolle and Symes affair and that he had connived in their protection. He and others implicated in the plot were dispatched to France while Nicolle and Symes, facing a court martial, were sentenced to death.

A much-chastened Sherwill was lodged in the Cherche Midi Prison in Paris. It was November and the start of an exceptionally cold winter.

I was pushed into Cell No. 38 on the top floor. It was pitch dark and I had to feel around to find my bearings. In doing so I fell over a slop-pail. . . . When stoves were lighted – in the corridors – life was slightly more bearable but never comfortable. . . . The cell doors were tight fitting and the only heat came in through the trap over each door which, while guards were on duty, was required to be kept closed. I have spent hundreds of hours standing on my stool, itself standing on my table, with my head touching the ceiling so as to get the benefit of the rather warmer air in the upper half of the cell.[22]

Sherwill and the other Guernsey prisoners could see no end to their misery. All they could look forward to was thin gruel, straw mattresses as hard as the boards on which they rested, loneliness and boredom. For one of them the strain was too much. Just before Christmas Day James Symes' father was found dead in his cell. He had slashed his wrists.

Six days later, on 29 December 1940, the Guernsey contingent was told they were to be released and that Nicolle and Symes would, after all, be treated as prisoners of war. Honour and expediency motivated this act of clemency. That an amnesty had been offered and accepted and its terms followed scrupulously by the islanders put von Schmettow and his staff in the position of having to argue against the ruling of the military court. Then again, as seen from Berlin at a time when there were still hopes of Britain suing for peace on German terms, there was propaganda value in acting compassionately. The official statement posted in Guernsey spoke of the conclusive guilt of the two spies and of those who had aided them but announced that despite 'aggravating circumstances' the German authorities had decided to be merciful. Sherwill, who was told he could no longer hold any public office, marked his return to private life with a New Year's party.

> My wife and I got out her last bottle of wine and we broke into tiny fragments (it was impossible to cut it) a chunk of stale dry Cherche Midi rye bread I had brought home to show what I had been enduring. We telephoned our nearest friends and bade them come to the feast, which they did.[23]

John Leale was his successor as President of the Controlling Committee.

The dramatic events in Guernsey were barely acknowledged in London, where plans for a major attack on the Channel Islands, known as Operation Tomato ('to destroy or make prisoner all the enemy in the Channel Islands'), had long since been relegated to the bottom of the pending file. The absence of reliable intelligence was one factor but another was the shortage of guns, an indication of Britain's precarious war footing. In late September, Churchill told Sir Roger Keyes, Chief of the Combined Operations Executive, 'Hold up the project for the present.' The last three words were critical. The Channel Islands were still very much part of the war zone.

8

PROPAGANDA WAR

It has been said that in war, truth is the first casualty.[1] This was certainly true of the Channel Islands under German occupation, with both sides spinning the news on thinly disguised propaganda. In the early days, the Germans had the best of it. The paradox is explained by their skill in deploying the most powerful propaganda weapon of all, that of undermining the propaganda of their opponents.

Scare stories of the bestial excesses to be suffered if the wicked Hun breached the British defences had led islanders to expect the worst. When, in the event, the advance party of the German military proved to be polite and considerate with many of the officers speaking good English, the general relief was such as to engender a false sense of security and even warm feelings for the intruders. True to the mentality of small, closed communities the islanders, for the most part, asked for nothing more than to be allowed to get on with their lives, a desire the Germans promised to respect.

Their best behaviour was not simply to impress the natives; it was also seen as a useful aid in softening up the citizens on the mainland who, in German eyes, needed only a few gentle nudges to dispense with their incompetent and corrupt democracy. So it was that on the

Channel Islands, whenever there was an encounter between the German military and local people, there was a photographer on hand to record the smiles and handshakes.

The image of a civilised interchange governed by sweet reason did not last for very long. Journalists on the *Jersey Evening Post* and the French-language paper *Les Chroniques de Jersey* and for the *Guernsey Star* and the *Guernsey Evening Press* soon realised that Nazi ideology was incompatible with the liberties traditionally enjoyed by islanders. Any hopes Frank Falla, deputy editor of the *Star*, held about getting on with his job unimpeded were dashed when, soon after the occupation began, his editor was fired for a minor indiscretion, and Falla was told to take over. His 'control' was Kurt Goettmann, a thirty-two-year-old Berliner with an excellent grasp of English. Though the latter was never going to be popular, the worst that Falla could find to say about him in hindsight was that he was over-fond of his own appearance ('A maid working at Goettmann's house told me that he pomaded and powdered himself and that his bathroom was like a woman's'[2]) and that his journalistic credentials were fabricated.

For some years, he proudly boasted he had been in Paris and London working for the German news agency, DNB. He was in fact neither a journalist nor a writer, but a 'cutter-up'. His function in Fleet Street – a connection of which he boasted at every opportunity – was that of sitting in DNB's office receiving tape news items from all over the world, searching publications in English and cutting out and sending synopses to Germany for republication.[3] . . .

Goettmann possessed one virtue: he was not a member of the Nazi Party and was fairly tolerant in his relations with local organisations and people who were responsible to him. Unlike most Germans, he did not force political jargon down your throat as long as you avoided discussion. But if you did choose to argue you found him quite as parrot-like as the next German in repeating the Nazi clichés.

They rubbed along together for nearly two years.

In his war memoir, Falla relates how, from the outset of their relationship, he scored points off the censor by complying with his instructions in a way that allowed readers to distinguish between propaganda and genuine news.

I had no option but to agree that the German war communiqué, news items and Lord Haw-Haw's daily outpourings should be given due prominence – the front page, nothing less! This I did with my tongue in my cheek and the front page was duly filled with Nazi-supplied news. We thus schooled our own public into accepting the front page as nothing but Nazi news in which we had no hand, and turned their full attention to pages two, three and four as exclusively ours in which we featured local news, official notices and civilian affairs. If the Guernsey reader did anything about the front page, he read it cursorily and laughed it to scorn.

Judged at a span of seventy years it is hard to take these claims seriously. None but the most ignorant of Guernsey readers would have needed to have been 'schooled' in detecting the German-inspired reports. Nor is there any reason to assume that Goettmann was unaware of the significance of the paper's layout. Naturally, he wanted German news to make the front page headlines. Falla might choose to believe that readers would turn away but discounting curiosity was not what journalists were supposed to do. It was also naïve of him to assert that 'pages two, three and four' were 'exclusively ours', given that local news was suitably doctored to exclude the slightest hint of anti-German sentiment. Elsewhere in his memoir, Falla concedes as much:

Any reference to food shortage was prohibited, and although we were allowed to listen to the radio at that time any chance mentions of BBC or British broadcasting personalities which we slipped in hopefully were deleted from the final proofs. For instance, while I was Acting Editor of *The Star* a reader wrote a letter to the Editor in which he praised 'a radio talk given by J.B. Priestley'. This was deleted without comment, as was the phrase '*chacun à son goût*' which appeared in another story. . . . Any direct insinuation that we were worse off under Nazi rule or bemoaning that we lacked many essentials of life was not tolerated.

None of this is to suggest that Falla was other than a patriotic reporter doing his best in adverse circumstances. Later in the war he was to show great courage in producing an illegal newsletter in defiance of the authorities. But it is easy to exaggerate the role of journalists in providing some sort of antidote to the all-pervading influence of Nazism. As long as anyone could remember, the presentation of news in Guernsey and Jersey had been a fairly placid affair. Like all small-circulation papers across Britain, there was more emphasis on births, marriages and deaths along with farm prices and other practical information than on any serious political or economic analysis. Community leaders were treated with the enormous respect they rarely deserved. There were no investigative reporters eager to expose wrongdoing. Rather, the existing tendency was to exercise restraint, a subtle form of self-censorship. German censorship was resented more because it was imposed overtly and by an outsider.

After the Battle of Britain upset Hitler's timetable for a cross-Channel invasion and he turned his attention to Russia, the propaganda bludgeon struck harder if less effectively. It was a general rule that British air attacks on German cities had to be downgraded to the space allocated to netball and friendly cricket matches while German advances against Russia received extensive coverage. An avid if selective reader of the *Jersey Evening Post*, Arthur Kent recorded a catalogue of obvious fabrications made more improbable by supposed links to Fleet Street newspapers.

Churchill banquets while millions starve.
King George VI of the Jews.
American troops want to fight England.[4]

That – remarkably – the Jersey censor spoke no English gave an advantage to the editor, Arthur Harrison, and the staff of the *Jersey Evening Post*, who exploited grammatical errors to neutralise German bluster.

> The English await the invasion with anxiety but not more so than the German people.
> During the day our planes shot down four hundred tanks on the Eastern front.
> In a raid on the east coast of England, the Luftwaffe shot down three planes and two harbours.[5]

It is possible that this news sabotage lost more than it gained since, having been caught out a few times, German vigilance intensified to a point where subversion was often seen where none was intended. When the *Evening Post* carried a household hint about tightening up a loose hammerhead, the censor demanded it be taken out. The item was to run alongside an advertisement urging readers to stock up on winter woollies. The heading 'Be Prepared' in conjunction with hammer tightening was interpreted as an incitement to attack occupation forces on dark winter nights.

Anything that might reflect badly on the Germans was rigorously excised. It was perhaps understandable that the censor should balk at printing the news from Sark that a senior officer had blown himself up on one of his own landmines (a British censor might have felt the same way) but it was surely obtuse to forbid publication of letters of thanks from local children to a French charity which had sent biscuits (a fondly remembered luxury in 1942) and to cut details of Guernsey's annual budget because it might reveal how much the islanders were paying to support their unwelcome guests.

German propaganda and censorship had two main objectives. The first was to persuade the islanders that they had no better choice than to stick with the occupying force. The second objective was to encourage their own troops in the belief that, however bad the news might be from mainland Europe, the Reich would eventually prevail.

With heavy casualties on the Eastern front and the boost for Allied fortunes when American entered the war, what might be termed internal propaganda took priority over any concerns about what islanders might think about their future. Both Jersey and Guernsey had a German-language newspaper – *Deutsche Inselzeitung*. Its early issues brimmed over with confidence, Erich Hohl, the editor of the Jersey paper, declaring that his was the first German newspaper in the British Empire 'for the moment'. He predicted the war would be over in three weeks, the vanquishing of Britain being 'just a manoeuvre'.[6] When he was disappointed he held fervently to the Führer's promises of victory, regaling his readers with images of a rosy future when secret weapons of devastating power were let loose on the enemy.

A subsidiary function of the German propaganda machine was to help boost morale on the home front. In the early days this usually took the form of happy family pictures. Escaping to the mainland, Fred Hockey told a *Daily Herald* reporter:

> The Kommandant made a little speech, and asked all those of French citizenship to raise their left hands. There were very few. Then he asked all those of British citizenship to raise their right hands, and we all put our hands up. It seemed a bit queer at the time, but it wasn't till afterwards that we found out what it was all about. As we raised our right hands a photographer snapped us – and pictures appeared in the German newspapers of the Guernsey islanders 'giving the Nazi salute, and heiling Hitler!' I'm told it's an old trick, and they did the same thing in Paris.[7]

More ambitious were the mock landings, intended to show the folks at home that Nazi invincibility was no myth.

> Early one morning about 50 German soldiers, all dressed up for battle and carrying their guns, went off with a few boats and a film camera to the little island of Herm, which lies off our east coast. They put the cameraman ashore on the deserted beach, and then the German soldiers made a gallant landing from their boats.

Then they got back into the boats, and made the landing again, and again. They landed on that beach hundreds of times that day, till they had a film which looked like thousands and thousands of German soldiers, fully armed, landing on a beach. I suppose they had already taken a film of German troopships leaving Germany.[8]

It must have occurred to those who participated in the fiction that what they were serving out could just as easily be served to them. How much, for example, of the German newsreels shown at the Regal in Guernsey and the Forum in Jersey could be believed? Precious little, if stories of the popularity among the troops of BBC transmissions are anything to go by.

Islanders had their own way of giving their verdict on German movie propaganda.

We might start with a cartoon or a Laurel & Hardy film, whatever we had, but when the German news came on, there was a lot of booing, and it got to a stage where the German guards put house lights on so they could see who was booing. But the next week when they showed the German news again and the house lights went on, everybody got up to go to the toilet. So they stopped that. You could only go out once the news was finished. . . . There was a film called *Victory in the West*, a German film, and of course it showed all their propaganda of our boys being captured at Dunkirk. But when the audience saw our troops at Dunkirk they clapped and shouted, 'Come on, lads! You can do it! You know you can get them!'[9]

From 1943, as the war began to turn against Germany, doctoring the news took second place to strident declarations of Nazi ideology. The forerunner of a succession of ludicrously misjudged plants, one that had those who came across it unexpectedly reeling in disbelief, was a *Guernsey Star* Christmas message as amended by Kurt Goettmann. In its original form, as composed by the vicar of St Stephen's, it concluded with the recognition that 'Christ was born into the world to save the world and bring peace on earth'. The printed version had more to say: 'The recognition that Christ was born into the world to save the world and bring peace on earth is the need of Britain and her Jewish and Bolshevik allies.'

Soon afterwards Goettmann left Guernsey, ostensibly to train for the Luftwaffe. However, his military career was cut short when his successor Horst Schmidt-Walkoff found evidence to suggest that Goettmann had been supplementing his army pay by siphoning off official revenues and engaging in the black market. He was eventually reduced to the ranks and sentenced to three years' imprisonment.

Goettmann may have been a bigot and a crook (it is interesting that Guernsey's eagle-eyed journalists failed to detect what he was up to) but Schmidt-Walkoff was the epitome of Nazi fanaticism, whose only excuse for his excesses was the mental instability caused by wounds he had incurred in North Africa.

Islanders were not entirely dependent on the German interpretation of current affairs. Until June 1942, most families had one or more radios tuned into the BBC. Granted, this was less than a guarantee of discovering the whole truth. While bad news could not be entirely obliterated from the airwaves, those responsible for official communiqués were shameless in adapting the news to give a patriotic slant. But there was at least a chance of weighing up one side against the other. This came to an end when the German military ordered the confiscation of all radios.

It had been tried before. In late 1940, radios were impounded to punish islanders for turning a blind eye to the commando landings. But that order was soon rescinded. This time there was no relenting, even though the Feldkommandant argued that this fresh imposition would lead to disaffection among islanders, not to mention heavy policing and administration, and thus be more trouble than it was worth. The army refused to back down. Senior officers tried to justify their intransigence by suggesting that receivers could easily be connected into transmitters for sending messages to London, but in fact they were less worried about what the islanders might get up to than the effect on the morale of their troops when they heard of the mass bombing raids on German cities. It was surely no coincidence that the decision to seize domestic radios followed closely on what Arthur 'Bomber' Harris, Commander-in-Chief of Bomber Command, had headlined as 'The Greatest Air Raid in History'. On the night of 30–31 May 1942, over a thousand bombers released 1,500 tons of high explosive and incendiaries over Cologne, all but wiping out the city centre. The effect on young soldiers, many with families in the heavily urbanised industrial regions of Northern Germany where the attacks were concentrated, can easily be imagined.

Collecting the radios was a large-scale operation. Eight thousand sets were gathered in from Guernsey alone. Any German hopes that the civil authorities might co-operate, and so shoulder part of the blame, were soon disappointed. Convinced that the Hague Convention was on his side, Coutanche refused to sign the confiscation order. Trying to put a gloss on the operation, the impounders assured families that their property would eventually be returned. They were not believed. Many responded with their first positive act of resistance: they held on to their radios.

Their ingenuity in creating hiding places for illicit listening would have impressed a stage illusionist.

Sets have been retained and erected in surprising numbers, and very ingeniously concealed. One man found that in two apparently identical cupboards in a bedroom, the roof of one was slightly lower than the other, so he fitted a false roof in the taller cupboard, which served the dual role of matching the two cupboards and concealing his wireless. The false roof simply pulled down on a hinge, and when in place defied detection.[10]

One popular ruse was to make a radio alcove which could then be plastered over. The only giveaway was the electric wire connecting to the nearest socket. There were drawbacks: after the radio was hidden away there was no chance to alter the tuning, and electricity cuts and a limited supply of batteries meant that the service could never be relied on. But it was amazing what could be achieved by improvisation.

You used about 100 jam jars and you put a copper plate on one end, a piece of wire and a piece of tin, and you did that through all the jam jars, with some water, and . . . a compound like a blue stone . . . 100 jam jars would give you approximately a 90 volts dry battery. Now 100 one-pound jam jars, they need placing somewhere. So we had a bedroom cupboard and these 100 jam jars just pretty well fitted on the floor; we worked it like that with the radio up in the loft. It was really silly. Anyway, one afternoon three Germans came down to search; my mother was alone in the house. It was a weekend I'm sure, because I wouldn't have been home otherwise. She came running to the field to tell my father that the Germans were in the house. They looked around and found nothing; they didn't go into the loft. But what amazed us was that they opened the cupboard, and there are these 90–100 jam jars, and they didn't suspect a thing. My mother actually passed out during the time they were there.[11]

The old trick of disguising an object by putting it in full view where no one would expect to see it was carried off with great aplomb by an elderly lady who covered her radio with a tea cosy. Careless of the likely consequences, one Jersey citizen kept his radio in a wardrobe in his back bedroom.

I had been listening to it and hadn't bothered to shut the door. All of a sudden we heard some shouting and in they came, a Sergeant and four or five troopers; we didn't know what the hell was going on. Eventually they explained, in broken English, that they were looking for someone; they went to look in the bedroom, and there was the wardrobe door wide open. As it was open they didn't bother, there was nobody in there if the door was open. For once being brainless was an advantage.[12]

The demand for news soon outpaced the supply of conventional radios. Fortunately, there was an alternative. Mechanics made scores of miniature crystal sets.

Here at once was the opportunity to listen in with the advantage of having so tiny a set that it would be a simple task to hide it quickly in an emergency. But one great snag arose, earphones were almost non-existent and a crystal set useless without. So, very mysteriously, dozens of telephone call-boxes around town and country, long since out of service, received stealthy visitors after nightfall, who emerged the wealthier by a telephone ear-piece, the latter being found an excellent improvisation for the headphones.[13]

Even the earphones for deaf people in the cinemas were 'borrowed' for the good of the cause and more than one telephone receiver was spirited away from German-occupied houses.

Arthur Linthorn Le Masurier knew how to make a crystal set, but he was also aware of the penalties for owning one.

He placed it into a Queen Mary cigarette tin. He then realised he would need to find a way of devising a method of warning when listening to the news to give him time to hide the set. The cottage had a long path from the front gate to the front door. Five feet away from the back of the cottage was a dry granite party wall covered in thick ivy. The kitchen door led onto the back of the cottage. Arthur invented an alarm system. When the latch of the gate from the roadside was lifted, a bell rang in the house. He had dug a trench along the pathway where the wire was hidden, and this wire led into the house which was attached to a bell. If the bell rang, Arthur had sufficient time to dismantle the set, go out the back door and hide the box in a hole where a small granite stone was easily removed and returned, then covered by the ivy.[14]

The other increasingly popular source of news was the underground press. One of the first newsletters in circulation was produced by the staff of the *Guernsey Star* where Charles Machon, a fifty-one-year-old linotype operator, had the idea of turning out a printed version of BBC bulletins. This was a direct and dangerous challenge to the authorities, who ranked the dissemination of news as a far more serious crime than simply listening in. Defiance was punishable by up to six weeks in prison and a heavy fine, though this was soon to be the minimum sentence. Machon had four co-conspirators, including Frank Falla, who recorded the news in shorthand for reproduction onto thin tomato packing paper.

L.E. Bertrand tempted providence by keeping a wireless in a garden shed no more than fifty feet from a German anti-aircraft battery.

As I was taking down the news I could see the Germans working, parading, kicking and beating the foreign workers. There were some Russian prisoners attached to the German Anti-Aircraft Headquarters. Many times have I seen the poor fellows taking the food from the rabbits which the Germans fed with crusts of bread. They were starved, but I never saw the Russian prisoners ill-treated by this German Battery.

All was going so well, with an ever-increasing number of readers, that Bertrand decided on an extension to his coverage.

The Home Service News came through well but not the Overseas. The fault was due to too short an aerial which was also too low. I had mixed it with other wires in a small greenhouse so as to evade detection. There were some telephone wires passing over my garden leading to the Anti-Aircraft Battery Office. I had often looked at these with envy, and then one night a storm came to my assistance by blowing one of these wires down right across my garden.

Early next morning I sabotaged 80 feet of it and left the remainder in a heap on the ground. An hour afterwards German linesmen were in my garden refixing their wires. They did not question me. At times some of them were within ten feet of my radio, and I was very much relieved when they had gone. The next day I put up this new wire and had better results with the Overseas Service coming through well.[15]

Bertrand's newsletter came out uninterrupted from June 1942, when radios were confiscated, to the liberation.

The Guernsey Underground News Service with its emotive acronym, GUNS, managed to escape detection for nearly two years. The successful run ended in February 1944, when over-confidence in distribution put the newsletter into the hands of a collaborator, an Irish national who had posed as a friend of Machon. One by one the undercover reporters were taken into custody. Denied an opportunity to speak in their defence, though it is hard to imagine what they could have said in mitigation, they received sentences ranging from two years four months for Machon to one year four months for Falla. Machon, who suffered from stomach ulcers and was denied treatment, died in a German prison. It was a fate shared by his friend Joe Gillingham.

There was a curious twist to the story. Awaiting deportation, Frank Falla took his daily exercise in the yard of the Guernsey prison. One morning he bumped into a German in the uniform of a private soldier. It was Kurt Goettmann, one-time censor in Guernsey. Before they were moved on Goettmann had time to utter a cry from the heart: 'It is all a dreadful mistake, Mr Falla.'

In parallel cases, sentences were equally harsh. In Jersey, Herbert and George Gallichan produced a newssheet called the Bulletin of British Patriots. To force the perpetrators to reveal themselves, ten hostages were taken. The brothers gave themselves up and were deported. George spent a year in Dijon prison – Herbert saw out the rest of the war in Wolfenbüttel concentration camp.

9

INTO EXILE

The order was published in the *Jersey Evening Post* on 15 September 1942 and in the *Guernsey Evening Press* on the following day. It was abrupt and to the point.

> By order of Higher Authorities the following British subjects will be evacuated and transferred to Germany (a) Persons who have their permanent residence not on the Channel Islands, for instance, those who have been caught here by the outbreak of war (b) All those men not born on the Channel Islands and 16 to 70 years of age who belong to the English people, together with their families. Detailed instructions will be given by the Feldkommandantur 515.

The name of the Feldkommandant, Colonel Friedrich Knackfuss, was attached to the order.

Bob Le Sueur was a close friend of a family in the second category. Knowing that they seldom read the newspaper before supper, he cycled over to their home to try to break the news gently and to help them get ready for the unwelcome journey.

When I got to the house, the paper had been delivered but she was getting a meal for her four children and hadn't read it. So I asked her to sit and I told her this news. Then the husband came home and he'd only just arrived when there was a knock at the door and there was this German soldier with orders for them to leave the next day with their children. I stayed with them helping them to pack. The next day they had to get down to the harbour.

There were no buses or taxis. We hired a farmer's horse-drawn van. We joined hundreds of people. The atmosphere was quite extraordinary. For one thing everybody was wearing their warmest clothes because they were going to a German winter and since they could only take what they could carry they put as much as they possibly could on their bodies. There were no tears. It was almost like Victoria Station on a bank holiday weekend. People were waving to each other 'Hello, you've had papers too', that sort of thing. We laugh about the British stiff upper lip, but I didn't laugh that day, I saw it, and it was true. It really was quite extraordinary. There'd been tears at home I'm sure, but there were no tears in public. And there were some women wearing dark glasses which I assumed was to hide the fact that they'd been weeping. The glummest faces, and I really mean this, the glummest faces there were those of the young German soldiers, who were probably quite decent individuals and were obviously terribly embarrassed at what was happening.[1]

Not everyone took the news of their impending embarkation quite so phlegmatically.

My husband was out, and a parish official came with a German, and he handed me a bit of blue paper. He said 'This is your instructions, will you please read it? And sign it?' And then my husband came in and . . . he was very cross and he read this notice and said, 'I'm not going to sign this. I don't wish to take my wife and family to Germany.' So our official, poor man, he was rather old, he said, 'Come, come, Mr Stevens, do be reasonable, don't upset things.' So my husband got even crosser, he said, 'No I will not sign this. I'm not going to Germany. I don't intend to go to Germany', and looked at the German and said, 'I'm not going to sign your paper. You can shoot me, if you like.' There was a tense moment, then this German said, 'I'm sorry, I'm not allowed to shoot you.' So I thought, 'To hell with all this', and I signed the form to get rid of them.[2]

Rather than face exile, a few went into hiding, as Reg Langlois recalled:

I asked my father what the noise was coming from the loft and he said that it was probably a bird that had got caught up there. A few days later I heard the noise again. I thought it was a mouse but I said nothing. We had a lot of mice around the farm and they did no harm. It was only at the end of the occupation that I discovered that Grandpa Hodgetts had spent three weeks up in our loft in the dark. He had been born in Birmingham and, had he been found, he would have been deported to Germany with all the others.[3]

Rules and regulations that challenged logic were not unfamiliar to islanders. But there were usually reasons given, however bizarre. The deportations, what Knackfuss preferred to call an evacuation, defied rational explanation. Why now, more than two years after the start of the occupation? What on earth was the point in spending time and money in relocating those who were already, in effect, prisoners of the Reich? It was not until some time after the German surrender that the real story emerged.

A year before the first deportations, some five hundred German civilians working in Iran had been taken into British custody. In retaliation for a breach of international law, Hitler ordered that, for every German held by the British, ten Channel Islanders should be exiled to the dismal Pripet Marshes in the eastern European war zone and their properties distributed among native-born islanders. A quick survey revealed that of the 66,000 wartime population of the Channel Islands, 6,000 had been born on the mainland. A hint of what was going on came with a postscript demanding a list of Iranian nationals. Incredibly, there was one: a sixty-nine-year-old man born in Izmir.

Also revealed was a Mr Churchill. Hitler was convinced that he had unmasked a nephew of the Prime Minister. This was not his only error of judgement. Having made his gesture, he left the Foreign Ministry and the Wehrmacht to carry out his order. But neither of the responsible bodies showed any enthusiasm for the task. The Wehrmacht had no wish to be saddled with settling deportees in an operational area, while the Foreign Ministry anticipated that a confiscation of property would incite the British to act in like manner against German internees, many of whom had substantial accounts with British banks.[4]

More as a delaying tactic than in any real hope of a deal, the Germans invited a Swiss plenipotentiary to negotiate with London, suggesting a deal whereby if the Iranian Germans were released the Channel Islanders would remain unmolested. The British response of 16 September 1941 drew attention to some unpalatable facts. While so far only men of military age had been detained in Iran, the great majority of the islanders threatened with deportation were clearly non-combatants. The argument was all the more forceful among those who championed the Hague Convention when it was realised that wives and children were on the deportation list.

Stuck for a solution, the German Foreign Ministry officials did what all civil servants do in time of trouble: they allowed the relevant papers to slip to the bottom of the tray. Meanwhile, eager to forget what it saw as a time-wasting distraction, the military likewise adopted a selective memory while counting on the problem fading by neglect.

And so it might have done had not a well-intentioned Swiss proposal for an exchange of seriously wounded prisoners incorporated those Channel Islanders who wanted to go to Britain, in exchange for the release of 5,000 German seamen in British hands. The alarm bells sounded in the Führer's bunker. If there were islanders available for a swap this meant that the Pripet Marshes had been deprived of their company. An explicit order from the highest authority had been ignored. No matter that the Iranian Germans were long forgotten; Hitler demanded to know how his prerogative as supreme leader had been circumvented.

An inquiry, led by General Warlimont, skilfully avoided apportioning blame, concluding that it was all a misunderstanding between the Foreign Ministry and the Wehrmacht, a fudge made more acceptable to both sides by a convenient fire that had destroyed most of the critical documents. But that was by no means the end of the matter. The only way to pacify Hitler was to revive the original order and, this time, to make sure that it was carried out. So it was that the Feldkommandant in Jersey was told to get on with the job.

As a start, 1,200 British subjects were to be deported. Coutanche and his senior colleagues, including the twelve Constables, were summoned to hear the bad news.

> We were shown into a room in which there were a number of German Officers. . . . The Feldkommandant, Colonel Knackfuss, then entered and, having taken the Chair, asked [the interpreter] to translate to us an Order. The translation began 'By the Führer' and dealt with the immediate evacuation from Jersey to Germany of certain classes of persons. We were not given a copy of the translation of the Order. We were told that twelve hundred people would be required to leave the island on the next day, that the Constables would be consulted as to the persons to be evacuated, and that the Constables would be required to serve the evacuation notices. I asked, at this juncture, for a private interview with Colonel Knackfuss. This was granted and we withdrew alone to the Feldkommandant's room.[5]

Coutanche delivered a strong protest, to which Knackfuss responded that the order came from the Führer himself, that no one had the power to vary it in any way and that it would be carried out to the letter whatever Coutanche said or did. But the Bailiff did gain one significant concession. He refused to allow the Constables to have anything to do with selecting or serving notice on the deportees. Their role would be limited to arguing the case for exemptions and for supplying a 'guide' to relevant addresses.

The Superior Council met the next day. Coutanche recalled:

Their first feelings were that we ought all to resign and refuse to carry on the public administration of the island any longer. However, calmer feelings eventually prevailed and we finally decided, and in this I still feel quite sure that we were right, that we could do far better by continuing to act as some kind of buffer between the Jersey people and the Germans.[6]

Coutanche has come in for heavy criticism for failing to hold his ground. It is true that if he had persisted in his opposition, he would have put Knackfuss in a difficult position. The Feldkommandant was not keen to take exclusive responsibility for defying the Hague Convention. An appeal to von Schmettow might have paid dividends.

How much could be achieved by this means was proved a year later, when Knackfuss unilaterally decided to cut islanders' rations as a reprisal for an RAF raid on supply barges from France. A vote in the Superior Council for a letter to be sent to the Swiss ambassador in Berlin, the first call for an impartial judgement, led to a confrontation between Coutanche and Knackfuss, who demanded that the appeal be withdrawn. Coutanche refused. Events then took a strange turn. Leaving the office of the Feldkommandant, he was told by Duret Aubin that they had to go immediately to see von Schmettow, who wanted to know what was going on. They duly obliged. Coutanche wrote later:

I have no evidence whatever of what then took place between the office of the Commander-in-Chief and the Feldkommandantur. I can only imagine that Helldorf [von Schmettow's Chief of Staff] told Knackfuss that a letter to the Protecting Power was not to be tolerated and that he had better do whatever might be necessary to induce me to withdraw it.[7]

In the event, the only important cut which was actually made was in the bread ration. Knackfuss also accepted that a genuine shortage was the sole justification for a reduction in any ration and that cuts in retaliation for legitimate acts of war defied the Hague Convention.

A similar intervention might have at least postponed the deportations. As it was, they were dragged out over two weeks, causing maximum embarrassment to those who, reluctantly, had to enforce the order. Moreover, by dealing directly with the anglophile Baron von Aufsess, Coutanche did manage to have withdrawn, if only temporarily, a demand for a supplementary list of candidates for expulsion.

Throughout the nights of 15 and 16 September, German cars chased about Jersey trying to find the addresses where deportation orders had to be delivered. This was followed by a rush of claims for exemption by those who were too ill to travel or who carried out essential work. Mothers with very young children were also struck from the list. In the end only 280 sailed on the first deportation, a figure a long way short of the 1,200 target.

Their departure did not pass without protest.

Four of our group, Frank Le Pennec, George Le Pennec, my sister Marguérite Mière and myself [Joe Mière] were among a crowd of about a hundred people standing looking across the harbour to the German transport ship berthed at the Albert Pier. The deportees were boarding the ship. My sister Marguérite, with the tears running down her cheeks, started to sing 'There'll always be an England'. . . We all joined in, singing at the top of our voices. . . . Then, across the harbour, came the voices of the deportees on the ship. It seemed that all of us had lumps in our throats. This was followed by 'Jersey Jersey', then 'God save the King', the deportees' voices blending with our voices.[8]

It was too much for one supervisor. Joe Berry was with a group on South Hill overlooking the harbour.

Along came a German officer on a bike, and he jumped off his bicycle and told us to get going, started shouting at us, and so everybody told him to get lost. So off he went. But a few minutes later he was back at the head of a squad of soldiers. He ordered them to fix bayonets and march us down the hill. Well, it took us about half an hour to walk down there. We were just about moving, you know, and we were all singing. . . . When we got to the bottom of Pier Road, another German officer came along on his bike. He was an older man. He threw his bike down and stood shouting and waving his revolver. And one of the youngsters in front of us laughed and he hit him over the head. And then I thought, 'This is it'. That was the only time I was really frightened. I got hold of my wife and said, 'Come on' and we went away. But there were several people picked up.[9]

Among them were Joe Mière and his sister who, with four others, were held in jail overnight. In his diary Leslie Sinel praised the German sailors for being considerate and sympathetic, especially with children and old people. He went on to report 'many marriages between young English women and men who are Jersey born' and a suicide pact between husband and wife at Beaumont.[10]

Victor Graham, a London-born conscientious objector who had volunteered for farm work in Jersey as an alternative to the armed forces, remembers the long walk through the streets of St Helier towards the harbour.

They were lined with people and for those of us who made our slow way past all these well-wishers, it was more like a royal progress. Every few yards or so, all the way down Queen Street and King Street and on as far as the barriers at the Weighbridge, we had to stop, put down a bag or case so that we could shake hands yet again, and then exchange farewells and good wishes. My thoughts continually went back to my arrival in Jersey such a short time before, when I got off the Mail Boat not knowing a soul on the island. Now, not only had I made good friends, I had a wife and child into the bargain. All round me were familiar faces that

I would know or remember for the rest of my life, both in the slow moving line of deportees that stretched ahead and behind us and on each crowded pavement in the narrow street.[11]

More deportation orders were served on 17 September. The terms were more explicit, with those named told to present themselves the next day along with their immediate families, parents, spouses and children of any age. Farmers and workers in essential services were given deferment.

Among those caught in this latest round were the fourteen-year-old Michael Ginns and his parents.

When we got to St Helier, the streets were lined with German troops with fixed bayonets, all looking very downcast. They didn't like this business either. . . . They couldn't understand it. Anyway, we arrived at the Jersey Bus Garage, and we had to report to a typist and another soldier who could speak English, who took down all our particulars, and then we had to sit and wait. My father, who was well into his sixties, fainted. He had a weak heart, but he was brought round and ordered to be put on the boat. So we were eventually loaded onto buses, taken down to the harbour, and we got down to the end of the Albert Pier. They'd been loading this old tender called *La France*, but it was nearly full, and an officer got onto a bollard and said: 'Everyone will go to the other ship.' Well the other ship was the *Robert Müller VIII*, a large cargo vessel which only that morning had arrived with a load of coal, and it was intended to put us in the hold. But a local doctor with St John's Ambulance protested and luckily Colonel Knackfuss was down there, and he backed him up and said: 'You can't put women and children in that thing'. So the officer got back on the bollard and said, 'Everyone back to the first ship'. So we went back to the first ship but by then it was full. We were on the last bus-load that was accepted. After that, nearly everybody was turned back.[12]

This second exodus brought yet more crowds out on to the streets to show solidarity with those forced to leave.

It was an amazing scene that I watched, from my office, not a dozen yards from the building into which the people were directed for a roll-call. As usual, the enemy failed to understand the British temperament. Hundreds of SS men [probably ordinary German soldiers], in full fighting kit, carrying sub-machine guns at the ready, patrolled the approaches to the harbour and were stationed at every corner. Machine guns were posted at vantage points to quell the rioting they seemed to expect. . . . What the Germans saw was a crowd of cheery-faced people joking with each other, exchanging handshakes and cheers with the Jersey people, and gaily singing patriotic songs.

Many ex-servicemen among the deportees proudly wore their war medals. I saw hats and parasols in the national colours. I saw families from the country drive up in farmers' vans, the horses gaily bedecked with ribbons. You would have thought they were on their way to some great cup-tie, instead of the unknown hardships of an internment camp in Germany. What admiration one felt for the English that day![13]

On 19 September, those who had been sent home after the second deportation were told to reassemble at the Weighbridge on the twenty-fifth, subsequently postponed to the twenty-ninth by severe gales. This time security was tighter, but while streets near the harbour were closed off, a crowd of young people gathered at the top of Pier Road to shout insults at the Germans and to cheer the 560 men, women and children who were embarking on two small vessels. As the boats set off on a rough sea, back on land fighting broke out with the German patrols. An officer was knocked unconscious and a football match was played with a German helmet. Fourteen boys were arrested; those over eighteen were handed down short prison sentences but Emile Barber, who was said to have instigated the trouble, was sentenced to three years in a German prison camp.

Guernsey's share of the exodus came to around eight hundred, with another eleven from Sark. Sherwill went with the Bailiff and John Leale to make their protest to Dr Brosch, said to be an 'excitable and neurotic man'.[14] Working under orders from Knackfuss, he clearly had no inclination to negotiate. By now there was a firm ruling on exemptions – women more than seven months pregnant, who were granted a reprieve until after the birth, families with one child not more than six weeks old and adults with 65 per cent disability. Deportees had to assemble at the Gaumont Cinema in St Peter Port on 21 September.

Since the original order appeared in the *Guernsey Evening Press* on 16 September, this at least gave a reasonable time to prepare. There were those in Jersey who had less than twelve hours to get ready for the journey. But when the Guernsey contingent did eventually assemble it was to find that the *Robert Müller*, the coal carrier so recently rejected for Jersey passengers, was again being pressed into service, the justification being that it had been suitably adapted by the addition of a few long wooden benches in its deep holds. Vociferous protests resulted in a return trip for the rather more seaworthy *Minotaure*. After further delays caused by rough weather, the Guernsey deportations eventually got under way on 26 September. The *Minotaure* was back the next day for the second batch of unwilling travellers.

Of the eleven English-born residents of Sark, only nine turned up at the harbour at the appointed time. Major Skelton and his wife were not to be found. Yet the Dame had seen them a day earlier.

> They called at our house for a few moments and asked me to take charge of three letters and some jewellery which, they explained in a perfectly normal way, they did not wish to leave in an empty house.[15]

When they failed to put in an appearance, a search started at the couple's house, only to find that 'Major Skelton was dead and his wife was in a ghastly state having stabbed herself in sixteen places.' She was taken over to Guernsey where for several weeks she was too ill to be questioned. Not so the Dame, who found three sealed letters at their home. Fearing that they were incriminating – the Germans seemed convinced that Major Skelton had been a British agent – she hid the evidence under the straw of her rabbit hutches. Later she found that the letters were farewell messages. They had to wait for the liberation to be sent to their addressees.

While the boats were being loaded a frantic search was going on for accommodation on the German side of the water. The least appealing destination for those deported was Dorsten, a former prisoner-of-war camp in the heart of the heavily industrialised Ruhr. Conditions were primitive. Women and children were put in barrack blocks but the men were crammed into wooden huts with holes in the walls stuffed with cardboard. Slow-burning coal stoves created a permanent fug with the result, one inmate recalled, that 'By morning, those sleeping in the upper tiers of bunks resembled smoked herrings.'[16] Outside, the air was just as murky. Local factories pumping out sulphur were responsible for the thick yellow blanket that settled over the town. Food was poor and in short supply.

The good news was in the relationship with the camp guards. The Kommandant, 'a small man who carried an enormous cavalry sword almost as big as himself',[17] was grateful for the humane treatment he had received from the English when he was their prisoner in the Great War. Now, he was keen to repay the favour. He used his own money to buy milk for the children and made sure that Red Cross food parcels were delivered without delay or pilfering. No wonder he was nicknamed Rosy Joe.

Dorsten was a transit stop. Six weeks after the arrival of the first deportees, the single males were packed off to Laufen in south-east Germany. A few days later, the married couples and families were sent to Biberach, a little town close to the Swiss frontier within view of the Bavarian Alps and not far from Laufen. A third destination was Bad Wurzach south of Biberach. In happier days, all three centres were rural idylls attracting tourists who wanted good clean air, hill walks and the quiet life. First impressions of Biberach were swayed by the fine weather. 'My parents remember how hot the day was, especially as everyone was wearing several layers of thick clothing which could not be packed. Exhausted, carrying heavy suitcases and two small children, they only just managed to climb the hill to the camp.'[18]

For Victor Graham, it wasn't long before thick clothing was very much appreciated.

Biberach was colder than anything I had previously experienced. . . . Not only was the fuel ration inadequate, but its period of issue was too short for the long winter and the cold spring that followed it. It was fortunate that the buildings, unlike those at Dorsten, were well made and insulated. The large windows were actually double-glazed, something unusual to most of us at that time, though it was not at all uncommon in Germany and elsewhere on the Continent. They were also peg-hinged, so that they could be lifted right out, when the weather was warm enough, to give our crowded room as much fresh air as possible.[19]

The camp consisted of twenty-three barrack huts surrounded by a barbed-wire fence with observation towers. It had previously held prisoners of war.

Our guards were German army guards. Of course we were all frightened. They used to do roll calls, making us stand outside to be counted. We used to say they just couldn't count because they always got it wrong. There were always one or two missing. And so they started all over again. And you can imagine women, children and men standing there . . . After a while, the men managed to persuade the Germans that it wasn't fair to make women and children stand outside for I don't know how long. So they let the men be counted and the women stay inside in the rooms, by their beds.[20]

It got better. Each barrack had its own water, electricity and communal bathrooms. Basic rations, typically cabbage-leaf soup, mouldy bread and ersatz coffee made from acorns, were soon supplemented by Red Cross food parcels containing such delicacies as margarine, cheese, biscuits and meat pies. The chief enemy was boredom, alleviated somewhat by home entertainments. Biberach had its own makeshift orchestra, a library, workshop and an active amateur dramatic society. The senior guard, Otto Leibe, did his best for his charges and was well liked. The inevitable depression among inmates was tempered by the positive thinkers.

> Room Nineteen was probably about fifteen feet by ten. It was furnished with three double-decker, wooden bunks, six steel cupboards, a table and six stools and it was heated by a round, iron stove . . . Compared to what we now know of other camps, ours was not a bad little nest. We had room to move about when we were all home and out of bed, and there was space enough for all our belongings, even after our left luggage arrived from the island and we began to acquire books, musical instruments, tools and other bits and pieces. In all, it was a good base camp in which to build a modest life together, and this we set out to do.[21]

After six weeks at Biberach, Pat Holt and her family – parents and two brothers – were put on a train to Bad Wurzach where home was a derelict schloss, an eighteenth-century, three-storey building in the centre of the town, straight out of a Franz Lehár operetta – 'all church bells and ox wagons'. One-time home of the local aristocracy, the castle had adapted to a Catholic monastery, a theological training college and, latterly, a prisoner-of-war camp for Corsican troops before being allocated to the Channel Islanders. 'It was dirty and horrible,' says Pat, but once inside she and a friend discovered 'the most beautiful painted ceiling.' The two girls started laughing 'because to have this painted ceiling and us there as prisoners was a strange contradiction'.[22]

'After Biberach, where there was only twelve to a room, suddenly we were in rooms of about thirty people,' recalls Michael Ginns.

> Big high ceilings, double doors at each end. And it was filthy, the beds were damp, we had to go to bed with our clothes on for two

or three nights. And then you had to go down three floors to the kitchen to get your food and bring it back up to the rooms.

My mother with her nursing experience went to nurse in the hospital, and my father in bad health couldn't manage all those stairs so he was a permanent resident in the hospital as well. So I was up in a room on the top floor. There were three or four others in our room of my age, Johnny Latter from the Beeches, Jack Case, John Burgess who's still around and lives in St Andrew's road. So we used to get the usual issue of soup twice a day. Red cabbage soup was known as Blue Danube because that was its colour, swede soup was called Glory, millet soup was called Black Forest because of the bits of twig floating in it. And pea soup, I wouldn't mind a bowl of that now. It was dried peas, soaked, and it was good stuff. If you were lucky you'd get a bit of what I suspect was horse floating in it. But you were hungry so you didn't mind and you ate it. We had German army black bread and an issue of margarine and substitute honey. And then the kitchen staff would put out potato peelings and we'd go and get a bowlful. If you sprinkled cheese powder on it and shoved it in the oven, it wasn't bad. We weren't desperate like concentration camp prisoners, but it was bad enough. Those were dark gloomy days.[23]

Also at Bad Wurzach was John Green, one of a family of six, the youngest of whom was three years old. John was just a few weeks short of his sixteenth birthday, which was fortunate for him since boys over sixteen were sent to Laufen. The daily routine at Bad Wurzach was an exercise in subsistence living.

The camp was guarded by elderly armed police – they weren't active fighting men. We had to organise ourselves. All the work attached to running the camp we had to do. We had to run the kitchen. We had to send working parties out to bring in supplies. Coal had to be brought in. We had an army doctor, a dentist and a very efficient nurse who was the mother of Michael Ginns. We ran a sort of hospital under the supervision of the doctor. One of the problems was that there were a lot of children there who had nothing to do. They were really at a loose end. We provided what we could in the way of schooling but it wouldn't pass these days as education. We did the best we could.

Hobbies became all-consuming passions.

I was amazed at the number of budding artists we had. . . . Some of the pictures were very good, and none of the painters had any training. We had a dance band – I don't know where they got the instruments from. We could have a dance in the evenings once a month or something. Amateur dramatics were always well-received because it took a lot of doing for people not used to it. There was a field attached to the camp where we could play football. Each of the men's rooms had its football team, so there was quite a bit of sport. We tried to do anything that would take our minds off the war.[24]

Friendships were made in the nearby village. Pat Holt's father, a plumber and heating engineer, got on so well with his local opposite number that he was able to borrow tools to unblock lavatories and repair the water boiler.

Not much news got through, though there were those like John Green who picked up hints that there were worse places for those deemed to be enemies of the Führer.

The Kommandant's secretary, who was an interpreter as well and spoke excellent English, said to us that we ought to be very careful. And we know now what she was talking about. But we didn't fully appreciate it. I think we knew about concentration camps but we didn't know then what happened there.[25]

Not until December 1944, when a group of Dutch Jews were delivered to Bad Wurzach. It took the islanders some time to work out why they were there. It turned out that each of them had a British grandparent which by some twisted bureaucratic logic gave them preferential treatment. And not before time.

> Now those people looked like everything you saw about people who'd been in concentration camps. They were really only skin and bone – very badly treated, very badly dressed. There was about thirty of them. Most of them could speak English. Naturally they kept a bit to themselves. For them, coming to the camp and receiving the food we had and the Red Cross food was tremendous. They talked about how they'd been treated and what conditions were like. So at that stage we were beginning to know what happened in those camps.[26]

*

The threat of deportation came back to haunt islanders in early 1943. A commando raid on Sark had stretched German nerves, coming as it did in the wake of the Allied victory at El Alamein. With such a boost for British confidence it seemed likely that there would soon be an attempt to retake the Channel Islands. The German inquiry into the raid revealed that the commandos had been given essential information about the defence layout by a Mrs Pittard, said to be 'a helpless and somewhat simple-minded woman'. At her interrogation a promise was made not to send her to Germany if she told the truth. This was altogether too soft-hearted for Berlin, but since the word of a German officer was sacred a means had to be devised of punishing the widow Pittard without appearing to have reneged on the original decision. This was achieved by ordering another deportation that happened to include the lady. Among those selected were retired officers who might be expected to lead a resistance. These included Ambrose Sherwill. Also in the round-up was the American husband of the Dame of Sark, who had served in the Royal Flying Corps.

> Once again all the sad preliminaries were gone through and 150 people assembled at the Gaumont Cinema. Exception had been taken by the Germans to the number of helpers attached to the

Red Cross who had been present at the first deportation, and very few of us besides members of the St John Ambulance were given permits to assist on this occasion.[27]

Thirty-five of the deportees were brought over from Sark.

Some of them apparently had had no idea that they were to be deported to Germany but were under the impression that they were coming to live in Guernsey and had no suitable clothing for their undertaking. Several of them had young children. Many of the Sark people came under neither the category of ex-officers nor of ex-criminals, and had not the faintest idea why they were being deported. The sad bewilderment of their faces was unforgettable.

Another piece of cruelty was the inclusion in this deportation of several wives and children of the Guernsey policemen who were already paying the full penalty of their wrong-doing by serving heavy sentences of imprisonment and penal servitude. One of the wives had three small children, including a baby in arms.[28]

All the men ended up in Laufen.

Twelve miles from Salzburg, Laufen is another tiny Bavarian town in the foothills of the Alps. The bridge across the River Salzac connects with the Austrian village of Obendorf, where the carol 'Silent Night, Holy Night' was composed. Schloss Laufen, once the summer residence of the Archbishop of Salzburg, was the centre for unattached male internees. Among the late arrivals was Maurice Hill, who had been caught demonstrating against the first deportations. 'I met a lot of friends who I had seen off from Jersey and, of course, as I walked through the gates and some of them saw me they thought it was a great joke.'[29]

The accommodation, 'huge rooms with high ceilings', was tolerable, though there was a problem of keeping the bugs under control. The Red Cross helped to make up the shortage of rations. Discipline was relaxed.

In charge of the Camp was a very decent German Colonel, a very pleasant Security Captain who had spent years in America, a Sonderführer who had been educated at Midhurst in Sussex and a dear old German military doctor who really did his best for the sick. The troops who guarded us were mostly very badly wounded soldiers quite unfit for the front line. The German Sergeant Major, Ertl, was a good soldier who put up with a great deal more than any English NCO would have stood. At the time I was interned, I never saw or heard of a German finger being laid on a single British subject.[30]

According to Victor Graham, the Germans gave less trouble than some of the more authoritarian inmates. Soon after his arrival Sherwill was elected camp senior. This did not go down well with the young Graham, a free spirit who did not take kindly to orders from above. Sherwill, he wrote, was 'a petty dictator who held his position by playing on the fears and hatreds of the more timid internees'. There is no mention of Graham in Sherwill's memoir but he does refer to troublemakers and the problems he had in keeping the peace, not least in reconciling the interests of disparate groups.

Most of our people were British subjects either from the Channel Islands or else picked up all over Europe, including a large contingent from Italy and another from Greece, hardly any of them speaking any English but, as the children and grand-children of Britishers who had settled in those countries and had married Italian or Greek girls, in possession of British passports. Then I had an Egyptian Jew, a Persian, and a native of Bethlehem and his two sons born in Berlin of a Viennese mother. One poor chap, who had been picked up in, I think, Czechoslovakia, was mentally deranged and caused me no end of trouble when, one morning, calling down to the German office for something or other, he snatched a picture of Hitler off the wall, threw it on the floor and jumped on it. Believe it or not, the German Commandant was quite annoyed but eventually accepted my explanation that the chap was mad. Perhaps he was saner than the rest of us.[31]

For the most part, the exiled islanders got on with their makeshift lives as best they could. The circumstances were a long way short of ideal but they knew that many others were less fortunate. They also knew, by now, that the war was moving in favour of the Allies. Everybody wanted to go home but, buoyed up by hope, they were content to wait.

10

FORTRESS ISLANDS

It has been said of the Atlantic Wall that it was the most ambitious building project in the western world for two thousand years.[1] Even by Nazi standards of mammoth constructions it was certainly a hubristic project. The statistics are barely credible. Anything from eight to ten million cubic metres of concrete and 1.2 million tonnes of steel, close on five per cent of Germany's annual production, were appropriated for an interconnecting line of fortifications along three thousand miles of coastline from Norway's North Cape inside the Arctic Circle all the way down to the French border with Spain. One of the strongest links in this chain of defences was the Channel Islands, which accounted for up to one-twelfth of the total resources devoted to the enterprise.

Those who gasp at such profligate misuse of men and materials are as one with the senior German commanders on the western front. If rational strategy had been the only consideration, German forces would have withdrawn from the islands to reinforce vulnerable points along the French coast. But common sense was not what Hitler wanted to hear. His instinct was to hold to the last man every inch of territory gained in the first flush of German aggression. He rationalised that the

Channel Islands served a military purpose as guardian of German shipping in disputed waters but, in fact, he was much more concerned with the symbolic value of possessing a part of Britain. To surrender or to appear to surrender the stepping stones to the enemy's south coast would, he knew, be seen as a confession of failure. This he was not prepared to contemplate.

The build-up of the Channel Islands' defences to a level guaranteed to deter or annihilate all intruders started with the commando raid on Guernsey in July 1940. An unmitigated failure from the British point of view, it indicated to the occupiers that other, more carefully planned assaults could be expected. Urging his troops to be extra vigilant, von Schmettow warned that in the event of a raid 'rapid support from the continent cannot be expected particularly during bad weather and darkness'. The only effective response was an immediate counter-attack to propel the enemy back into the sea. How precisely this was to be achieved was left to subordinates to work out.

This vague directive served well enough while Britain was weak and on the defensive. But after the threat of invasion was lifted and Britain began to fight back, Hitler worried that the islands were vulnerable. His fears were confirmed in February 1941, when better-armed and better-trained commandos launched an attack on the Lofoten Islands where the major part of Norway's fish oil was produced. The destruction of the factories interrupted the supply of glycerine for German explosives, a morale-boosting success for the Allies. That the Channel Islands would be the next soft target in line for commando attention seemed only too apparent.

On 10 June 1941 an order came from Berlin that Jersey and Guernsey should each be reinforced by an additional regiment along with tanks and heavy artillery. Come October, Hitler was again demanding a strengthening of defences, including more troops and artillery, heavy armoured tanks, assault guns, anti-tank guns, searchlights, flame-throwers and mines. The stockpiling of ammunition was to be such that 'each gun can be fired until its barrel is worn out'. In addition, 'our defences must be combat-ready for a defensive battle lasting at least a fortnight'. Food reserves for sixty days were approved along with an allocation of six million tons of construction materials for the expansion of the Guernsey and Jersey airfields.

More than ever Hitler was convinced that the British must yield to the political pressure of the Russians and attack somewhere. The re-conquest of the Channel Islands was one of the few practical propositions.

On 20 October Hitler gave the go-ahead for a construction programme that would make Guernsey, Jersey, Alderney and Sark 'the mightiest fortress' in an eight-year plan. There were to be between 200 and 250 strong points on the larger islands with walls from two to three-and-a-half metres thick. The idea of a static defence front having taken hold of Hitler's imagination, he began to think more grandly of a protective barrier along the entire western European coast. Frustrated in his expectation of an easy victory over Russia and with America's entry into the war at the end of 1941, he deemed a bastion against a reinvigorated Britain and its powerful western ally essential.

In March 1942, Führer Directive 40 set out the broad policy for creating what was soon to be known as the Atlantic Wall. Attention was focused on statements of the obvious such as: 'The distribution of forces and the building of defensive works must be carried out so that our strongest defence positions are located in those sectors most likely to be selected by the enemy for landings.' Field Marshal von Rundstedt, commander of Army Group West, was delegated to fill in the details and to implement the building programme. And this is where the problems started. Hitler had called for 'especially close and complete cooperation between all three services'. But the Kriegsmarine, the Wehrmacht and the Luftwaffe were not noted for their easy relationships. There was an added complication in that much of the building work was to be the responsibility of the Organisation Todt, a state construction agency that was virtually independent of the military.

In his fiftieth year when war broke out, Dr Fritz Todt was the model technocrat, an engineer with the managerial skills to give practical shape to grandiose schemes. A supporter of strong, centralised government as the only means of getting things done, he was an early convert to the Nazi Party. Devoted to Hitler, his loyalty was rewarded with lucrative commissions, the most enduring being the autobahns, a national dual-carriageway road network that was the envy of Europe. As Inspector-General of the German Highway System, Todt aimed at maximum efficiency by standardising equipment and by dovetailing the phases of construction so that none of the quarter-million men in his employ were ever left wondering what to do next. From 1936, a thousand kilometres of autobahn were opened every year. Such was his reputation that in 1937 he was invited to London to share his expertise. *Time* magazine described Todt as the Nazis' 'busiest beaver'.[2]

Awarded the honorary rank of general in the Luftwaffe, Todt began work on the West Wall or Siegfried Line, the defence system along the German sector of the Rhine, Hitler's first attempt at an impregnable military barrier. He was also responsible for Berchtesgaden, Hitler's mountain hideaway. By now Todt had brought together all the engineers and managers of the German construction industry into a single enormous entity known, inevitably, as Organisation Todt.

When war was declared the OT was still engaged on putting the final touches to the West Wall. By now, Todt, a quiet, retiring man, the very opposite of the typically bombastic henchmen surrounding the Führer, had become armaments minister as well as head of construction and maintenance for highways, waterways and power plants. Though clearly overstretched, Todt was the first person Hitler turned to when he wanted to make real his plans for defending the French coast and the Channel Islands against all comers. Originally staffed entirely by Germans, as the OT extended its activities it came to rely on conscripted workers and forced labour from the occupied territories. By 1943 its total strength was over one and a half million. But that was after Dr Todt had departed the scene.

On 7 February 1942, after a meeting with Hitler, Todt was scheduled to fly from Rastenburg to Berlin. When he arrived at the airport early the following morning it was to find that he had been allocated a Heinkel He III twin-engine bomber instead of his usual aircraft which was still being serviced. The Heinkel took off at 0800 hours. A few minutes later, it exploded. All on board were killed. Sabotage was suspected but never proved.

Hitler's sadness at losing a close associate was short-lived. A great believer in fate, he took it as a sign that Albert Speer, his favourite architect and a gifted administrator in the Todt mould, should have been on the same flight but, after a late night, had decided to postpone his journey. Speer was duly appointed Todt's successor.

By this time the fortifications on the Channel Islands were already beginning to take shape. Thousands of tons of cement and other building materials had been shipped from St Malo for the fortress bunkers that were to disfigure many of the best sea views. Open beaches were cut off by stretches of ten-feet-high solid concrete blocks capable of stopping tanks in their tracks, while whole fields were requisitioned for artillery batteries or festooned with barbed wire and jagged steel teeth that could make matchwood of troop-carrying gliders.

At a conference with Speer in May 1942, Hitler made clear that on no account should the demands on resources for the continental stretch of the Atlantic Wall be allowed to detract from work in the Channel Islands. Speer thought both objectives could be achieved, though he must have had second thoughts later in the year when Hitler was more specific in his demands for an extended defence network starting with 15,000 bunkers and emplacements to be manned by 300,000 troops, all this to be ready by 1 May 1943, just seven months ahead.[3]

Though Speer missed his deadline by a mile, progress in the Channel Islands was impressive. The fortification programme peaked between April and September 1943. By then, relative to size, the islands had a greater concentration of emplaced artillery than anywhere in Western Europe. The most powerful guns were those of the Mirus battery at St Saviour's on Guernsey, whose range of 50 kilometres brought the gulf of St Malo into range.

The barrels had a remarkable history. They began life on a Russian battleship, which was taken over by the Germans in 1918, returned to the Russians, and broken up in 1935, when the guns were removed and stored in Bizerta. In 1939 they were sent to Finland to be used in the Russo-Finnish War by the Finns, captured

en route by the Germans, returned to Germany for recon-
ditioning, and sent to Guernsey.[4]

It took a year and a half to build the emplacements which accounted for
45,000 cubic metres of concrete. An underground barracks could
accommodate 400 men.

In the spring and summer of 1943, the island ports were unloading
steel and cement at a rate of 20,000 tons a month. Stone was quarried
locally while the beaches offered a ready supply of sand. In Jersey alone,
by 1944, a million tons of sand had been excavated. To move heavy
materials, light railways were built. In Jersey, a line ran from St Helier
to Corbière in the south-west, where a second line connected to the
Ronez quarry on the north coast. Smaller-gauge lines traversed the east
and west coasts. In Guernsey, a railway covered about two-thirds of the
coastline from St Peter Port to St Sampson's, then to L'Ancresse Bay
down to the west coast to L'Erée. In addition to building materials, the
railways carried military hardware including thousands of land mines.
When a calculation was made in April 1944, Guernsey had 54,000
mines, Jersey 39,000 and even Sark had 4,500. Alderney, bereft of almost
all its native citizens, was circled by over 30,000 mines. An added
strength for Alderney was the old fortifications, with granite walls up to
twenty feet thick, built to protect against Napoleonic incursions.

Underground, large caverns were dug out for storage and shelter –
23,495 square metres in Jersey, 19,216 in Guernsey and 4,795 in Alderney,
with space for reserve troops and vehicles. Plans for creating underground hospitals were abandoned after it was found that wounds did
not heal easily in conditions of high humidity. 'Even patients admitted
with relatively minor ailments looked and felt worse after discharge.'[5]
Both the major labyrinths are now war museums.

For work on such a massive scale, Organisation Todt relied on the
muscle power of imported civilian labour, some of it voluntary but a
high proportion, possibly as much as two-thirds, press-ganged into
working for the enemy. At the peak of activity there were close on 15,000
foreign workers on the islands, 7,000 in Guernsey, 6,000 in Jersey and
2,000 in Alderney.[6] They were a mixed bunch. The first arrivals were

French colonials, unemployed Algerians and Moroccans rounded up by the Vichy government and handed over to the Germans. Leslie Sinel described them as 'very poor specimens, badly clad and shod and all of them terribly hungry; some were seen on Christmas Day eating raw limpets and acorns while, if they get the chance, they are always ready to beg for a bit of bread'.[7]

The subservience of the Vichy regime was demonstrated again with the dispatch to the Channel Islands of Spanish refugees who had fled Franco's Spain. Republican and thus staunchly anti-Fascist, many joined the French Resistance (war memorials in or close to the Pyrenees invariably mix French and Spanish names), but those who ventured into urban areas were liable to be interned and then sent either to work for the Germans or back to imprisonment or worse in their own country. They came from a wide range of backgrounds, and those who were well educated or skilled tradesmen were highly valued by their captors, who offered better pay and living conditions to those who were co-operative. After participating in the construction of submarine pens on the French Atlantic coast, a Spanish contingent, several thousand strong, was posted to the Channel Islands. They worked alongside Dutch, French and Belgians who had been persuaded that signing up with the OT was better than the alternative. Of course few of these artisans wanted to be anywhere except at home with their families, but most were reasonably treated, and, though their leisure hours were few and far between, they were free to move about and to spend whatever money they had, usually on secondhand clothes.

Anyone who doubted that the rewards and punishments meted out by the OT were largely dependent on nationality was jolted into reality with the appearance of Russian or, more specifically, Ukrainian slave workers. If the North Africans looked destitute, these unfortunates seemed almost beyond help. They made their first appearance in Leslie Sinel's diary on 13 August 1942.

Hundreds of Russians arrive for work in the western part of the island; they made a pathetic sight, and many of them were mere boys, the majority of them with no footwear and many with bleeding feet; they were under the escort of the Todt Organisation and were badly treated, being hit with truncheons.

Michael Ginns has traced their origins.

Some had already been working in remote villages when the Germans demanded a certain quota for labour in the West; whilst others had been rounded up in 'street sweeps' in their home towns, which accounts for the presence of young scholars (14 or 15 years old) caught while on their way home from school. . . .They had been packed into railway cattle trucks for some weeks for their journey from the Ukraine to St Malo with no sanitary facilities whatsoever; occasionally some form of sustenance was thrust in to them, but that was all.[8]

A few were prisoners of war, identified with the letters SU across their backs. 'These were better clothed and shod than their fellow country-men but all of them looked dejected and suffering from lack of food.'[9]

Nazi racial prejudice categorised people of Slavic origin as *untermenschen*, subhuman, fit only for the most basic labour. They were, said Frank Kieller, 'the living dead'.

The first I saw were in rags. Some wore cement sacks over their heads and shoulders, like monks' hoods. They were gaunt, and grey all over, coated with cement dust. Some were only children. Many had no shoes, or only bits of sacking tied around their feet. The Germans herded them like cattle. OT guards beat them with whips or sticks. They were ruthless and immediately attacked anyone who fell or failed to keep up.[10]

Joe Mière recorded what happened when a young girl dropped her little bundle of possessions.

She ran back to get them and this Organisation Todt chap struck her on the head with a pick-axe handle. You could see the blood come down over the grime on her face; he went to strike her again and she screamed. Being young and not even thinking and I'm no hero, I went to go forward to stop him and the boss and the staff threw me back into the shop. Poor old Mrs Garnier who used to do our floors saw all this going on, she lifted her eyes up to the sky and said 'oh my God, where are you'.[11]

In another version of this story[12] the writer has Mrs Garnier reflecting on the way ordinary German soldiers seemed devoid of pity. 'Some laughed at what they saw.' It is not to split hairs to note that she was almost certainly pointing the finger of guilt in the wrong direction. 'Ordinary German soldiers' had little to do with the marshalling of OT workers or, after an initial period, with the management of the building of the fortifications. Starting out as a purely civilian institution, the OT had gradually adopted a military veneer. Todt's assumption of high rank was followed by military-style khaki uniforms for overseers, who saw themselves as part of the fighting forces. That they were very often precisely the recruits the regular army could well do without only served to inflate their pretensions. Brutality overlapping into sadism was their claim to strength and a demonstration of their devotion to Nazi ideals.

If there was any restraint on the OT supervision of its workforce it was exercised by the army, though only in a haphazard way and usually by the initiative of individual soldiers. Heinrich Candells was on sentry duty at St Ouen's Bay when he saw an overseer beating two Russians with a pick handle. He ordered him to stop, which the man did. However, the following day Candells had to apologise to the overseer. 'It was a good thing that my company commander was not a Hitler fanatic or I would have been in serious trouble.'

A former medical orderly, Otto Schmiegler, spoke of the 'huge brute' of an overseer at St Brelade's Bay. Schmiegler related how he was sickened by the sight of Russians being beaten by this overseer, and announced that he was going to report the matter. His friend advised caution, 'No, Otto, say nothing, you will be in trouble'. Schmiegler insisted that as a medical orderly, he could not stand by.

Schmiegler went on to claim that at his instigation the

Feldgendarmerie set up an observation post. Having seen all that they needed, the overseer was arrested and taken away in handcuffs. Michael Ginns, who conducted the interview, questions the details of the story.

> It is hard to believe that the military police would be so concerned about Russians being beaten; perhaps the truth is that they did indeed come to observe, but saw 'the huge brute of a man' involved in some black market dealing.[13]

If challenged, German commanders would doubtless have claimed there was little they could do to alleviate the suffering of the slave workers. The OT was independent of the military with a direct line to Berlin. If von Schmettow or others had weighed in against the OT they would have been pitting themselves against Albert Speer, who was judged by Hitler to be more competent and dependable than most of his generals. Hitler wanted his Atlantic Wall and his Channel Islands Fortress and while Germany still had the upper hand in Europe, there was no gainsaying his order or the means for achieving it.

But if there was little that could be done to change the brutal regime that passed for man management in the OT, external pressures brought some relief to those worst affected. According to Leslie Sinel, in November 1942 the Red Cross mounted an investigation into the treatment of Russian workers. It would not have taken long to arrive at an approximation of the truth. The death rate alone was a clear pointer to what was going on. There were no fewer than sixty-three burials in the eight months after the arrival of the first Russians. Following the Red Cross visit, those in poorest physical condition were sent back to France, where it is said that they received medical attention.[14]

The better treatment of the Russians in Jersey was also noted by J. Cutler Vincent who, on 26 April 1943, wrote that, 'the Russians are all better clad now and some of the lucky ones with suitable size clothes might be mistaken for Spaniards'. And again, on 23 June, 'We have noticed lately how much the Russians are working. There is little slacking now. One has heard that they are better fed; they are certainly better clothed.'[15]

There were many attempts to escape but since it was almost impossible to get off the islands the labourers' best chance of avoiding recapture was to merge in with the local community as, most commonly, farm workers. The least fortunate tried to live off the land, which meant either begging or stealing or both. As one islander put it, 'You could be feeding one lot at the front door while another lot robbed you at the back'. After a spate of burglaries at St Ouen, the farmers set up an early version of Neighbourhood Watch. Whoever was first to hear prowlers would bang metal against metal to start a din that would be taken up by neighbours until the whole area was alerted.

All that the OT represented in the Channel Islands hit its nadir in Alderney. Thérèse Fréjus was aged fifteen at the beginning of the war. She and the rest of her Brittany family were in Jersey to help bring in the potato harvest. With no prospect of returning home their last hope was to keep clear of the occupying forces. Thérèse was unlucky as her son, Vincent, relates:

> My mother was taken by the Germans and put into a forced labour camp on the island of Alderney. She had no family or friends with her. She suffered rape, starvation, beatings and had both legs broken to stop her trying to escape. She said she was better off than the white Russians, who were left to die in camps they called 'the maggot farm'. My sister was born in the camp in 1944, her father was a German soldier.[16]

Stories of the harsh treatment of Alderney's press-ganged workforce are legion.

> Every day the Camp Commander made a habit of beating any man he found not standing properly to attention or who had not made his bed properly or did not execute a drill movement properly. The beatings were carried out on the head, face or body with a stick about 2.5 centimetres in diameter. The Camp Commander's assistant also beat workers daily with a stick of the same thickness on all parts of the body until their faces were

covered with blood and they could not rise from the ground, when he would call on the prisoner's mates to carry the prostrate body away.[17]

The first arrival of OT expendables, some 1,000 East European captives, appeared in July 1942. Their number grew until May 1943 when there were around 4,000 labourers spread over twenty-seven nationalities. There were also 300 or so 'half Jews', the offspring of mixed marriages, who qualified for degradation if not for annihilation. Their joint task was to equip the island with three heavy coastal batteries along with concrete emplacements, anti-tank walls and the usual components of static defence, including 30,000 mines. Accommodation was in four camps named after German North Sea islands – Helgoland, Norderney, Borkum and Sylt. The best of these was Borkum which housed up to 1,000 volunteer skilled workers, mostly from Germany and Holland. Their treatment was in stark contrast to conditions in the other camps where hunger and beatings were part of the daily routine.

In October 1942, there was an occasion when a carrot was thrown from a window by one of the cooks and was picked up outside by a Russian who was beaten mercilessly with a stick and then kicked while lying on the ground.

This was an account by a Pole and a Russian of life in Norderney Camp. It was no better in Helgoland:

If ever a man was reported to the Camp Commander for taking food from the garbage pails, he would summon the offender to his office, beat him with a length of stick or length of rubber hose filled with sand until he fell to the ground, kick him and order him to leave the office.[18]

Worst off were the occupants of Lager Sylt, which in March 1943 was taken over as a concentration camp by SS Construction Brigade 1, an offshoot of Heinrich Himmler's paramilitary force. As in other more notorious concentration camps, the inmates of Sylt wore striped floppy uniforms with their identifying numbers prominent on their backs. Each had a coloured patch to show why he had been incarcerated – red for political, pink for homosexual, purple for conscientious objector. True to the SS principle of divide and rule, selected prisoners were given authority over their fellows. These sad creatures were called Kapos. From the ranks of the SS guards and the Kapos, there was no shortage of volunteers to exercise their sadistic tendencies.

Often the men were beaten so long that they fell down from sheer weakness . . . We were beaten every day. My friend Antoni Onuchowski died that way. He was from my native village and of course I knew him well. Onuchowski had stayed behind in Sylt Camp for a few days because of illness. He had swollen feet. Afterwards he got a bit better, but he was still very weak and could not walk properly. One day, after work, when our squad was marching back to camp, he could not keep up and fell behind. I saw the *Truppführer* remain with him and get to work with his truncheon. Later we lost sight of him. All the evening we kept waiting in the camp for him, but he never returned. The next morning after reveille, when I went to the latrine, Onuchowski lay there on the other side of the barbed wire at the side of the camp. His face was covered with red weals and when we later brought his body into the camp and undressed it, we could distinctly see the weals and blotches on his body.[19]

The camp commandant at Sylt, Karl Tietz, was top of the hate list for the Alderney underdogs. He was not himself a dispenser of punishment; he left that to his henchmen, notably a black French colonial who took to his work with more than usual relish. The spectacle was too much for one German naval officer, Paul Markert, who was shocked, not so much by the suffering inflicted but by the colour of the person administering it.

I only knew that they were labourers from the east, Ukrainians, and only some time later I saw that they were vegetating under the most miserable conditions, really you couldn't call it living. There was a guard, a black, who beat them up, mercilessly. I then had the leader of the camp ordered to me, and I told him that if this would happen ever again, I would shoot the negro, regardless. I also told him that I couldn't stand it that a black person should beat up a white man, and he should know that and act accordingly. So that was stopped, as far as I know.[20]

In fact it is inconceivable that Markert threatened Tietz or anyone else bearing the SS insignia; fired up by his own prejudice and with the passage of time, he may have confused what he wanted to do with what really happened. He must have known that the consequence of any protest on his part would be a posting to the front line of a war zone. It is thus hardly surprising that acts of compassion were rare and those of any avail rarer still.

Once, on 6 January [1943], whilst we were loading heavy wooden boards, a Russian was hit by a hook that slipped during the operation and he fell into the ship, roughly 6 metres down . . . I lowered two more Russians on a platform into the hold of the ship and lifted the victim with the crane. I told [the OT *Truppführer* present] to call an ambulance at once. He went away but no ambulance turned up. Then a truck arrived for an officer, whom I asked to remove the wounded man to a hospital. But even when I threatened to stop loading he would not remove the man. After 30 minutes I got two Russians to drive the wounded man back to his camp. Two days later, on enquiry, I was told that the man had died.[21]

Another German working at the harbour found a way of supplementing the rations of slave workers.

Every eight days or so, a boat went to the Casquets with food and it used to bring back the stale bread they had not eaten there. I used to take this bread and divide it up among the Russians.[22]

For servicemen, the worst enemy was not overwork or malnutrition but sheer, unrelenting boredom.

Soldiers had to be drilled, that goes without saying. They had to be familiar with their weapons and so on, but you couldn't do that twenty-four hours a day. I tried hard to educate the men through courses and study groups. I had a lecturer from the Hanover University, who was an industrial engineer and economist, and he taught the soldiers the basics of his subject. . . . Others were kept busy with medical studies. And then I had a landscape gardener, who designed and laid out gardens. One day he came up to me and said: 'There are these old casements; they are always damp and tend to keep the same temperature; they are ideal for growing mushrooms.' I said: 'Where do you want to get the mushrooms from?' 'Send me home on leave, and I'll bring back enough spores.' And so he did. We got some horse manure, put it into the casements, sowed the mushrooms, and later on we had enough mushrooms to feed all of our 360 men once a week.[23]

The daily routine for the guardians of Alderney started at six in the morning with an inspection an hour later. The rest of the on-duty hours were devoted to weapon training and exercise. Tedious it may have been but it was preferable to that experienced by Otto Spehr, a German prisoner whose crime had been to distribute leaflets calling for the overthrow of the Nazi regime.

In the morning we got up at five o'clock, cleaned the barracks, had breakfast – those that had anything for breakfast. Then, next was the line up. We were counted to see whether we were all there. That usually took a while. And then we went to work at six – either six or seven o'clock, depending on the time of the year. There was a watery soup for lunch, a bit of cabbage or turnip in it or something else, a bit of bacon, a few potatoes. And when we got back in the evening, about six o'clock, there was a check again to see whether everything was there – all the tools. That always took hours. Then supper was given out. Everyone got a piece of bread – that is, one loaf was divided between six people. That had to do for the whole of the next day. And then there were ten grammes of margarine and sometimes a slice of sausage or a slice of cheese. At the end – something to drink that was called coffee.[24]

Maybe it was some comfort all round that the infamous Karl Tietz had his comeuppance. Court-martialled in April 1943, he was sentenced to eighteen months' penal servitude. But it was not for crimes against humanity that he was found guilty. In the eyes of his superiors his offences were far more serious. Tietz had been caught black marketeering in cigarettes and the 'illegal purchase' of watches and other valuables from Dutch prisoners.

11

RAISING THE STAKES

The pace of defence construction slowed appreciably in the summer of 1943. Workers were posted over to Germany to repair war damage such as that caused by the Dam Busters' Raid, while Allied advances into Italy called for strengthening fortifications along the Franco–Italian border. It is a fair guess that the change of emphasis was kept from Hitler, though criticism of his preoccupation with the Channel Islands rose by several decibels when, in November, Field Marshal Rommel was transferred from Italy. His new role was commander of Army Group B in France and The Netherlands with special responsibility for defences.

Rommel's first inspection of the Atlantic Wall left him unimpressed. Less than a third of the planned gun emplacements and bunkers had been completed. Moreover, despite the huge allocation of steel and concrete, many of the redoubts were scarcely more than earthworks. The strong points were often miles apart. Rommel was also critical of the Todt engineers, whom he described as 'neither tactically nor strategically proficient', with no knowledge of the general war situation and no experience of co-operation with the armed forces'.[1] Confident enough to give Hitler unwelcome advice, he delivered a list of strongly worded demands including an immediate withdrawal from the Channel Islands. The 30,000 or more troops stationed there could, he argued, be more effectively deployed manning the defences in Normandy. His prescience was rewarded by a severe rebuff. Hitler had made up his mind. The Channel Islands were sacrosanct: there was to be no further discussion.

Rommel's task of strengthening critical sectors of the Atlantic Wall was not made easier by differences with von Rundstedt, who was not at all convinced that static defences served any useful purpose. His preference was for mobile units that could quickly be brought into action wherever the invasion was concentrated. Rommel's response was to point out the risks from the superior Allied air power. In his view the enemy had to be destroyed before the heavy armoury got off the beaches.

The debate was complicated and tensions heightened by a command structure which allowed Rommel to report directly to Hitler while technically being answerable to von Rundstedt as the overall com-mander in the west. The result was muddle and confusion with Rommel barely able to contain his anger whenever he thought of the 'useless garrison'[2] across the water, waiting for an attack which never came.

But it would be wrong to dismiss the elaborate and costly protection of the Channel Islands as a total waste of German military assets. On the assumption – a rather big assumption, it is true – that the islands were worth defending, the coastal barricades acted as a deterrent against large-scale Allied operations. Hitler was right in believing that the British would, if given the chance, strike at the occupying force if only for propaganda purposes. From the early stages of the war, plans for retaking the islands were discussed at the highest level, amended and discussed again without resolution.

As Chief of Combined Operations, Sir Roger Keyes did his best to divert Churchill's attention from the Channel Islands. The risks of an attack going disastrously wrong were simply too great to contemplate. Keyes was backed up by a Joint Planning Staff report which pointed out that while the capture of any one of the islands was feasible, holding it for any length of time was near impossible. The enemy was likely 'to bring a heavy scale of bomber attack to bear which he could do with the greatest of ease; causing not only casualties to our garrison but heavy losses in life and property to the British population of the island'. Little could be done to prevent this since the islands were outside the range of fighter cover.[3]

The alternative was a quick in-and-out raid on Alderney, the only feasible destination, which 'would have the advantage of inflicting casualties on the enemy, upsetting his sense of security and possibly causing him to reinforce the islands'. But raids against 'important objectives' on the French coast would be far more productive. 'Moreover, the necessity for leaving the islands again would be most discouraging to our own people living there' who might well suffer reprisals.[4]

The Chiefs of Staff soon weighed in against what was now codenamed Operation Attaboy, arguing that 'however carried out, [the operation]would not serve the purpose which the Prime Minister has in mind'.[5] Two objections were raised.

> To land a sufficiently strong force to capture the island, it would be necessary to use the beaches on the North and North West coasts. Landing on any of these beaches, however, is controlled by weather conditions; unless there has been a spell of calm weather lasting three or four days, landing is impracticable owing to swell. Statistics show that a calm spell of the required duration is unlikely in March or April, and it is improbable that landings would be practicable on both sides of the island on the same night. In addition, even if the weather conditions permitted a landing on the North and North West coasts, the outlying navigational dangers would necessitate a lengthy approach at slow speed across strong tides.

More significantly:

> The enemy has been in occupation of the islands long enough to have organised a complete system of defence and experience in

landing agents has proved that the enemy is on the alert. The warning system in the island is known to be particularly efficient and it would be impossible to land undetected.

Churchill agreed, reluctantly, that Attaboy should be filed, at least for the time being. But his minute to General Ismay, the senior military adviser on his personal staff, suggested that far from changing his views, he believed that eventually he would be proved right.

I thought it would have been possible to take [Alderney] in one night, hold it the next day under strong air patrol, and leave the following night. I understood that the Air Force might be able to give the air support during the single day, and that this would bring about many fruitful engagements with the Germans, such as are now sought over the Pas de Calais.

I do not know why it should be supposed that the French coastline is not so well defended as ATTABOY. There is this difference also; whereas the numbers in ATTABOY can be out-matched by us, those available on the mainland have measureless superiority. I shall await the new projects mentioned.[6]

The Channel Islands were back on the agenda in early 1942 when, taking over from Sir Roger Keyes as Chief of Combined Operations, Lord Louis Mountbatten was charged with preparing the way for the invasion of Europe. If Mountbatten and Churchill had one thing in common, it was their love of Boy's Own adventures. Goaded by the Prime Minister, Mountbatten came up with ever more fanciful schemes for sending Hitler into one of his tantrums. He scored occasional bull's-eyes, notably the raid on St Nazaire on 28 March 1942 which deprived the Germans of the only dry dock on the French Atlantic seaboard big enough to accommodate the battleship *Tirpitz*. This was achieved by the bold, but simple, procedure of loading an antiquated US destroyer with delayed charges and ramming the lock gates. Casualties were heavy: all but twenty-seven of six hundred commandoes were killed or captured. But for military and propaganda purposes, the enterprise was

After the raid. Some of the damage caused by the German air attack on St Peter Port. *Imperial War Museum/HU25922*

German troops on parade in St Peter Port. *Imperial War Museum/HU25977*

A victory parade in Jersey. *Courtesy of the Jersey War Tunnels archive*

A British flag on its way to Germany. *© 2000 Topham Picturepoint*

Picture section designed by David Fletcher Welch

The Swastika flies over St Helier Town Hall. *Courtesy of the Jersey War Tunnels archive*

Major Lanz, first German Kommandant of the Channel Islands, is helped from his car by a British bobby. *Imperial War Museum/HU3616*

Bailiffs Alexander Coutanche of Jersey and Victor Carey of Guernsey are watched over by Admiral Friedrich Hueffmeier as they talk with Red Cross officials. *Imperial War Museum/HU5967*

How to handle the islanders. German soldiers are given an open air lecture. *Sueddeutsche Zeitung Photo/Lebrecht*

Together on opposite sides. A German sentry with a British bobby. *Courtesy of the Jersey War Tunnels archive*

Sign of the times. *© 2000 Topham Picturepoint*

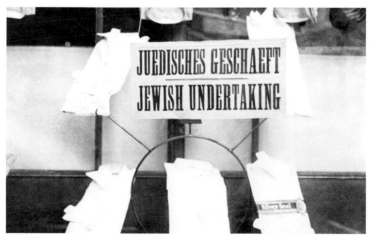

JUEDISCHES GESCHAEFT
JEWISH UNDERTAKING

Nazi race laws reach out to Jersey. *Imperial War Museum/HU25933*

Big Brother is watching you. A portrait of the Führer adorns Guernsey's Palace Cinema. *Imperial War Museum/HU25980*

GAUMONT PALACE

German tanks on the move in Guernsey. The photograph was taken by Frank le Page from an upstairs window. *Imperial War Museum/HU25951*

For most of the war it was only German passengers who used Jersey airport. *© 2000 Topham Picturepoint*

German observation tower at Les Landes, Jersey. *© 2000 Topham Picturepoint*

A motorcycle patrol checks out the Jersey coastline. *© 2000 Topham Picturepoint*

"La Gazette Officielle"

Feldkommandantur 515.

Jersey, den 15. September, 1942.

BEKANNTMACHUNG

AUF höhere Anordnung werden folgende britische Staatsangehörige evakuiert und nach Deutschland überführt.

a) Personen, die ihren festen Wohnsitz nicht auf den Kanalinseln haben, z.B. vom Kriegsausbruch dort Überraschte.

b) alle nicht auf den Inseln geborenen Männer von 16–70 Jahren, die englischer Volkszugehörigkeit sind, mit ihren Familien.

Nähere Weisungen ergehen von der Feldkommandantur 515.

Der Feldkommandant,

gez. KNACKFUSS,
Oberst.

NOTICE

BY order of Higher Authorities the following British subjects will be evacuated and transferred to Germany

(a) Persons who have their permanent residence not on the Channel Islands, for instance, those who have been caught here by the outbreak of the war,

(b) all those men not born on the Channel Islands and 16 to 70 years of age who belong to the English people, together with their families.

Detailed instructions will be given by the Feldkommandantur 515.

Major Friedrich Knackfuss, Feldkommandant of the Islands from 1941-1944, standing with an islander on a promenade in Guernsey.
Imperial War Museum/HU25932

In July 1949, belated recognition came for Ambrose Sherwill, by now Bailiff of Guernsey. During the occupation he was deported to Laufen Internment Camp in Germany. He is pictured here with his wife after receiving his knighthood at Buckingham Palace.
© 2000 Topham Picturepoint

Baron Max von Aufsess, Chief of Administration at the Feldkommandantur, Jersey, 1942-1945.
Imperial War Museum/HU25912

With no petrol for islanders, this ambulance had to rely on an older form of horse power.
Imperial War Museum/HU25930

The first of the Red Cross food parcels arrive on the Vega.
Imperial War Museum/HU25968

Mothers and children collect their food parcels in Guernsey.
Imperial War Museum/HU25920

Road sign in St Helier daubed by islanders, who faced fines and imprisonment if caught. *Imperial War Museum/HU25934*

General Heine proves his identity on boarding the *Bulldog* to sign the surrender. © *Bettmann/CORBIS*

Liberating forces land at St Helier. *Imperial War Museum/HU66318*

Task Force commander, Brigadier A.E. Snow, announces the creation of a short term military government. *Imperial War Museum/HU25937*

Lieut. Colonel E.D. Stoneham of the British Task Force is welcomed by the people of St Peter Port. *Imperial War Museum/D24596*

The Dame of Sark outside her home on liberation day. *Imperial War Museum/V201*

The first British supplies are welcomed by hungry islanders. *Imperial War Museum/V182*

Mrs A.J. Bell of Mount Arrive, Guernsey, smiles for the camera as she shows off the contents of her full shopping baskets. *Imperial War Museum/V197*

A big cheer from the people of St Peter Port for the British Task Force. *Imperial War Museum/D24590*

judged a huge success. Triumphalism led Mountbatten to be yet more ambitious.

On his desk was the aborted Attaboy. Churchill was intent on finding means of inflicting maximum damage on the Germans at minimum military cost. Any attempt to retake Guernsey or Jersey might have put unwarranted demands on the armed forces. But Alderney was surely worth re-examining as a workable proposition. Mountbatten agreed. In his view, the recapture of the island could be used as a base for attacking German convoys, as an emergency landing ground, as an advanced station for Fighter Command's radar coverage and as a springboard for future operations against the Cherbourg peninsula. There was also the opportunity for 'bringing enemy air forces to battle under reasonably favourable circumstances'.[7] The downside of Mountbatten's plan was his inventory of the men and weaponry needed. This included a force of 4,800 infantrymen and paratroopers, six destroyers, five assault ships and eighteen tank landing craft.

To win over the Chiefs of Staff to allocate such generous resources to what was clearly a limited objective, Mountbatten needed powers of persuasion he simply did not possess. Aside from Churchill, the Chief of Combined Operations did not have many fans among senior commanders. A patrician by birth and by nature (he was a great-grandson of Queen Victoria), he condescended to all save the Prime Minister and the King. As Chief of the Imperial General Staff, General Sir Alan Brooke admired Mountbatten's energy but had no faith in his judgement, dismissing him as a bad influence on Churchill with his 'wild proposals' which had more to do with personal aggrandisement than with winning the war. No one trusted Mountbatten. The ascetic Brooke would have agreed with the sentiments, if not the earthy language, of General Sir Gerald Templer, a later adversary of Mountbatten, who in 1956 told the by then First Sea Lord, 'If you swallowed a nail you'd shit a corkscrew.'

Predictably, the Chiefs of Staff savaged the new plan, known as Operation Blazing, which, they argued, called for too many scarce troops for what was essentially a diversionary operation. Weighing in with the opposition was Air Marshal Sir Arthur Harris, Chief of Bomber

Command, who was called upon to prepare the way for an air and sea assault with low-level bombing aimed at taking out the major defences. Harris had two objections: his aircraft would be vulnerable to counter-attack from the French coast (Alderney was only fifteen miles out to sea) and, even assuming a clear run, only a few of the bombs dropped could be expected to hit a target as small as Alderney. The rest would fall harmlessly into the water.

In fairness to Mountbatten, Harris's reluctance to engage the enemy in the Channel Islands was, as much as anything, politically motivated. Almost certainly unwittingly, Mountbatten had based his estimates of bombing accuracy on figures provided by Professor Solly Zuckerman, a Churchill adviser who urged precision targeting on such as transportation centres to inflict maximum disruption on the enemy. Harris wanted none of that. More to his liking was the strategy urged by Professor Frederick Lindemann (later Lord Cherwell), another Churchill confidant, who favoured the 'barn door' bombing offensive against German cities to destroy civilian morale. With Churchill leaning towards Lindemann's strategy as the only immediate way of showing Germany that Britain was capable of fighting back, Harris was on safe ground in standing firm against a project that might otherwise have secured the Prime Minister's enthusiastic endorsement. He was backed up by Air Marshal Sir Sholto Douglas of Fighter Command, who could not imagine how a garrison on Alderney could be protected against the Luftwaffe when the nearest British fighter bases were seventy miles away, while Major General F.A.M. Browning feared that the paratroops of his new Airborne Division and their carriers would be decimated by anti-aircraft defences.

A modified plan for a one-day occupation of Alderney by a smaller force, none of them paratroops, was similarly rejected, though the Chief of Staffs reluctantly agreed to reconsider the matter later in the year. Meanwhile, methods of attack other than 'indiscriminate air bombardment' would be considered.[8] Mountbatten knew when to withdraw. While an attack on the Channel Islands was put on the back burner, he turned his attention to the French ports, hoping for a repeat of the commando performance at St Nazaire.

In August 1942 six thousand mostly Canadian foot soldiers, with naval and air-force support, made an assault on Dieppe. The objective was to unnerve the Germans and to boost confidence at home by capturing and holding for a short time a major French port. Instead the attackers were repulsed with a casualty rate that accounted for well over half the infantrymen killed or taken prisoner.

Casting about for a project that would reburnish his reputation after this unmitigated disaster, Mountbatten once again focused on the Channel Islands. By now aerial reconnaissance together with intelligence from escapees had put together a pretty accurate picture of Channel Island defences. Though Dieppe had proved there could be no easy walkover of the German fortifications, Hitler, ironically, took the opposite view, maintaining that the mere fact of the raid taking place justified a yet higher priority for coastal impregnability. Mountbatten argued that while the capture of Guernsey 'would be highly desirable' and of Jersey 'desirable but by no means essential', the assault and capture of Alderney would be 'essential . . . prior to an assault on the beaches of the Cherbourg Peninsula'.[9] In other words, in Mountbatten's view, the successful invasion of Europe depended on gaining a foothold in the Channel Islands.

In the hope of achieving this, Mountbatten made concessions to the Harris school of thought by proposing an air assault so massive that an attack from the sea would meet with little opposition. Invited to come up with figures, Mountbatten proposed dropping on Alderney 4,600 tons of high explosives carried by 1,500 medium and heavy bomber sorties over three nights. Having whacked this ball towards the net, Mountbatten followed with a volley for the other Channel Islands, with the hardest hit for Jersey. Operation Condor (some suggested unkindly that it would have been better codenamed Operation Dieppe) anticipated a blanket bombing of the east and west coasts of the island followed by commando and infantry landings at strategic points with paratroop drops on the racecourse and the airfield. After three days of consolidating the beachheads, there would be a three-pronged attack on St Helier. There were no estimates of civilian casualties, but no one doubted that they would be heavy.

On all counts Mountbatten failed to get his way. Despite his deference to 'Bomber' Harris, the top-level consensus was against an operation of such limited objectives and with such high risks of severe losses of men and military hardware. Alan Brooke recorded meetings where Mountbatten 'drove me completely to distraction . . . [he] . . . is quite irresponsible, suffers from the most desperate illogical brain, always producing red herrings'.[10] A month later, he was again railing against 'Dickie', who 'gave me a heap of trouble with a proposed attack on the Channel Islands which was not in its proper strategic setting and tactically quite adrift.[11]

Alan Brooke told Mountbatten that the proposed scale of air bombardment, heavy though it was, 'was most unlikely to destroy the defences' while Air Chief Marshal Sir Charles Portal pointed out that Alderney was in range of field batteries on the western tip of the Cherbourg Peninsula, which meant that British troops on the island would be under constant attack.[12] Though Churchill kept aloof from the dispute between Mountbatten and the Chiefs of Staff, there can be no doubt as to which side he was on. As late as the summer of 1944 he was expressing disappointment that having 'pestered repeatedly about operations for the liberation of the Channel Islands', no assault had been mounted.[13] His frustration was in no way relieved by sporadic air attacks on harbours and airfields and by hit-and-run commando raids such as that on Sark in October 1942, which led to the second wave of deportations of British-born citizens.

After Germany's surrender there was much speculation among islanders as to why their homes had escaped the devastation visited on Caen and St Malo and other French towns. One popular theory had it that a British government could not be seen raining bombs onto British subjects. But this was to credit political and military leaders with sensitivities they could not afford to possess. Indeed, one of the few indications of account being taken of the civilian population was an American declaration that air attacks on the Channel Islands would be without the participation of the US Air Force. But even here the fear of German propaganda making a meal of what nowadays would be called death by friendly fire took priority over any real concern for the welfare of the islanders.

There can be little doubt that the deciding factor against Mountbatten was the scale of his operations against the likely costs and the risks of failure. In this last context, the strength of the German defences was a major consideration. If the islands had been lightly defended with a smaller concentration of German troops, an attempt at recapture, with Bomber Command leading the way, could almost certainly have taken place. Here then is one of the great ironies of the war in the west. The Channel Islands were saved from destruction not by their own efforts or by the actions of their protectors and allies, but by the paranoia of the Führer and the exertions of the Organization Todt.

12

RESISTANCE AND RETALIATION

The first response to bravery is to praise it. Marie Ozanne and the Reverend Clifford Cohu died for their beliefs and for the right to free expression. They were, in their own ways, indomitable spirits who were ready to make the final sacrifice. But over their harrowing stories hangs the question: what did they achieve?

Marie Ozanne was a major in the Salvation Army, a proscribed organisation under the occupation. Defying the ban, she continued to appear in uniform and to preach from the steps of the Nocq Road Citadel in St Sampson's in Guernsey. This put the Germans into a quandary. To arrest her would have been seen as an overreaction to the activities of someone they regarded as a religious fanatic. On the other hand, her defiance was setting a precedent that others might follow. After numerous cautions, Ozanne pushed her luck beyond tolerable limits with voluble protests at the treatment of slave workers held in a compound close to her parents' home. Arrested and imprisoned without trial, she fell desperately ill, and died of peritonitis on 23 February 1943. Few attended her funeral, which was not publicised.

Canon Clifford Cohu, though much older than Ozanne, was equally zealous in advertising his independence. A leading participant in an underground news network, he took to cycling through St Saviour, ringing a bell like a town crier, and shouting, 'Wonderful news today', before delivering the latest BBC bulletins. His inevitable arrest led to a rounding-up of eighteen of his fellow conspirators including John Nicolle, a farmer, Joseph Tierney, a parish cemetery worker, and Arthur Dimmery, an English-born gardener.

Cohu was sentenced to eighteen months, to be served first in Dijon then in Preungesheim prison in Frankfurt, where for long periods he suffered cold and hunger in solitary confinement. The last his wife heard of him was in July 1944. Two months later he was dead. Nicolle, Tierney and Dimmery also succumbed to starvation and ill-treatment. Their names, along with that of Marie Ozanne appear on the Jersey Memorial, unveiled on 9 November 1996.

That it took over fifty years for their defiance of the occupation to be publicly recognised speaks volumes for the confusion among islanders when it came to deciding whether or not resistance had been justified. One side of the argument held that Marie Ozanne and Clifford Cohu had given their lives needlessly, that Cohu, by his foolhardy actions, had been culpable in leading others to early graves, and that it would have been better all round if they had redirected their religious fervour into supporting those in authority who were trying to minimise the damage caused by the occupation. The counter argument was that in refusing to submit to tyrannical rule, the resisters, however bizarre their activities, were sending out a message that was impossible to ignore.

The contradiction was endemic to the curious situation in which the islanders found themselves. Urged to stay at their posts and to do their best for their countrymen, the bailiffs and, by implication, others of the civil administration had to try to minimise the impact of the occupation by working alongside the Germans to maintain the social fabric, while doing nothing that would adversely affect the war effort of the mother country. It was a perilously thin line they had to tread. For hard-pressed officials, fearful of any action that might invite reprisals, the resisters were simply trouble-seekers causing misery for all. Intent on pressing their argument, at times they made the case against resistance bluntly and injudiciously. Ambrose Sherwill, who at the beginning of the occupation gave unintentional comfort to the enemy by speaking on German radio without sufficient thought to the likely reaction, was surely equally misguided in declaring that escapees who had braved treacherous waters had committed a 'crime against the local population'.

It is easy enough to be wise with hindsight but then, as now, the achievements of the escapees, many of whom carried valuable intelligence on the Channel Islands' defences, were beyond praise. One of the first was Denis Vibert, who demonstrated 'remarkable endurance and daring' in his determination to reach the mainland. Interestingly, in his subsequent discussions with the intelligence services, he gave full credit to Coutanche who 'has shown up very well during this trying period' and whose relations with the Germans 'has averted many possible unpleasant situations'.[1]

Vibert's first attempt to escape was by rowing boat, in November 1940.

> He had planned to row from Jersey to certain rocks south of Guernsey on the first night, with the intention of hiding there during the succeeding day. The first part of the adventure was successful, but unfortunately the wind changed the next day and it was impossible to continue the journey the following night. He waited four days but the conditions did not change. During this time he developed influenza, and finally he decided to abandon the attempt and return to Jersey. The return was not uneventful as his boat was wrecked and he had to swim a quarter of a mile to shore. His absence had not been discovered by the Germans.[2]

More preparation went into his second attempt. In the autumn of 1941 he acquired a small boat, two outboard motors and a quantity of petrol siphoned off from a German truck, and set out at night.

> The first bit of bad luck occurred just after leaving; two German 'E' boats passed about a hundred yards away and although he was not seen the wash half filled his boat making his little store of food

uneatable. He rowed some four miles out to sea before making use of his outboard motor. He drank all his water supply that night. By daybreak he was some fifteen miles west of Guernsey, and he replenished the petrol tank. At this stage the sea was rather choppy and water got into the engine making it unserviceable. He then fitted the spare engine but had the misfortune to let it fall into the sea. He rowed for three days, sleeping part of the nights. He had no food or water. On the evening of the third day he had reached within two miles of Portland Bill when a British Destroyer picked him up.[3]

The best estimate of the number of escapees is 225 (150 from Jersey, 75 from Guernsey), of whom at least a third were captured or drowned. Anecdotal evidence bears witness to their great courage in defiance of heavy odds. Arthur Kent's diary records an attempted escape from Jersey that had tragic consequences.

> Three youngsters between the ages of 15 and 18 [Peter Hassall, Maurice Gould and Dennis Audrain] put to sea one night in a frail craft on the south coast of the island. The boat struck a rock half-a-mile out and sank, one boy being drowned [Audrain], the other two reaching the shore exhausted. The German Court Martial, ruling that photographs of military objects had been found on the boys, sentenced the survivors to nine months each; six months for themselves; and six months shared for the boy who was drowned! – such is the curious working of their minds.[4]

What Arthur Kent could not have known at the time was that the boys had been given away by a member of Peter Hassall's family, one who presumably went along with Sherwill's doctrine that escaping was a crime against the people. Maurice Gould died in prison, a victim of tuberculosis aggravated by ill-treatment. Hassall survived three years' hard labour. When he returned to Jersey after the war he spoke little of his ordeal until, a few years before he died in 1998, he shared memories which have 'not given me a proper night's sleep since May 1942'.

Guernseyman Fred Hockey, who was determined to join his wife and child in England, nearly didn't make it. He and seven comrades were in an open boat when a German aircraft flew over and dropped a flare.

> Terrified, the men lay flat on the bottom of the boat and held their breath. It was like daylight until the flare burnt out and the men could not understand why they were not seen. They continued on their hazardous journey and at 4 a.m. their engine broke down. This was repaired and on they went. It was foggy which made navigation difficult, but on the credit side the fog was a cloak that hid them from the enemy.
>
> They sighted land at Start Point in Devon and anchored at Berry Head at 6 p.m. the following day after a nineteen-hour journey.[5]

Inevitably, the undertaking had repercussions.

> The Germans were furious and stopped permits for fishing. An order was published in the 'Press' stating that all boats in the island had to be in the town harbour by a given date. This was particularly hard on the west coast fishermen who had to bring their boats across the island to the harbour as best they could. A warning was published stating that, should there be any more escapes, reprisals would be taken against the Guernsey people, and males of military age would be taken to France.[6]

It was this that prompted Sherwill's denunciation.

If anything that worked against German interests counts as resistance, the help given to slave workers must qualify even when the motivation was purely humanitarian. It certainly took courage. Dr Noel McKinstry, the Jersey Medical Officer of Health who was tireless in promoting the art of preventive medicine, was also instrumental in protecting deserters from the ranks of forced labour. There was invariably an ambulance on hand to pick up a young Soviet on the run and one of them was cared for in the McKinstry household for five months while he recovered from a breakdown.[7]

But the chief impetus came from the members of the Jersey Democratic Movement, a group of young radicals who, bored with endless discussion on what would happen after the end of the occupation, wanted action now. Among the founder members were Leslie Huelin and Norman Le Brocq. They created a network of support for escapees, helping them to find refuge in farms and other safe houses in the north of the island which were generally free from German surveillance. A contact in the Town Hall in St Helier supplied blank identity cards while another friend at the Food Control Office provided a stack of ration books. Collections of food and clothing were organised. One benefactor was Len Perkins, whose Co-op bread round took on quite a few non-paying customers.

One of the safe houses belonged to Jack Le Breton, a farmer whose wife, Phyllis, recorded her memory of a young Russian who arrived one night, half-starved and weak from exhaustion.

> I was in the kitchen when he tapped the window. We knew at once that he was another of those prisoners. My husband always gave them something to eat. I used to say to him – you're playing with fire. And my father-in-law was worried, too. He said – you'll get us all sent to Germany. I was very nervous but this particular one came to live with us. He was filthy dirty when he arrived but my husband gave him some clean clothes. In the evenings he would sit with me in the kitchen, learning English. He would say – what means this? What means that?
>
> At night he slept in our old car in the garage which we locked up permanently but there was a secret door. He was the sort of man we could trust. The children loved him and when he could understand some English he used to read them fairy stories.
>
> Sometimes we would be here in the kitchen and we would see the Gestapo out of the window. Our Russian would go running out of the back door to hide. There were a lot of close shaves like that. The Gestapo often used to come. They didn't knock. They

walked straight in. When our Russian felt that to stay with us any longer might attract attention he'd move on to another of the houses where he'd be safe.[8]

Mrs Le Breton was wrong on one detail. The islands were free of the Gestapo, although Karl-Heinz Wölfle of the Secret Field Police (GFP) buttressed his power of intimidation by announcing himself as 'Wölfle of the Gestapo'. But the GFP were frightening enough. Another Russian slave worker found shelter with Louisa Gould who had a grocer's shop in St Ouen, Jersey. One of her own sons having been drowned at sea, Mrs Gould found consolation in caring for the young man.

She decided to keep him for the rest of the occupation. Of course, it was an indictable offence to hide an escaped prisoner. Unfortunately, she was given away by an informer. That's what was suspected – someone who held some grievance or was jealous and wanted to get her into trouble from some feeling of spite. Louisa was taken off to the town prison and interrogated. The truth soon came out and Louisa was sent over to a German prison in France and finally to Ravensbruck concentration camp. The devils put her into a gas chamber and that was the end.[9]

One of the biggest challenges in giving aid was linguistic. A Ukrainian lodging with the parents of Len de Poidevin was known simply as Alex.

There was a dried-out brook by the side of our house and garden and I was there digging away at something and this chap popped his head up out of the ditch and frightened the life out of me. He was in a terrible state; beaten and starved. Of course, my family took pity on him. He couldn't speak English, but he always used to call me 'boy'; I was only a boy then anyway. But my sister is very good at picking up languages and she could converse with him far better than I could.

Alex was given a bed in the loft. He was in hiding for three years.[10] In all, around one hundred islanders played a part in sheltering Russian prisoners.

Few if any of these activities were known to the civil authorities. It was best that way since there could be no conflict of interests. The problems started when a senior official was faced with a stark choice between patriotic instinct and the demands of his German masters. Investigating a robbery in May 1943, the Jersey police came by the incidental knowledge – passed on by a vindictive neighbour – that Frederick Page's nearby house contained two illegal wireless sets. Centenier Garden, the officer in charge, consulted the attorney-general, Charles Duret Aubin. What should he do? He felt sympathy for Page, and for James Davey, in whose house the listeners had gathered. But if the Germans discovered that he had falsified his report, retribution would be swift and innocent people might suffer. Duret Aubin dodged the issue, telling Garden that he 'must decide with his own conscience where his duty lay'. He made clear, however, that if a formal report came his way he would have no choice but to pass it on to the occupiers. Having consulted his colleagues, Garden decided that the community came before the individual. Page and the others were promptly arrested, tried and sentenced to twenty-one months' imprisonment. Page died in Germany four months before the end of the war.

No doubt Garden and Duret Aubin felt great remorse. Doubtless also they told themselves that what they did was better than the alternative, a German-dominated administration that would give scant consideration to the welfare of the islanders. The ever-present risk was that, in trying to preserve a thin veneer of sovereignty, they would sacrifice too many of their compatriots. This dilemma was characteristic of other essentially law-abiding societies such as The Netherlands, Denmark and Norway, where the long absence of war had left citizens vulnerable to bullying tactics. Acquiescence in German demands led to further demands and to a humiliating deference to the reigning authority. In the Channel Islands this reached its nadir with the acceptance of the notorious Order for the Protection of the Occupying Authorities, which compelled island officials to report to the Germans any civilian wrongdoing. This and an overscrupulous regard for the law is what led to the death of Frederick Page.

*

Even recognising the agonising problems of living with the enemy, it came to be a matter of regret and recrimination that no formal protests were made over the confiscation of wireless sets in June 1942, the deportation of English-born islanders to internment in Germany in September 1942 and, most particularly, over the register of Jewish residents in the autumn of 1940.

The post-war revelation of the horror of the concentration camps and the barbaric quest for the 'Final Solution' have, quite properly, led to a heightened awareness of the preliminaries to the Holocaust which were not recognised at the time. How many of the Dutch civil servants who signed the 'Aryan declaration' in October 1940 knew that details of family history were to be carefully scrutinised for signs of Jewish ancestry? Even if they were aware, it may have seemed a matter of small significance until colleagues of Jewish descent were summarily dismissed.

In the Channel Islands there was even less reason for immediate concern when an order was posted for Jews to identify themselves. The general impression was that there were no Jews in the islands, since the few who might have qualified had taken the opportunity four months earlier to evacuate to the mainland.

This was how Sherwill excused his easy acceptance of the order which came at the time when he was negotiating with the Germans over the Nicolle and Symes affair. 'I had as much as I could take for the moment,' he wrote later.[11] Nonetheless he came to feel ashamed that he had submitted so easily, not least because subsequently it was discovered that there were in fact five Jews living in Guernsey and that as a direct consequence of the anti-Jewish orders (there were nine in all), three women were deported in 1942, the first of thousands from the occupied territories in Europe. The deaths of Thérèse Steiner, Auguste Spitz and Marianne Grunfeld were registered in Auschwitz.

Of the members of the Royal Court who had to approve Sherwill's recommendation to accept the first anti-Jewish order for it to be registered as an enforceable law by the civil authority, only one, Sir Abraham Lainé, refused his assent. Sherwill paid tribute. 'As I sat listening to him, I realised how right he was.'[12] But it was not enough to turn any votes.

In Jersey too, the first order was assumed to be an ideological formality with no practical application. Drawing on the memories of Betty Bair, the official interpreter for the States, Bob Le Sueur records that while there was no formal protest, attempts were made to avoid the issue. A German demand for a list of resident Jews was met with assumed incomprehension. There was no such list. What about the census returns? These were held in London and, in any case, did not specify religious affiliations. Then a list had to be compiled, based on local knowledge. Surely, the Bailiff knew of Jewish families? Coutanche felt on safe ground in giving names of those who had already left the island. But he then went on to say that to the best of his knowledge there were no Jews remaining in Jersey. It was a claim too far. If Coutanche was right, argued the Feldkommandantur, then why would he object to the Order being registered? The matter was conceded without further discussion. In the event, though Jewish families were caught up in the general deportation of aliens in 1942, only one Jew was deported from Jersey simply because he was Jewish, a Romanian engineer who felt safe as a neutral then got caught when Romania entered the war on the German side.[13] But that was one too many.

Without offering excuses, the anti-Jewish legislation has to be seen in context. Recent delvers into the records have accused Sherwill, Coutanche and the rest of covert anti-Semitism. If treating the Jews as a race apart is anti-Semitic, then there is some justice in the argument. But with the notable exception of the Nordic countries, this was the prevailing attitude across Europe, not least in Britain, and America.

The Jewish question had been in the news ever since Hitler had come to power in January 1933. If, seven years later, the Nazis' genocidal intentions were not yet fully understood, the persecution of Jews was well attested by such as Kristallnacht (the night of broken glass) and the subsequent round-up of 30,000 German Jews. Yet almost every country considered safe for refugees imposed strict limits on Jewish immigration. In Britain, the revealing excuse for keeping the lid on refugee numbers was fear of stirring up anti-Jewish agitation. By way of a gesture, the government was ready to offer a 'temporary refuge' to ten thousand Jewish children as long as they came without their parents. It was hoped that what became known as the Kindertransporte would be replicated in the United States, where a figure of 20,000 was projected. The proposal did not get beyond a congressional committee. One of the counter-arguments held that accepting children minus parents was contrary to the laws of God. Even well into the war, anti-Semitic sentiment was commonplace in the letter pages of the American and British press.

In this murky light, the response of the Channel Islands to Nazi racism appears relatively benign. Coutanche made a stand against Jewish persecution in refusing to endorse the penultimate Order, confirmed in Guernsey on 30 June 1942, which ruled that Jews had to identify themselves by the six-pointed star. It is, therefore, surprising that Coutanche did not do more to rein back on the activities of his Aliens Officer. Clifford Orange was the archetypical petty bureaucrat for whom compiling and filing were deeply satisfying tasks. Who he worked for was less important than the work itself which he performed assiduously – in this case, to identify twelve Jews living in Jersey and to threaten their survival. In Guernsey, this role was assumed by the equally dedicated William Sculpher, the chief police officer.[14]

If any defence can be mounted for Orange and Sculpher, it is in the refrain heard frequently at the Nuremberg trial of Nazi war criminals: 'I was only obeying orders.' This was seen at the time as a peculiarly German excuse for the abuse of human rights; it was surely inconceivable that British public servants would ever be faced with the dilemma of enacting policies which they knew to be morally dubious.

Not long after the war, however, this situation did arise. In the Suez crisis of 1956, civil servants across the great departments of state were convinced that the attack on Egypt was horribly wrong in principle and in practice. No one of any consequence resigned but many came to reproach themselves for acting against their instincts and against the best interests of their country. One commentator on the profession of government concluded that, 'Neutrality in public office tends in the end to moral corruption.'[15] Whatever we feel about this, it is undeniable that Orange and Sculpher, however despicable their actions, were behaving true to the form of the British as well as the German civil service. They were only obeying orders.

One of the saddest cases with anti-Semitic undertones was that of Lucille Schwob and Suzanne Malherbe, half-sisters who faced the death penalty for incitement to mutiny; they had distributed pacifist and anti-Nazi slogans with a strong religious flavour, in areas where they would be seen by young soldiers deeply troubled by news filtering through of the destruction wreaked on their homes in Germany. Both talented artists, with Malherbe fluent in German, these single-minded resisters got away with it for so long because they worked independently without support from other islanders who knew them simply as 'the French ladies', eccentric but harmless. When eventually, the Feldpolizei caught up with them, so effective had been the counter-propaganda it was at first assumed that they headed a whole network of dissenters.

On their arrest in July 1944 they joined in a suicide pact, overdosing on gardenal. They failed and woke up in prison. Ironically, their effort to end it all saved their lives because by the time they had recovered sufficiently to stand trial, the Allied invasion of Europe had put a stop to deportation. In the event the death sentence was pronounced but with a strong recommendation for mercy, to which Coutanche added his name.

Interviewed after the war, Judge Harmsen was keen to stress his own role in standing down the firing squad.

> I said to the defending counsel, a German officer who was a lawyer, he should file a petition for mercy. And he said to me, 'Why? It is right that they are being sentenced to death.' And I said, 'But you are their defending counsel. Of course you must file a petition for mercy. I hereby give you an official order to file a petition for mercy.' And the Bailiff also filed a petition for mercy, and in it he maintained that for a hundred years no man on the island had been executed, and since time immemorial, no

woman. And so the files were tied up and packed, a plane arrived from Germany and took the files away, and I hoped I would never see the files again. The war would soon be over anyway. Just imagine: the files came back. I did a tour round my desk before I opened them to see what was in them. And so, great relief, they had been pardoned. Ten years' penal servitude.[16]

Eager to reaffirm his friendly relations with the civil authorities, Harmsen went on to claim that Attorney-General Duret Aubin, in a plea for the release of the two prisoners before the surrender, agreed that 'they are bad women' and promised 'when peace comes, I will make sure they leave the island'.[17] Unconventional perhaps. But bad? It is hard to believe that Duret Aubin was serious. Unless, of course, he had been talking to Baron von Aufsess, who liked to parade himself as the epitome of sophistication but whose prejudices, aired in his *Occupation Diary*, were close to the surface.

There are very few Jews in the islands. The two Jewish women who have just been arrested belong to an unpleasant category. These women had long been circulating leaflets urging German soldiers to shoot their officers. At last they were tracked down. A search of the house, full of ugly cubist paintings, brought to light a quantity of pornographic material of an especially revolting nature. One woman had had her head shaved and been thus photographed in the nude from every angle. Thereafter she had worn men's clothes. Further nude photographs showed both women practising sexual perversion, exhibitionism and flagellation. I declined with distaste the loan of a book on cubism written by the father.[18]

When, after nine months in prison, Schwob and Malherbe were sent home they found that they had been stripped of their possessions, including their valuable collection of Expressionist paintings. In every respect they had paid dearly for their resistance.

Others endured even greater torments. Arrested for helping to set up a transmitter for sending messages to a listening post in the south of England, Maurice Green's father Stanley was imprisoned in France before being sent to Buchenwald. There he was beaten and tortured and suffered mock executions. At the end of the war he weighed just four-and-a-half stone. Maurice Green remembers:

He never did [adapt back to normal life]; if he'd see something on television . . . the camps, you know . . . he would sit there crying his eyes out. One day I asked, 'Why is it you always cry Dad? Haven't you got over it?' He said, 'No. You know what job they gave me in Buchenwald? Loading bodies onto a horse and cart; four of us, each one take a leg and each one take a hand. Throw them on the cart; some of these were too weak to move, but they weren't dead. We took them along and they went down the shoots into the crematorium; we never heard anymore.' He said, 'What are they going to think in heaven when I die?' He was never the same. I could never recognise him as my Dad. He was a totally different person . . . [Later] he had a couple of minor strokes which the doctor said was from the beatings he'd had on the head. Evidently he had marks on his back. He had a bayonet put through his foot when he was in Buchenwald. He didn't obey quick enough; it was actually a Jewish boy who saved his foot. He was a doctor; he lit a fire, burnt some sticks and put the stick right through the hole where the bayonet had been, and that saved Dad's foot. He also had a bayonet scar [on his side]. They said he was lucky to have survived.[19]

A hundred or so islanders saw the inside of a concentration camp. William Symes, landlord of The Dive in St Peter Port, smuggled out information to the Resistance in France. He too ended up in Buchenwald. Clarence Painter and his son Peter, found in possession of a Mauser, a souvenir of the last war, went to Natzweiler-Strulthof camp.[20] And so the roll-call continues.

Over the entire war, there were four thousand arrests across the Channel Islands. Most were for relatively minor offences such as possessing an illegal wireless or daubing anti-German graffiti. But the terror of discovery should never be understated, least of all by those who have not felt the tap on the shoulder or heard the slam of the prison cell door.

As the German reputation for invincibility crumbled away, resistance hardened. Even if the islanders could not muster the raw power to inflict heavy damage on the interloper, there were countless ways of making his life difficult. This absence of co-operation, which stopped just short of active hostility, could be just as effective in undermining German authority as sabotaging railway lines or sniping at patrols. Opposition of the sort known in the British military as 'dumb insolence', hard to pin down but effective for all that, opened up cracks in the German power structure.

Defiance was implicit in the solidarity shown at any public event where crowds gathered. Arthur Kent was at the final for the Jersey Occupation Cup which marked the end of the football season.

> Nearly five thousand supporters flocked to the ground with almost everyone sporting their favourite's colours – red and white, and blue and white; moreover, a score or more of the farmers drove their vans in from the country, each one crammed with enthusiasts and the horses trailing team ribbons. . . . Rattles sounded, bugles blared, bells were rung and motor horns wailed; the whole contributing to the noisiest, gayest assembly in the four years of occupation. . . . The Germans, frowning their disapproval at this wild exuberance, made it clear that the people had gathered, not so much in support of the football teams, but as a demonstration for the fall of Rome which had occurred the same day! In consequence they vetoed any further advertising of sporting fixtures likely to induce crowds to gather.[21]

Anti-German sentiments were also on display at the funerals of Allied sailors and airmen. In June 1943, when a British plane was brought down over Jersey, the burial of the two airmen at Mont-à-l'Abbé was held at dawn. The expectation that this would deter mourners turned out to be wide of the mark. Hundreds lined the mile route from the hospital chapel to the cemetery.

> A great many beautiful wreaths were sent, mostly made with red, white and blue flowers with ribbons and sympathetic inscriptions attached, and for several days schoolchildren and their elders continued to enlarge the mass of wreaths and flowers upon the grave – large crowds also attended the funeral shortly afterwards of an American airman who had crashed into the sea off the island.[22]

When, in October 1943, HMS *Charybdis* was sunk by German torpedoes west of the Channel Islands, the funeral of twenty-one seamen washed up on Guernsey's shores was organised by the authorities as a low-key affair. In the event 5,000 people turned up at the Foulon cemetery, a never-to-be-forgotten demonstration of solidarity. It was not long before a ban was imposed on civilian attendance at servicemen's funerals.

Earlier, in the summer of 1941, there was an overwhelming response to the V for Victory campaign launched on the BBC. The Churchillian sign was soon appearing on walls and doors. Bernard Baker was initially dubious as to the purpose of this campaign. 'What possible good can it do? What possible harm can it do to the enemy war machine?' But he was soon persuaded that the V battle was worthwhile.

> Yesterday, enrolment day for the 'V' army, saw quite a number of 'V's put in various places around the island. A flight of some twenty steps leading to the upper gardens at Westmount (and quite a favourite spot with the Huns) had 'V' on every step. 'V's were painted in the roadway at Mont au Prêtre and chalked up in several other places.

The sound version of the V was in Morse code, as heard in the opening notes of Beethoven's Fifth Symphony.

You can hear cyclists doing it on their bells, the telephone rings –
three sharp rings and a long one, door bells and knockers suffer
from the same malady, and the 'V' greeting is becoming more and
more common. That such a childish thing should have come to
mean so much is really one of the remarkable things in this 'crazy
war'.[23]

The German response was to adopt the V for themselves.

Their cars and lorries all carry the 'V'. The only difference between
the 'V' for victory and the 'V' for 'vernichtung' which I
understand means disaster or annihilation, is that the German 'V'
is surrounded by laurel leaves. The great people are just
surrounding themselves with them in an effort to ridicule the
campaign. I wonder if they realise just what an admission this is
on their part that the 'V' is getting them down.[24]

Dr Wilhelm Casper, the chief civil administrator in the Channel
Islands until 1943, later claimed that the idea for the German V came
from John Leale, Guernsey's President of the Controlling Committee
after Sherwill, who apparently suggested, 'If you don't like the Victory
sign, make it yourself, then it will cease soon.'[25] This is hard to believe,
the more so because Casper's testimony of his time in the Channel
Islands is at best selective. But Leale was responsive to German
sensitivities. It is at least possible that he saw the V for Victory campaign
as a dangerous irritant that had to be neutralised.

For young people otherwise constrained by the deprivation of war,
the occupation was a licence to behave badly. When Mum and Dad
railed against that terrible man Hitler and all his works, childhood
inhibitions were cast aside. Breaking the curfew was the most common
offence. In 1941 seventy-two cases came before the Jersey Royal Court.
Food was stolen from military stores, fires were started, cables cut, rocks
left on railway lines.

We pinched German signposts like at Robin Hood one evening 12 signposts were missing, they burnt well in the fire mind you, because they were dry wood. The Germans had to go round in circles, and in the end the Bailiff put a notice in the paper saying not to touch these German signs because they were getting very upset about it, and they had to spend hours looking for particular places.[26]

Short-tempered Germans could be driven into paroxysms of rage, as Fred Gallienne discovered when he decided to ride his bicycle on the left of the road.

Of course at that time we had to cycle on the right-hand side of the road, and the horse and carts had to go on the right, everything had to go on the right-hand side of the road. I was going along there on the right-hand side of the road, then I suddenly thought: 'Oh sod this, I'm going to cycle on the left.' So there I was, cycling away on the left, when the road suddenly goes downhill. It sweeps down at the bottom, and goes up the other side, and there was a high hedge on both sides in those days. I was going merrily down on the left-hand side, but what I didn't know was that there was a German soldier on his bike coming down the other side of the hill on the right-hand side!

Well, I think the inevitable happened, we collided at the bottom. . . . I quickly got up and ran up the hill and hid in a gateway, where I could look down and see what he was doing, and he was in a furious, absolute rage. He picked up my bike, hurled it against a granite wall, then he grabbed hold of the tyres and started pulling at the valves and releasing the air from both my tyres. And then he saw my packet with the valuable shirt inside it, and I thought, 'please don't take that'. Anyway, he didn't even open it up, he just hurled it over a hedge.[27]

Some teenagers like Richard Williams raised the stakes with violent confrontations.

On one occasion we were arrested by two Germans after breaking into Commercial Street food store. They must have thought that because we were quite young they could handle us so one passed the other his rifle and he grabbed us by the scruff of the neck. As he marched us up the street we turned and gave him a good whack in the stomach with all our force which put him down and as the other fumbled with both the rifles we jumped on him and threw him to the ground and gave him a good kicking and made a run for it. We managed to creep into West's Cinema through a fire exit and mixed with the crowd which certainly saved us.[28]

Others took to more ambitious forms of resistance.

Getting towards the end of the war, there was a camp opposite the Links Hotel where they had a lot of Poles and slave workers, but a lot of Germans as well, and we decided that one day we would burn it down. So my cousin and myself one night, got some paraffin from the shop my aunt owned, and we crawled underneath the barbed wire and put it in the shed and set fire to the whole camp. We ran off like rockets, we were up the lane and hiding in the golf course at Grouville and we could see all these flames coming up and we could hear them all shouting. I did my bit for the resistance that night! Well, of course they tried to find out who had burned it down but they never caught us. Every time I phone my cousin up in London now he says remember the night we burnt the camp down – we never got caught![29]

As the incidents of delinquent behaviour – so judged by the military and civil authorities – increased, so too did the severity of punishment, as Arthur Kent recorded in his diary.

Every cell in the local prison is filled with political prisoners arraigned on a score of different charges: pilferers of German stores; lads who refused to do work for them of a military nature;

people caught disseminating the news; others found with wireless sets.

A young lady, pestered daily by two Germans as she attended her horses in their stables could no longer stand their observations and, with considerable accuracy, threw a handful of manure at the amorous Huns. The sequel was a two months' sentence. She appealed and it was increased to five.

A young boy, working as a messenger in our office, did not step off the pavement quickly enough when two German officers were approaching and brushed against the shoulders of one – he got fourteen days' imprisonment.

The son of an elderly and greatly esteemed gentleman, Major Ogier, was arrested in possession of some drawings of the island's defence system. Both he and his father who was in very bad health were taken to Paris for trial. The youth was certified as simple-minded by German doctors who put him in an institution but Major Ogier was sentenced to a period of imprisonment. Upon release he was sent back to Jersey in a very weak condition, but he was not permitted to stay here with his wife to recuperate in health. Within a fortnight they had him transported to Germany where he died after a few weeks in an internment camp.[30]

Two boys who stole explosives were lucky to escape the death sentence. Their intention, it was said, was to destroy the States building. It was another difficult case for Judge Harmsen, who had no wish to be saddled with the responsibility for executing two juveniles. Having decided that they were too young to be responsible for their actions, the charge was reduced to one of theft. Found guilty there was then the question of where they would be held, the adult prison being deemed unsuitable. Not for the first time Attorney-General Duret Aubin came to the rescue of his German overlords, as Harmsen recalled:

He said, 'I know a farmer in the north of the island, who gives a strict upbringing to young boys who have behaved badly. I suggest that the two boys are taken to him and taught by hard work not to do such a stupid thing again.' I said, 'OK, let's do that.' And so the matter was settled.[31]

Whatever the boys learned from the experience, it must have occurred to them that the margin between resistance and survival was terrifyingly narrow.

13

BEGINNING OF THE END

Leo Harris was in a wardrobe when he heard about the invasion. That was where his father had hidden the radio. After the D-Day announcement of Allied landings on the French coast, the family went out on to a balcony to watch for the German reaction at Havre des Pas.

> What greeted us was a very pleasing sight as they rushed around putting up great coils of barbed wire which they pulled across the streets. You can still see the hooks in the walls where they dropped the wire. They had machine guns out on street corners with sandbags around them, a couple of men lying behind them, all wearing helmets obviously ready to repel any attack. The shell guns were manned. At Green Street, we could see that the gunners were all there, the little shell gun freshly lubricated and ammunition brought up for it. And there was a lot of activity, men marching up and down and orders being shouted.[1]

On the front pages of the daily press there was a stark warning from Colonel Heine for civilians not to get involved:

Germany's enemy is on the point of attacking French soil. I expect the population of Jersey to keep its head, to remain calm, and to refrain from any acts of sabotage and from hostile acts against the German Forces, even should the fighting spread to Jersey.

At the first sign of unrest or trouble I will close the streets to traffic and will secure hostages. Attacks against the German Forces will be punished by death.[2]

None of this came as a surprise. Anticipation of great things about to happen had taken hold in the spring of 1944. Anyone with access – first or second hand – to the BBC knew that an Allied invasion of occupied Europe could not be long delayed. On the eastern front, the Soviet army was driving the German invaders back towards their own borders. One by one German cities were imploding under saturation bombing. When flying at full strength the aerial procession across the North Sea was an awesome sight extending up to seventy miles, all the way from the east of England to the Dutch coast. The Luftwaffe was exhausted of men if not machines. Most of the veteran pilots were dead and their replacements, hurriedly and inadequately trained, lacked the skill to make best use of the new fighters coming off Albert Speer's production lines. By mid-1944 the life expectancy of a German pilot fresh out of flying school was just thirty days.

If the onslaught on occupied France was expected, its precise timing was a well-kept secret, not least from von Schmettow, who was in Rennes for invasion war games when the real thing got under way. His visit was memorable on two counts. It came as a shock to him to find that the section of the Atlantic Wall he was invited to inspect was well below the standard of his island fortifications. Yet more surprising was to be told by his immediate superior, General Erich Marcks, that in his view the main thrust of the invasion would be directed at his troops at the mouth of the Seine, an opinion that contradicted Hitler's reasoning. When von Schmettow eventually managed to return to Guernsey it was to hear that his chief had been right. Not that Marcks had long for self-congratulation. A week later he was killed outside his command post.

Fed on rumour and speculation, the Channel Islanders could only hope that this really was the beginning of the end. The signs were positive. Swarms of bombers passing overhead, columns of smoke and flame a mile high over St Malo and Dinard and the sound of heavy gunfire along the French coast spoke of a major engagement. And if that was not enough there were the frenetic efforts of the occupiers to prepare for an immediate attack.

> Open areas including fields, even those with growing crops, and what was left of Jersey's three golf courses, were covered with anti-air landing devices such as steel girders and concrete posts ... The most vulnerable beaches were liberally sprinkled with obstacles, many fitted with explosive devices.[3]

Bombs fell on the Guernsey and Jersey harbours and those manning the gun emplacements were kept on their toes by fighters using them as target practice. All beaches were put out of bounds to the civilian population and the telephone exchanges closed.

Desperately trying to turn a disastrous situation to their own advantage, German propaganda became so twisted and perverse as to produce an effect quite the opposite of that intended. As the armada of planes passed overhead and the big guns blazed again along the French coast, islanders were able to raise a smile at their diet of misinformation.

> Many of the crews of ships approaching our coastal defences and coming under their withering fire, shewed white flags, jumped overboard, made their way to land and gave themselves up.
> . . .
> British soldiers, learning of the devastation caused by our new explosive, in which whole towns on the south coast are laid waste and London itself a mass of flames, in consternation ceased to fight for several hours yesterday on the Normandy bridgehead. American troops, on the other hand, not caring tuppence for the great damage caused to English towns, continued to give battle.
> . . .
> United States artillerymen have caused great indignation among

the womenfolk of a certain part of England. After artillery practice with live ammunition, the brave Yankees send out little girls and boys to find and carry in shells that have failed to explode, paying them so much for each shell recovered.

The first two reports were said to come from Paris newspapers; the third was credited to the *Daily Telegraph*.[4]

German propaganda made the most of Anglo-American casualties, all done skilfully with the open admission of bitter fighting ('Hell is raging on the Normandy coast') quickly followed by claims of 'unshakeable resistance'.

The Anglo-American losses are heavy. Of many enemy forces on the second day of the invasion hardly a third of the men are still alive. The losses of the airborne troops are particularly heavy. Hardly had the glider formations, scattered by AA fire and fighters, landed than our reserves came into action. The parachutists were often wiped out before they were able to assemble for defence. Other gliders were lost with their crews in the minefields. The German counter-blows struck with destructive force the enemy units landed east of the Orne and on the Cotentin peninsula the American landing troops found themselves surrounded and despairingly had to fight their way through from coast to coast.[5]

American and British casualties continued to be reported in exaggerated detail, while German losses were barely mentioned. Blame for the destruction of ancient cities such as Caen and Cherbourg was laid squarely on the Allies. Readers were meant to conclude that benevolent German protectors of French interests had suffered an unprovoked attack. Meanwhile, the citizens of London were said to be fleeing 'new German projectiles'.

Following the order of the Government the evacuation of London is in full swing. Thousands of mothers and children, and people who are not urgently wanted, are leaving the deadly danger zone of the city. Trains are overcrowded and large queues of people are waiting at the stations to get away from London.[6]

Why British civilians were legitimate targets was not hard to explain by those used to twisted logic. Apparently, the treatment being meted out by V2 rockets was also the fault of the Allies who had inconsiderately made London 'the commanding centre and the brain of the invasion'.[7]

The inevitable counterclaims were heard on the BBC. London was not in panic, far from it. As for the invasion, it was more or less on schedule. Cherbourg fell on 27 June. Three days later American forces were able to claim control of the entire Cotentin Peninsula. Making sense of all this was for islanders an inexhaustible source of gossip and debate. Overall the mood was optimistic. If the Allies had gained a secure foothold in France, and even German reports conceded as much, surely liberation could not be long delayed. 'We thought this was the end,' recall John and Carette Floyd. 'We would soon be free.'[8] No such luck.

The Allied decision to leave the islands in German hands was the consequence of weighing up priorities. The prime objective of the invasion was to drive German forces back across the Rhine, the last great natural barrier barring the way to Berlin. At this vital stage of the war, to divert troops for what was essentially a mission of mercy could not be justified. It might have made a difference had the islands been less heavily defended. As it was, those in charge of the war effort reckoned that at least three fully trained and equipped divisions would be needed to retake Guernsey and Jersey. And for what? The islands' strategic value was limited to the cable telephone link between France and Britain, useful but by no means essential. The German war machine owed nothing to the islands in terms of raw materials. Moreover, there was the heavy cost in civilian casualties to be considered. The American representatives on the Joint Chiefs of Staff wanted no part in killing British subjects. They made clear that if a rescue was mounted, responsibility would rest exclusively with Churchill and his war cabinet. It would be better all round, went the argument, if the occupiers could be persuaded by victories in Europe that an honourable surrender was the better part of valour.

It was not until late August that the time was judged to be right for an appeal to common sense. By then Germany had suffered a succession of catastrophes. Caught in a pincer between American forces curving round from their advance south and Canadian and British troops moving down from Caen, the German Fifth and Seventh Armies had been trapped and destroyed. By 17 August St Malo was cleared of enemy troops.

On 20 August, General George S. Patton, the most energetic and impatient of Allied commanders, led his Third Army across the Seine, creating a bridgehead at Mantes-Gassicourt, a mere thirty miles north-west of Paris. Four days later, the French Second Armoured Division entered the capital. Meanwhile, to the east, the Soviet offensive had annihilated three German army groups to forge bridgeheads over the Narew River, north of Warsaw and the Vistula, south of the Polish capital. The talk in London and Washington was of the war being over by Christmas. In Jersey, Baron von Aufsess admitted to his diary, 'We are finally cut off. . . . We can hold out until the end of December, after that famine is inevitable'.[9]

Reports coming in from escapees confirmed that conditions were dire and that German morale was in free fall.

Many individual Germans have announced to the British their intention to surrender as soon as the Tommies come. Informant says the morale of the Germans does not appear good. Their sentries are strained and jumpy, officers on patrol in the streets are more bloody-minded than usual, while other ranks make vain efforts at fraternisation with the civilians. Fraternisation has for long been attempted with remarkable little success except with a certain type (*not* class) of girl.

The circumstances were ideal for psychological warfare.

The Germans in the Channel Islands have for long regarded

themselves as lost men. They always thought that the islands would be isolated. Informant suggests therefore that we deluge the island with leaflets graphically showing the Germans by maps and diagrams how hopeless is their position and how complete is the blockade. If enough leaflets are dropped in all the areas where troops are concentrated some will certainly get read and informant is sure that many troops will decide not to throw away their lives for a lost cause.[10]

It was thus in euphoric mood that Britain mounted a propaganda campaign to convince the German garrison on the Channel Islands that it was pointless to hold out against the inevitable. Bombs were dropped which, on impact, released nothing more dangerous than large quantities of printed material. The leaflets, headed *Nachrichten für die Truppen* (News for the Troops), listed German reverses and appealed to readers to surrender. It was not the most efficient distribution system (many of the letter bombs fell into the sea while others failed to explode) but it was reckoned by the experts in psychological warfare that enough had been done to get across the message.

The follow-up, on 1 September, was another air drop, this time to deliver an invitation to von Schmettow to make contact by telephone to arrange a meeting under a flag of truce. There is some doubt as to whether the letter was ever read by the Commander in Chief. A repeat of the message was dropped by parachute on the twenty-first, only for the mailbags to be lost at sea.

By now, Major Alan Chambers, the Canadian intelligence officer lined up to negotiate with von Schmettow, was losing patience. With a senior German officer in tow (the compliant Major-General Gerhard Bassenge, who had been captured in North Africa), Chambers was confident that his overture would be greeted positively. The challenge was to avoid being misunderstood. An approach to Guernsey by sea without prior warning was to risk being blown out of the water by a trigger-happy shore battery commander. Chambers was ready to take his chances. The opinion of General Bassenge was presumably not sought, though he might have been forgiven for not warming to a plan that could easily have led to his death by drowning or by firing squad.

On 22 September at 1045 hours, a launch with Chambers and Bassenge (codename Mr Black) on board, and sporting a prominent white flag, set off from Carteret. Their route to Guernsey took them close to Jersey's north coast, where there was more than enough heavy weaponry to bring their mission to a premature close. Their luck held as the launch came in close to Guernsey. An exchange of flares brought out a German patrol boat to investigate. It soon became obvious that not only was von Schmettow unaware of the attempts to contact him but that he had no intention of beginning a dialogue with the uninvited British party. When Chambers was allowed to signal to the shore that he wished to discuss the military situation 'in general', back came a sharp putdown: 'General von Schmettow is fully informed as to the military situation and therefore declines any discussion.'

Chambers could scarcely believe that the meeting on which he had staked so much would not take place. Returning to France (having come under fire from Alderney, where the gunners had not been warned that a flag of truce was passing by their shore), he cobbled a report together in an attempt to make the best of a bad job. He offered two likely explanations for von Schmettow's unco-operative attitude: either he was under threat from Berlin that at the first sign of weakness his family would be made to suffer or he was hedged in by Nazi fanatics who were not keeping him fully in the picture.

Subsequently, the only evidence to emerge to back up these assertions was linked to the malign influence of Vice-Admiral Friedrich Hüffmeier, who could certainly be described as a Nazi fanatic. Hüffmeier was a threat in that he was plotting to succeed his boss whom he regarded as being insufficiently dedicated to the cause. But at this stage, von Schmettow did not see himself as a sacrificial victim. On the contrary, he had every reason to look to the future with some optimism. His rebuff to Major Chambers coincided with the first signs of a German recovery on the western front.

Operation Market Garden, a combined ground and airborne attack mounted in September 1944 across sixty miles of German-held territory, was intended to bring the war to a speedy conclusion. As conceived by Field Marshal Montgomery, parachutists would drop on Arnhem where they would secure a Rhine crossing. An infantry follow-up by Thirty Corps was scheduled within forty-eight hours of the first landings. After that it should have been full speed to Hitler's power-house, the great industrial cities of the Ruhr. In the event, the tanks of Thirty Corps fell easy victim to German gunners, with the result that Allied supplies failed to get through. After nine days of close fighting in Arnhem, which virtually wiped out the British First Airborne Division and inflicted heavy casualties on the American parachutists, the operation was called off. Clearly, the Wehrmacht had a lot of fight in reserve.

There were other indications that the Allied optimism was on the wane. Supply lines from the captured Channel ports were dangerously extended. There was a desperate shortage of human energy. Battle-weary troops were in need of a rest. The three US armies came to a halt some sixty-four miles short of the Rhine. Patton's Fifth Armoured Division took the prize for getting furthest fastest, by liberating Luxembourg to penetrate ten miles into Germany. But then even Patton's battle express ran out of steam.

It was the same story in the east, where Soviet forces were dug in at the river barriers. With the approach of winter, it was plain to both sides that the stalemate would not be broken easily. It was equally plain to the German military leaders, including von Schmettow, that a premature surrender would play into Allied hands without any corresponding advantage.

It must also have occurred to von Schmettow that while he, as a soldier of the old school, was in no way enamoured with Hitler and his gang, the failure of the July assassination plot had left the Führer stronger than ever. For Joseph Goebbels, the master propagandist, Hitler's survival was a 'miracle of providence' justifying a 'total mobilisation for the war effort'. Even if he had been so inclined, von Schmettow was bright enough to know that a surrender was no way to make friends. Moreover, it could have been counterproductive, encouraging Hüffmeier to try his luck.

Come September 1944, German forces had, for the most part, been cleared from France, Belgium and the southern region of The Netherlands. The Reich still held sway over Denmark, Norway, those densely populated parts of The Netherlands isolated by the failure of Arnhem, the Channel Islands and, in another campaign, northern Italy. If there was disappointment that Germany had not crumbled before the onslaught, it was mitigated by the popular conviction that, at last, the tide had turned. That the Allies had cut into German defences, something Hitler had sworn would never happen, and in such massive strength, put paid once and for all to the myth of Nazi invincibility. Germany would fight back, of that there was no doubt, but the odds against a Nazi victory were lengthening by the day. Gone was the arrogance of the conquerors. Everywhere, Hitler's enforcers felt at risk. Where once they had strutted proudly, now they looked nervously over their shoulders.

This shift in the balance of power was like a bolt of energy to all forms of resistance. Reaction to the ever more onerous burdens of occupation became increasingly violent. In Denmark, for example, of the 2,600 or so recorded acts of sabotage, 90 per cent took place in late 1944 or 1945. Railways and arms factories were a favourite target, with the best hit scored against the Globus plant in Copenhagen which made parts for V2 rockets.

In Norway, where sabotage was rarely attempted until late 1944, a group known as the Oslo Gang used incendiaries and plastic explosive to destroy an oil depot that accounted for fifty thousand gallons of precious fuel. The Oslo Gang went on to disrupt production at the Korsvold aircraft factory, the acid factory at Lysaker and the locomotive works at Kragerø. A destroyer was sunk at the Horten naval yard and the factory making anti-aircraft guns at Kongsberg was blown up, as too was the headquarters of the German-controlled state police in Oslo. By way of an encore, another resistance group, based in the Akers dockyard, put themselves out of regular jobs with a detonation that sank fifty thousand tons of shipping.

When the Gestapo started closing in on resistance leaders, London was quick to respond with bombing raids on German intelligence operations. On 31 October, RAF 2 Group went into action against the Gestapo base at Aarhus University in Denmark. An attack lasting eleven minutes had a devastating impact. The Gestapo chief for the region had chosen that day for a briefing session. Two hundred and forty Gestapo officers gathered at Aarhus; not one survived. The success of the operation prompted an even more ambitious plan, no less than the destruction of the Shell House, the Gestapo's national headquarters in the heart of Copenhagen. Eight bombs hit the Shell House, setting it on fire. A high price was exacted. Over one hundred children and teachers died when a school was hit. But however terrible the consequences were for innocent civilians, the boost to morale for the resistance was undeniable. A renewed offensive against German organisations and military installations ranged from the destruction of a prototype U-boat engine to stripping out the German Chamber of Commerce to collect evidence against business collaborators.

This catalogue of remarkable strikes against the enemy by essentially peace-loving peoples inevitably raises the question of why the Channel Islanders were unable to aspire to the same power of destruction. There is a simple answer. At no point during the war were islanders encouraged in any way to rise up against the occupiers. After D-Day the Special Operations Executive (SOE), charged by Churchill to 'set Europe ablaze', sent in arms and agents to The Netherlands, Denmark and Norway, the aim being to shape the resistance into a unified fighting force. Results were mixed, ranging from disastrous in The Netherlands, where the Gestapo penetrated and virtually destroyed the entire resistance network, to the highly successful sabotage operations in Scandinavia. But the Channel Islands were alone in their efforts to oppose German rule. No arms were dropped and no agents arrived.

Geographical and logistical facts spoke against a citizen uprising. There were no mountains and forests where partisan groups could hide out. The generation of fighting men had been much depleted by the ten thousand or so who had left the islands to join the British armed forces. Moreover, relative to population and land area, the Channel Islands hosted a heavier concentration of German troops than anywhere else in Europe. In Guernsey, soldiers and civilians were almost one to one. It is thus hardly surprising that while resistance intensified in occupied Europe as a whole, in the Channel Islands, demonstrations of patriotism were largely non-violent, of the sort common in The Netherlands and Scandinavia before the stakes were raised by the Normandy landings. This might have come as a relief to those islanders who, like most of us, were not marked out to be heroes, but a more common reaction was frustration at inactivity and a sense of being forgotten in the Allied rush to get to Berlin.

However, with the end of the war in sight, islanders became ever more imaginative in finding ways to damage or disrupt the German administration. As a junior in the Jersey sorting office, Frank Connor was quick to spot letters from known informers or collaborators to their German masters. 'I used to take them to the head clerk and say, "I found these on the facing-up table" and he'd say "OK, give them to me Connor" and they were gone, straight into the fire.'[11]

Siphoning off petrol from German vehicles was a popular activity. One Jerseyman reported that on a good evening at the Forum Cinema or at one of the hotels he could fill a two-gallon can – the maximum amount unlikely to be missed – several times over.

For young people frustrated by passive resistance, the boldest and most effective means of signalling their independence was to escape to liberated France. The risks were great; the consequences often tragic. Leslie Sinel's diary for October 1944 is a litany of attempts to link up with Allied forces.

The Germans have extra patrols around coastal districts in the evening, but in spite of this a party of four young men got away from a point in Grouville Bay. Sentences have been passed of six and twelve months respectively on the young girl and a Dutchman who made an unsuccessful escape from the island on September 16. A sentence of 15 months had previously been imposed on another would-be 'escapee' who got into difficulty off the Paternosters on September 11.[12]

In early October, a boat carrying four youngsters was swamped.

When they had got ashore at Anne Port they managed to save the motor and other equipment, but the Germans, hearing movements, sent up Verey lights and challenged the figures on the beach. There was no reply and shots were fired. Nineteen-year-old Douglas Le Marchand was killed. The others were arrested and put in prison. A few days later Sinel noted that the jail now had 105 occupants, many of whom had tried and failed to escape.

John Floyd was one who felt that his teenage years had been wasted. Now, aged twenty-one, he determined to break out from the island fortress. Two school friends, one of them Peter Crill (later Sir Peter, Bailiff of Jersey), agreed to go with him. On a cold November night, John's sister Carette came to see them off. She recalled:

> There was no trouble in handling the boat, getting it off the lorry and down onto the beach. But the Germans had issued a notice that they were going to shoot anybody seen on the beach, and when we told our friends we were going . . . we didn't know it was going to be so serious. We could see the fortifications on La Rocque Point and we knew that German troops were there. We had to push the boat down the beach; every time we hit a stone it sounded like a drum. We were about an hour late so the tide was further out than it should have been, so we pushed the boat about a quarter of a mile. Then we came back and picked up the outboard and the petrol and off we went.

Peter Crill takes up the story.

> There was another boat leaving at the same time – a much larger boat which also had an outboard motor. We did not use the motors at first in order not to make a noise but rowed some distance out to sea. Outboard motors in those days were pretty temperamental. If they got wet they were a devil to start again. We started ours and it went all right but the motor in the other boat did not start so we came alongside to throw them a tow rope. Water came into our motor because the two boats were side by

side and we shipped water when manoeuvring them so our motor stopped. Whereupon, without another word they hoisted their sail and disappeared.

There were further mishaps:

We broke the compass and then we thought we would anchor because it blew up a bit but we could not use the anchor because the rope was tangled. That probably saved us in a sense. If we had anchored we would probably have been caught. So we decided to carry on. We hoisted our sail and I sailed by the wind. If the wind had changed we would have gone around in a circle. Fortunately, it remained North-West and by keeping the wind in my left ear, we were more or less straight towards France. At the place where we came ashore there wasn't anyone in sight so we dragged the boat up and went on to find a local bistro. Inside, one of the men said – 'Which way did you come?' We pointed to where we had left tracks in the sand. They then said 'you are very lucky because that section of the beach hasn't yet been cleared of mines'.[13]

After seeing the adventurers safely away Carette walked home, expecting any moment to meet a German soldier on the look-out for offenders against the curfew. She too was lucky. After recovering from their ordeal, her brother and his companions were handed over to American intelligence for a lengthy interrogation on Jersey's defences.[14]

A stolen boat served its purpose for George Houghton and four other runaways.

When we left, the sea was flat, there wasn't a ripple on it. But during the night the wind got up and the boat was bouncing up and down like a cork. The fuel ran out on the outboard, and it took us half an hour to get some more in the tank because the boat was jumping up and down and I was standing, one foot on the back seat, trying to get this fuel in. I don't know how much went in the sea, but we got enough into the tank to fill it and that took us across to France. We landed and pulled the boat up and left the girl with it while we went to see where we were. We climbed over a barbed wire fence, looked down and realised there were tripwires. We were in a minefield. You've never seen people get over a barbed wire fence so quickly in all your life.

Then we saw a farmhouse. We went and knocked on the door and the farmer gave us some food. He brought a plate out, piled up with butter, it made me feel sick. You know what the rations were like at that time. He called the police who wanted to know the names of our great-great-grandmothers and the whole rigmarole before he took us to the Americans. They offered us food and again our stomachs couldn't take a lot of it, things had been that bad. Eventually, we were taken to Cherbourg where we stopped for about a week before being sent to a rest centre in Southampton. While there they found out where my mother was in London. When I joined her I weighed under ten stone. I must have looked like a bag of bones.[15]

The young Frank Keiller (he wisely changed his original name, Killer, when he decided to be a doctor) recorded the problems he had to overcome before even contemplating an escape.

The first and perhaps the most difficult was to find a seaworthy boat. The waters around the islands are among the most dangerous in the world. On spring tides, the sea level rises and falls as much as forty feet. At certain times of the year, when wind and tide combined, water overflowed the old harbour and, if not prevented, swept up Conway Street and Mulcaster Street into town. Workmen built sandbag levees to keep the water back.

You had to find a safe place to work on your boat, to caulk it and make it waterproof, and if possible to paint it a dull colour. You needed a reliable engine and a good supply of petrol. You had to find a gap in the German defences at a point where you could get the craft into deep water and navigate it between the rocks and other hazards to the open sea. You needed some form of transport to get the boat to the shore and helpers to lift it over the seawall, or to carry it over the sand or between the rocks to where she would float. You had to do all this in complete silence, and with a constant watch for patrols.

Getting petrol wasn't easy. Sometimes it could be siphoned from enemy transport, or stolen from a fuel dump or bought on the black market. But all these methods were dangerous.

You needed food and water for a journey of unknown length and time; and a compass and bailer; and some form of communication, such as a torch, to signal with. In 1944 we took a bugle![16]

In all, forty-seven islanders arrived safely on the French coast. Few of them would have made it without the courageous support of those who stayed behind – such as William Gladden, an elderly boat builder; Bill Bertram and his family who farmed in easy distance from the sea and Noel McKinstry, whose medical duties gave him access to petrol that he diverted to fuel outboard motors. But whatever help was on hand, it was never enough to guarantee success against reefs, treacherous currents and vigilant sentries. Of those who were ready to chance their lives, six were drowned and another six were shot or captured.[17]

14

THE HUNGER WINTER

After three months of incessant rain came the hardest winter in fifty years. In occupied Europe and in Germany itself, essential supplies were down to bare subsistence level and still falling. Contemplating an increasingly fragile administration in the Channel Islands, Baron von Aufsess looked to a mercy rescue from Britain. Many others voiced the same hope.

The prospect of total destitution had been a talking point ever since D-Day, when the Allies had regained effective control over the Channel. In early July the number of hungry mouths was reduced by shipping most of the remaining OT workers back to the mainland. A month later, food reserves were said to be down to less than three months and there was already a desperate shortage of coal, sugar, salt and soap.

'Ever since early September,' wrote Horace Wyatt, 'the great majority of us have been habitually hungry, increasingly cold, generally wet and never clean.'

And nearly every week something else is missing from the very short list of the comforts that remain. The gas mains were finally emptied as long ago as September. The water mains only function for two or three hours a day. The supply of current from the electric power stations has just ceased and the telephone service is to stop in a few days' time. The island's stock of coal and coke is exhausted and there is no longer any household ration of wood fuel. The steam laundries are closed down and hand laundries cannot work, for want of soap and fuel. Personal cleanliness is out of the question.

Clothes were worn thin and beyond mending. Boots and shoes that kept out the wet were a rarity beyond value.

Those whose houses are not fitted with electric light – and they are many – have nearly all been condemned to darkness from sunset to sunrise for months past and now all of us are in the same boat. Oil is nearly unobtainable; a few candles have changed hands at as much as £1 apiece; to get a small box of safety matches one must pay at least a shilling and flints for lighters are even more difficult to obtain than petrol.[1]

Hardly anything was coming in by sea and there were only very occasional deliveries by air. Von Aufsess bemoaned the prevailing 'sense of bankruptcy and disaster'. Stealing was endemic. 'There is no small corner to which one can creep away and escape the wretchedness.' Anything that might cheer up the fireplace was coveted like precious metal.

Today a branch of a tree in our garden was blown down by the storm. It had scarcely touched the ground before an army of women and children hurled themselves upon it, hacking and tearing at the coveted firewood. Schoolchildren drag home great lumps of timber which they have hunted out somewhere or other, loads beyond the puny strength of such small fry to carry. Well-dressed ladies stoop to pick up every twig in their path. In the evening there is a veritable pilgrimage of people coming back to town from the country, with all sorts of mysterious bundles, on their backs, on rusty old bicycles, in home-made pushcarts or, most often, in ancient perambulators.[2]

Communal cooking and eating became the norm. Each household was entitled to one hot meal a day from the oven of the nearest bakehouse, reported Arthur Kent, adding that the food had to be in a tin 'measuring no more than a foot square and, be there a dozen in the family, only the one tin can be allowed'.[3]

The Germans were not much better off. When Major Alan Chambers made his attempt to secure an orderly surrender, his party was met offshore of Guernsey by a German launch whose crew did not look to be in good shape, as Tim Rogers recalls:

The official party went on board the German vessel while we on the 2632 had the company of two German armed guards who were very young and quite pleasant.

I know it was quite cruel, but we started eating our rations on deck, the weather was great. We had American rations which we proceeded to eat in full view of our guards; the ration packs contained a whole roast chicken each, white bread and oranges and bananas. But you should have seen the faces of our guards. Eventually we relented – they were only a couple of kids – and we gave them a bit of everything including some cigarettes. I am quite sure that they would have gladly exchanged their weapons for a full ration pack.[4]

The first cut in German rations came as early as August 1944, with another cut a month later. There was talk of conserving resources by a mass deportation of civilians, but beyond the question of breaking the Allied blockade was the inability of the occupying force on its own to maintain and run essential services, not to mention managing the farms that produced what little home-grown food was available. A more realistic alternative favoured by Berlin was to hold back those civilians needed for the war effort while telling the British that it was now their responsibility to look after the rest. Using Switzerland as the neutral intermediary, the German Foreign Ministry announced that it was graciously prepared to allow British ships to evacuate all those except the men of fighting capacity or to send in food. Meantime, civilian rations would be reduced to the 'minimum existence level'.[5]

The ultimatum circulated Whitehall, with the relevant departments agreeing that to do nothing would be to hand a powerful propaganda weapon to the Germans. When it came to a choice between evacuation and dispatching supplies, the latter was favoured by the Chiefs of Staff as a saving on shipping.[6] They were backed up by the Home Secretary.[7] The recommendation landed on Churchill's desk. He was not best pleased. He had made his uncompromising views clear three weeks earlier, on 2 September, when he had endorsed a plan to isolate the Channel Islands, leaving the garrison to contemplate its fate on empty stomachs. In a famous annotation to the plan he had declared unequivocally, 'Let 'em starve. No fighting. They can rot at their leisure.'

In the official history of the occupation, Charles Cruickshank claims that when Churchill scribbled his intemperate comments, 'He was, of course, thinking of the Germans'.[8] But there was no 'of course' about it. The war leader was focused on a single objective, the defeat of Germany. All else was secondary. Civilians might suffer – they were suffering all across Europe – but that was the price of ultimate victory. Only then would all troubles be over.

Later in the month, when any hopes that the Germans would quickly recognise the futility of the cause had been lost in the tragic fiasco of Arnhem, Churchill's mood was more benevolent. He was now ready to contemplate the evacuation of women and children, though he was still ill-disposed to make up the islands' nutritional deficiencies. He had two good reasons for this. The first was a worry that the occupiers would grab the lion's share of whatever was going, leaving only scraps for the hungry civilians. Evidence to back this argument came from The Netherlands, where Reichskommisar Dr Artur von Seyss-Inquart had retaliated following a national railway strike by confiscating canal barges and other transport including bicycles and by holding back on food supplies.

The second reason for refusing aid was the fear of opening the flood-gates to the many other legitimate claims on Britain's limited resources. On the very day – 27 September – that Churchill agreed in principle to a selective evacuation of the Channel Islands, the American war correspondent Walter Cronkite, reporting from the liberated sector of Holland, declared unequivocally, 'There is not enough food in The Netherlands'. He went on, 'People are living almost wholly on cabbages, turnips and backyard vegetables'. And that was only the start. Amsterdam was literally falling apart. As the weather hardened, empty houses were stripped of floorboards, staircases and beams; trees disappeared from the roadsides and parks; even the sleepers between tram lines were torn up to be burnt. Fear of epidemics took hold as hospitals ran out of basic medicines. For many the only meal of the day was a half-litre of cabbage and pea flour soup.

Along with appeals for help from the Dutch came equally deserving calls for aid from Greece and Poland, both on the edge of famine. With the British mainland also on short rations there was simply not enough food to go round, and certainly not enough to risk it falling into German hands. For the Channel Islands, the only way to Churchill's heart was via the Red Cross. Here was an organisation that by its very nature was dedicated to impartiality. Food parcels delivered under the auspices of the Red Cross usually got to the people for whom they were intended.

For several critical weeks, however, the Prime Minister was still intent on forcing the German Foreign Ministry to accept that under international law it was the responsibility of the occupying force to feed the civilians. But what if the larder was bare? Surely, then, the obligation was lifted. That was the German position. The circumstances were complicated by the absence of precise information on food stocks, estimates of which varied with whoever was writing the latest report. The Chiefs of Staff were certainly of the view that the threat of widespread starvation was exaggerated.

As supreme commander, General Eisenhower wanted to be kept informed. On 19 October, he was told by the Chiefs of Staff:

The information available to us leads us to the conclusion that if the needs of the civilian population were met by the despatch of relief supplies, the effect would be to sustain the German Garrison for four or five months longer than would be the case if no supplies were sent and to postpone the surrender of the Garrison possibly until the summer of 1945.

We are therefore advising the War Cabinet in this sense and recommending that no food supplies should be sent to the islands at this stage. We have no objection, however, to the despatch of medical supplies and comforts such as soap.[9]

But pressure was building up on Churchill to change his mind. At the end of October, Brendan Bracken, a close Churchill ally and Minister of Information, advised that telling the German commander to do something he was unable to do, 'to feed the population when he has no food for them and is unable to import any' was demonstratively a strategy for using 'the sufferings of the civilian population as a lever to compel surrender'. This would put the government at a propaganda disadvantage.[10]

Now it was the turn of Ernest Bevin, Minister of Labour, to add his considerable weight in support of a mercy mission. He circulated to the War Cabinet a letter, brought over by an escaper, from Edward Le Quesne, his opposite number in Jersey, written just before the latter went to prison for being found in possession of an illegal wireless. He reported:

The condition of the poorer section of the population is getting near the breaking point. We have no gas, no coal, sometimes one hundredweight of wood fuel per month. Medical supplies and anaesthetics are practically non-existent. There is no soap, no sugar, no tea or coffee. The meat ration is 4 oz per head once a fortnight. Potatoes, Jersey's principal product, is rationed at 5 lb per week. What little there is of Black Market is unobtainable by any but the wealthiest. . . . The German troops, under the very strictest discipline, have behaved well, but, similarly to ourselves, they are half-starved and are robbing everything they can find. . . . We have refrained up to date from appealing for help, feeling that in no way must we hinder the war plans of the British Government, but things are getting desperate, especially with that section of the community with which I, as Minister of Labour, have to deal.

What we require most desperately are medical supplies, soap and fats (soap is absolutely non-existent). I saw a piece of Lifebuoy soap sold last week for £3. We are all waiting anxiously for the day of release from our island prison, and especially for news of our friends and relatives on the mainland and in prisoner-of-war camps in Germany. Planes have dropped thousands of leaflets in German, presumably for propaganda amongst the troops. We often ask why not some giving us news in English from our own people?[11]

The Home Secretary took the opportunity to deliver another plea for common sense. Addressing the War Cabinet, Herbert Morrison warned that 'we have not unlimited time to come to the relief of our fellow countrymen'. He hoped that his colleagues 'will agree that the time has now come to put arrangements in hand at once for the dispatch by Red Cross ships of the supplies which are being held in readiness'.[12]

Churchill gave in, on condition that the Germans agreed to Red Cross supervision of the distribution of food parcels.[13] The decision was made known to the Germans on 7 November. Two weeks later Berlin accepted the terms. But there was still a period of waiting before relief came.

By now the feelings of the islanders had crossed from anger to despair and back to anger again. The apparent impotence of the British government was incomprehensible to people who, understandably, assumed they had been forgotten in the wider scheme of things. In early December, a letter from a Jersey citizen to her mother in London found its way into the news columns of *The Times*.

The rations will amuse you. Meat (once a fortnight), 4 oz each. Sugar, 3 oz per week. Flour, 7 oz per week. Salt, 2 oz every four weeks. Substitute coffee (acorns), 4 oz every six weeks. Jam 1 lb every six weeks or so (no more). Potatoes, 5 lb per week. Methylated spirit, half-pint daily. Bread, 3½ lb per week (two-thirds is bran and dirt); no yeast now so quite uneatable.

I buy all I can in the black market, and it is black. Meat, £1 1s. 4d. per lb. Sugar, ditto. Butter anything up to 20 marks, and is practically unobtainable. Jerries are paying 50 marks per lb so I am told. We once managed to get some Cognac at £3 per bottle, and two of them were bad and had to be thrown away! Tea is unobtainable, but I managed to get 2 lb last year at £7 10s. per lb. I heard of someone who paid £24 last month. Mad! We have not had any for ages, but kind friends gave us one or two ounces sometimes in exchange for eggs.[14]

Throughout the islands people felt that they were cut off from normal life, that they were being forgotten in the great scheme of things.

We would willingly put up with bombing and would help all we can if only we could be free again and could get into touch with England once more. We have had our fill of Germans and their evil ways, and never want to see or hear of them again. We all feel that we have been abandoned by the Mother Country and can't think why. There has never been one message over the BBC or anything in four and a half years. It seems so strange and shows great lack of imagination on the part of the Ministry of Information and BBC. If we had been French, Polish or any other nationality, we would have been showered with messages and pamphlets. But because we are British we are thoroughly neglected and no one at home seems to care a hoot that we have struggled to keep our end up, and the German in his place.[15]

Even if it was unlikely that the bombs would have been welcomed, the lady's frustration can be easily appreciated.

Both bailiffs made strong representations to von Schmettow, more in the hope of keeping up islanders' morale than in the expectation of gaining anything practical. They received a dusty response. Von Schmettow:

> told us that we had no idea what other populations had suffered; that, by comparison with many other places, the islands had not even felt the breath of war and he finished up by saying that in future it might be necessary for him to draw indiscriminately on our stocks of cattle, flour, potatoes and all other island supplies, because Germany did not build fortresses of the kind which Jersey had become in order to surrender them.[16]

Convinced that the British government did not realise how serious their situation was, islanders hatched plots to make direct contact with London. Coutanche himself offered to go, promising to return when his mission was accomplished, but understandably this proposal was rejected by von Schmettow. However, in Guernsey, Victor Carey, after much lobbying of his German overseers, was allowed to make a direct appeal to the Red Cross:

> Conditions rapidly deteriorating here. Will soon become impossible . . . bread will last till 15 December. Fat production much below consumption. Soap and other cleansers . . . exhausted. Vegetables . . . inadequate. Salt . . . exhausted. Clothing and footwear – stocks almost exhausted, wood fuel . . . inadequate. Many essential medical supplies [and anaesthetics] already finished.

Vociferous critics demanded tougher action. Among those who had long awaited their next square meal there was a conviction that their representatives were soft on the oppressors. A group letter to the Guernsey Bailiff demanded that the Germans be forcefully reminded of their responsibilities, pointing out that unless this was done there could be unfortunate recriminations when the war was eventually won.

The response, equally intemperate, suggested unhelpfully that the Germans had no need to be instructed on their duty to the islanders. At which point the patience of the malcontents gave out. One of their number, Fred Noyon, a retired merchant navy captain, took advantage of a fishing expedition to sail way off limits, where he was picked up by an American warship and towed into Cherbourg. He arrived in London on 12 November. It was undoubtedly a courageous act and there were those who subsequently gave him credit for initiating the Red Cross mercy mission. In fact, the British go-ahead for relief to the islands had already been given.

Among the senior German officers, Baron von Aufsess took a severely practical view of the prospects for holding out in their island fortress. As early as mid-September he was warning von Schmettow:

> Germany is already partially occupied by the enemy, and this process is likely to continue. It is therefore vital that we deal in proper legal fashion with this sole small corner of the British Isles to be occupied by German forces, if only from sheer common sense.[17]

At this point, the policy favoured by von Aufsess was to offer concessions to encourage the British to take responsibility for feeding the islanders, even if this implied weakness on the part of the occupiers. His aim was to tone down the Anglophobic rants heard in some quarters, taking particular exception to the views of a young lawyer who represented 'all the bias and bluster that make Germans hated round the world'. In a circulated document the diehard, 'a sinister looking man, completely bald despite his youth', advocated the rounding-up of the civilian population into camps where they would be cut off from further food supplies until Britain agreed to terms.[18] Von Aufsess learned that one of the Commander in Chief's closest advisers was arguing along the same lines. A recipe for 'victory or death' for all Germans was hardly appealing when victory was unattainable.

Or was it? For the first time in months came encouraging news for the Wehrmacht. On 22 October Hitler called together his chiefs of staff to announce a counter-attack in the west. His strategy, to sweep through the Ardennes forest on a sixty-mile front along the Belgian and Luxembourg frontiers and then, having crossed the Meuse, make straight for the Channel coast to retake Antwerp, was one of the most audacious action plans of the entire war. The objective was to disrupt the Allied supply lines, extend German control of The Netherlands and split the British and Canadian armies in the north from the Americans in the south, allowing both to be encircled. With Antwerp recaptured and other Channel ports still in German hands there could be no Allied escape by sea.

Hitler's generals were incredulous. Their remaining troops were inexperienced, inadequately trained and short on essential equipment. Only a quarter of the fuel needed could be guaranteed. All else had to be captured from the enemy. An attack through the Ardennes, a heavily wooded and mountainous region, was challenging enough. But in the middle of a hard winter? It was a 'nonsensical operation' argued von Rundstedt, while Field Marshal Walther Model, commander of the troops straddling the western front, declared that the plan 'hasn't got a damned leg to stand on'.

But the Ardennes offensive, codenamed Autumn Mist, was not without its merits. In 1914 and again in 1940 the Ardennes had given cover to a lightning surprise attack, and Hitler was convinced it could be done again. His only concession was to postpone the attack until 16 December, when long hours of darkness and morning fog would offer protection against aerial bombing.

A week before Christmas, at 0530 hours, German artillery opened up a forty-five-minute barrage, destroying communication links between Allied commanders and their forward observation points. When the guns stopped, searchlights pierced the night sky, the beams bouncing off the clouds to create artificial moonlight. Made ghostly by their white combat gear, the ranks of German infantry, fourteen abreast, rushed the American lines. The surprise was total.

Whole units of 'fresh, green and utterly untested' GIs were thrown into panic. Across an eighty-mile front, Allied forces crumbled. Fifteen thousand of their number were captured and thousands more lay dead or wounded in the snow. In Belgium many of those so recently liberated joined the straggle of tired and dispirited troops heading west.

'The Americans are on the run,' wrote a German soldier to his wife. 'We cleared an enemy supply dump. Everybody took things he wanted most. I took only chocolate. I have all my pockets full of it. I eat chocolate all the time, in order to sweeten this wretched life . . . Don't worry about me. The worst is behind me. Now this is just a hunt.'

The Battle of the Bulge, as it came to be known, gave a huge uplift to German forces while disheartening everyone else, not least in the Channel Islands where readers of the German-controlled papers were presented with a blow-by-blow account of the counter-offensive. 'The initiative in the west has completely passed to the Germans,' crowed the *Jersey Evening Post*. 'They have penetrated deeply into Belgium and are engaging the allied forces in a series of battles of attrition.'[19] Or, rather, this was what the German communiqué meant to say. Instead, by way of a Freudian slip, 'battles of attrition' came out as 'battles of nutrition'.

It was not long before a more sober assessment was called for. Up against superior air power, the German offensive petered out over Christmas. By the end of January all the territory taken in the Battle of the Bulge had been regained by the Allies. But while Hitler failed to achieve the great victory he had counted on, the Wehrmacht's extraordinary power of rejuvenation wiped out the last remnants of Allied complacency. Nobody now imagined that crossing the Rhine would be any easier than breaching the Atlantic Wall. There was to be no quick end to the war.

However, some succour for the islanders had finally arrived. The *Vega*, a Swedish vessel sailing from Lisbon, docked at St Peter Port on 27 December before moving on to St Helier, where unloading of the precious cargo began three days later. Leslie Sinel remembered that the *Vega* had been a frequent visitor to the islands before the war when it had carried hay and straw.[20] Few then had noticed its presence; now everyone cheered its arrival. Every citizen was entitled to a food parcel. Sinel carefully noted its contents:

6 oz chocolate, 20 biscuits, 4 oz tea, 20 oz butter, 6 oz sugar, 2 oz of milk powder, 16-oz tin marmalade, 14-oz tin of corned beef, 13-oz tin of ham or pork, 10-oz tin of salmon, 5-oz tin of sardines, 8-oz tin of raisins, 6-oz tin of prunes, 4-oz tin of cheese, 3-oz tablet of soap, 1 oz pepper and salt.[21]

In all, the *Vega* delivered over 100,000 food parcels and 4,200 invalid diet parcels, along with batches of soap, salt, medical supplies and cigarettes. The operation was closely supervised by the military, who were on the look-out for arms and equipment that might be used against them. With extraordinary insensitivity, the German command also demanded its own men should be responsible for the unloading. With no expectation of any benefit to themselves, the emotions of hungry young servicemen, labouring under the watchful gaze of crowds of islanders, can be easily imagined. If the Red Cross bounty had lifted the Christmas spirits of its beneficiaries, it had the reverse effect on German morale. As Arthur Kent observed, 'soldiers and sailors here in occupation now find themselves faced with a food shortage as acute as we ourselves have endured for so long'.

Only Jerry sympathisers and the more soft-hearted among us cannot but derive a certain grim satisfaction at their predicament. It is not easy to forget their ribald laughter as our womenfolk in the past queued for hours for a few pennyworth of vegetables or a pound or two of apples, nor their undisguised amusement as we thousands were forced to parade with – and bid adieu to – our radio sets back in 1942, when the last remaining link with a happier world we once knew was severed on some paltry excuse. Neither, for that matter, can we forget the innumerable restrictions imposed upon us, apparently because of our British origin, for so long, that the word 'liberty' is but a dim recollection of something synonymous with, and once enjoyed – it seems a lifetime ago – under this same British flag.[22]

For the first time in nearly four years, the nutritional relationship between 'them' and 'us' was evenly balanced. Either way it was not much to write home about. A soldier's typical lunch, his chief meal of the day, was sausages made from horse hides with a potato and green vegetable soup. After this diners were advised to conserve energy by taking two hours' nap.

> The bread got worse as substitutes were mixed with the flour. We began to eat stinging nettles, and grew to like it. In spite of orders to the contrary, everybody tried to find something edible in his vicinity. There was hardly any farmland in our area. The few farms were small and the farmers could not sell us much, although they were always ready to barter (by the end of the war most of us had lost our watches). Potatoes in the soup were replaced by turnips. Finally we got potatoes only on Sundays, otherwise only turnips, turnips.[23]

Culinary ingenuity knew no bounds. Recipes for unlikely dishes were exchanged between housewives like treasured possessions. Dorothy Pickard Hicks was rightly proud of her sugar-beet syrup.

> To make the syrup I cut the roots in cubes, covered them with water and cooked till tender, taking five or six hours. This I strained through a linen bag, squeezing and pressing out as much juice as possible. Then the liquid simmered in an open saucepan till thick. It needed constant watching and stirring, especially towards the end to prevent burning or boiling over. The finished product was something between golden syrup and treacle in appearance.[24]

There were those who made a business of preparing syrup in coppers, which they then sold or bartered. 'Great was the grief when a batch was burnt.' Jam tarts were made by mixing the pulp with bottled fruit but the jam only kept for a few days.

A sailor from Hamburg on one of the harbour defence ships in Guernsey felt that the navy was hard done by, since its members could not scavenge in the countryside. What they had was what they were allocated.

> 110 grams of oatmeal bread in the morning. Have you ever eaten oatmeal bread? Revolting! For lunch there was a Swiss chard soup, that is, Swiss chard leaves boiled in water without anything added – potato, meat or lard. And that was every day. And on Sunday, three potatoes and a bit of meat, with perhaps something still on the bones. I was very lucky. I once brought in some drifting lifeboats from a ship which had been sunk by a U-boat. And these lifeboats contained a large quantity of emergency provisions. There were milk drops, biscuits, pemmican and chocolate. And that was a very nice acquisition for us. The route from our accommodation along the beach promenade to the harbour was easy to recognise by the wrapping paper of the milk drops.[25]

Not that scavenging produced much in the way of edible food. Frank Hubert had already harvested his broccoli but that did not deter foragers from gathering what was left.

> We cycled to Les Fauconnaires, in St Andrews (about 2 miles away) and I showed them the vinery, which had about 700 feet of glass and where the broccoli grew. The stumps were more tender and thinner grown under glass. The soldiers sat on pipes in the greenhouse, exhausted and once they got their breath back, they pulled up a few stumps each, peeled them and promptly started eating. They must have been so desperate for food I felt some pity for them. When they had eaten all they could, they gathered the remainder and left.[26]

Household pets were fair game.

> My sister, Vivienne, was walking our black Scotch Terrier when a car pulled up and a German soldier just picked him up and drove off with him. She returned home very upset. On another occasion,

I saw two German soldiers walking near our house and one picked up a cat that was sitting on a wall and pushed it under his cape type jacket and walked on. I was about 14 at the time and rushed to a neighbour and told her and we both ran after them and demanded them to return the cat. At first they pleaded innocence but the cat was struggling under his jacket and eventually they let go of it. A very lucky cat![27]

Hans Glauber remembered how the unlucky ones ended up in the pot.

One day I caught a cat and we prepared it in a two-gallon zinc bucket. We skinned it, and of course we cut the head off, and you have to boil it for about two hours in order to get rid of the bugs which cats have, and it was boiled with some nettles and a few potatoes, in a sort of a stew, and a few parsnips. And then it was put on a beautiful white tablecloth laid out with proper knives and forks, you know, like the proper way to do it, and there were wine glasses and we washed it down with champagne, and afterwards coffee and so on. It was a real feast. And there was one person who had said he'd never eat cat or dog, he'd eat rabbit. And after we finished, I asked him, 'How did you like your rabbit?' He said, 'Oh, wonderful, I think I'll have to catch some myself now.' I said, 'Well, you've just eaten a nice big tom cat.' He said, 'Oh, come off it,' in his German way. So I said, 'You don't believe me?' He said, 'No, that was rabbit.' So I said to my friend Eric, I said, 'Go and get the skin.' And of course when he saw it, he went outside and brought it all back again. It was really cruel of us to do it to him, but that's the sort of thing you had to do in order to stay alive. I even shot two seagulls and ate them, and for a German sailor to do that – because there's superstition in the German navy that in the seagull there is the soul of a drowned sailor – shows how desperate we got to stay alive. I lost seven-and-a-half stone in nine months.[28]

Hunger bred violence. In Guernsey, Elizabeth Doig recorded a succession of robberies which led to at least one death, that of a farmer who 'heard Germans taking away his potatoes and went to chase accompanied by his son. The Germans shot him in the stomach and he died almost immediately. The son was shot in the ankle.' By December 'robberies go on wholesale'. Mrs Doig reported two instances where farmers were bound and gagged and all their food stolen including their Red Cross parcels. In another more elaborate stratagem, 'The people were ordered by letter to attend at Grange Lodge Hotel, German headquarters. This was a lure to get them out of their homes. When they returned, all their food was gone.'[29]

Rarely were the police, civilian or German, active in tracking down the perpetrators. Suffering the same pangs as everybody else, they were not at their most alert or energetic. As in some lawless frontier town, self-protection was the only remedy. Ruth Walsh's family 'lived in a terrace house with living rooms at the front, a kitchen at the back and a long passageway that went around from the front door'.

You could get into the kitchen from either side and father, who was quite a short man, a proper little Guernsey man, was out there making a cup of tea or doing something at the cooker. He looked around and there were two tall German soldiers there and of course as you know, they were always fully armed all the time, bayonets and daggers and guns in their holsters and everything.

There was a couple of carrots on the kitchen table and they were making to my father they were hungry and wanted some food and could they have those carrots. That's all there was in the house for us to eat and my father, he was so angry I can remember him to this day! What he did next, he just let rip on them, and well, I don't know if they could understand all the English, but I think they could tell. He said 'No, you can't have those, that's all I've got to feed my family on today, if you're hungry that's your fault, you came here!'

And he got them, he had to reach up to get hold of them by the scruff of the neck and he physically pushed them all the way the length of the house down the two steps onto the footpath. He said 'Now get out, and go, look what you are doing to my family.'[30]

What happened to Frank Browning and his family reads like something out of a Wild West novel. It was in early January.

They got into one of the barns on the farm. We decided that we were going to barricade up as much as possible, to make it more difficult for them to get in. There were two windows leading into this barn, but there were also three doors. Well, one door we'd nailed galvanised iron over, that one they couldn't open. The other one, that we used if we carted anything in, it opened inwardly, so we put a couple of pipes from the floor up to the lintel. And the other one, which had a Yale lock on it, we used to lock that up of a night. We could go through from the barn into the house, so once we were finished outside in the evening, one of us would go up and over the steps, and lock the door, and prop some props against the door so it couldn't be opened or forced open. On top of that we put a little bell so that the top door – it was a two-door, one top and bottom, like an old stable door, you see – had a bell on it. One morning, I heard this bell ring, and I called my father and brother, and I told them that we had visitors. So I said, 'Look, I'll go up as though from outside, you come from inside.' So we tried to trap them, but when I got to the top of the steps, this German was standing on the steps and he had his rifle pointing at me, he was pointing it towards my stomach. I couldn't see him because it was pitch dark, but he could see me. So I caught hold of it with my right hand and pushed it down, and at the same time he tried to get it away from me, and he pulled the trigger, and the bullet hit the step and smashed. I had the blast and parts of the bullet in my left ankle. Well, the other one was inside filling his bag with different things, I suppose. I know there were potatoes, onions and apples stored there. Then my father and brother came through from the house, where they'd lit a hurricane lantern. The German had a torch hanging on his tunic button, he had his holdall in his left hand and his revolver in the other hand, and he backed to the door. He swung his body to make a dive down the steps, but we were both still there, so he turned and fired, and he caught me in the upper part of the leg and broke my leg. Of course I fell down the steps, but I still had hold of his rifle when I got to the bottom of the steps, and he pulled it away from me and ran off over the yard.[31]

On this occasion the German police emerged with credit. A clear footprint in the soft soil under a window led to the arrest of the chief culprit.

For the military, hunger was not the only problem. When letters got through, the news was uniformly wretched, with homes destroyed and friends and relatives dispersed to unknown destinations. To go on leave had once been a much sought-after privilege. No longer. One German officer, 'a quiet, understanding man speaking fluent English whose help,' wrote Arthur Kent, 'I found invaluable in many trying interviews with the Commandant', returned, having witnessed the devastation of Hamburg, to sink into deep depression. The end was a bullet to the brain.[32]

Mental illnesses were almost as common as physical ailments. Unpredictable behaviour was put down to 'Island madness'.

One day one of my best non-commissioned officers ran out of the bunker to a heavy machine-gun and without any reason, without saying anything to anyone, loaded the gun and fired off a whole box of five-hundred rounds out to sea. Half the island was in a state of alarm, and an investigating officer from headquarters wanted to arrest this man. But the army doctor said that the man should not be punished. He probably couldn't help what he did.[33]

Even as the Channel Islanders savoured their first Red Cross provisions, the prospect dawned of several more months of hungry subservience. The parcels 'even with the greatest economy could not be made to last out a fortnight'.[34] The *Vega* was not expected to return for another month and, with the Germans purloining most of what was home-produced, deprivation was still widespread.

Christmas dinner for Kaye le Cheminant's family was: 'a medium-sized cauliflower between 6 of us (friends joined us for all 'holidays'), a large rather 'woody' swede, and a small piece of belly pork which gave each of us a piece the round of a teacup. We cooked it all in the copper of a nearby abandoned nursing home, whose one-time matron was a family friend, as we had no fuel for a fire by this time and there was no gas or electricity.'[35]

In the new year the War Cabinet returned to the question of food for the Channel Islands. Prompted by a Red Cross report that 'the shortage of supplies for civilians is becoming increasingly acute as local stocks run out', the Cabinet agreed to a delivery of 3,000 tons of coal but with no guarantee of further supplies. Churchill wanted it to be made clear to von Schmettow that if he failed in his obligations to the civil population he would be added to the list of war criminals.[36]

The Commander in Chief was not to be intimidated. 'The besieger alone bears the responsibility for his compatriots,' he wrote, adding, 'the German army does not build fortifications without holding them ... until the exhaustion of its powers of resistance.' Churchill was urged by the Home Office to be less bullish. 'To threaten the German Commander before there is any evidence of criminal conduct ... might exacerbate relations between the German garrison and the civil population and might tempt the Commander to take the line that he may as well be hanged for a sheep as for a lamb.'[37]

Churchill continued to grumble, the Cabinet turned to other matters and the Channel Islanders stayed hungry. In mid-February the bread ration was suspended. Rations for the week ending 17 February comprised 5 lb of potatoes, 2 lb of root vegetables, 2 pints of skimmed milk, no greens, no bread, no meat and no butter or other fats.

Illnesses aggravated or caused by malnutrition included tuberculosis, whooping cough and diphtheria. Children and old people were the most vulnerable.

We started to suffer from skin diseases. I can remember having scabies when I must have been about six years old. Then just before and just after Christmas 1944 I started with impetigo and eczema.

The only available treatment was distinctly unpleasant.

I used to go every morning to the Town Hospital. The sister with a pair of surgical scissors cut the heads off and let the poison come out. Then of course it spread to my hair. I had very long curly hair and I had to have half of my head shaved and I was really worried about this because my mother and her friends were saying 'Oh, hair shaved off at that age, I don't think it will grow again, what will happen? So I thought, I'm going to be half bald when I grew up, which was a load of nonsense because it did grow again, but, of course, people weren't so wise about things as they are now.[38]

Many families had hard emotional decisions to make.

My grandmother was 90 and not quite able to grasp the reason for why the shops contained almost nothing, but she was a quiet accepting little lady and accepted that this had to be our way of life. She ate the same amount as we did and at her age should have been having nourishing food as she was active and walked out each day for exercise. When she became ill through lack of nourishment and had to stay in bed, my mother gave her each day half of my pint of milk which I was allowed as a child. Then the doctor came to hear of what she was doing and said that this must not be – I was growing and had my life before me – Gran had had her life.

This must have been a terrible decision for my parents to make – to sacrifice one member of the family for another. Gran died peacefully in her sleep in her 90th year, just 3 months before the war ended. Her 4 sisters in England lived well into their 90s and

I am sure Gran would have done so too if she had not been so ill-nourished.[39]

The verdict of an inquest into the death of a woman aged seventy blamed 'cardiac failure supervening on pulmonary congestion'. She weighed just three stone.

15

A LAST STAND?

In his new year's message to his troops, von Schmettow warned that sacrifices must be expected in 1945. Little did he know that one of the first would be his own. Doubtless he felt that his close family connection with von Rundstedt, the most powerful field commander in the west, guaranteed him protection against those of his colleagues who wanted him to take a more aggressive line; but it was not to be.

Foremost of his critics was Admiral Friedrich Hüffmeier who, ever since his arrival in the Channel Islands in July 1944, had plotted to undermine von Schmettow's authority. Hüffmeier's strongest asset was his political skills. Proud of his unswerving faith in Nazi ideology and devoted to Hitler, he attracted praise and avoided blame for egregious errors that would have seen others reduced to the ranks. As one-time commander of the battle cruiser *Scharnhorst*, he had profited from the exploits of that most successful of convoy raiders (twenty-two ships sunk or captured), although his contribution had in fact been non-existent. Contrary to the story he assiduously cultivated, he was not in any way involved in the celebrated 'Channel Dash' when *Scharnhorst* and its sister ship *Gneisenau* ran the gauntlet through the Straits of Dover, having outwitted the British navy in its home waters. That was in February 1942, when the much-admired Captain Kurt Hoffman was on the bridge. Only two months later, after Hoffman's promotion to rear admiral, did Hüffmeier took over.

There followed a chapter of accidents that would have been hilarious if the circumstances had been less pressing. 'Poldi', as the new commander was nicknamed, began by running *Scharnhorst* aground off Hela. After she was refloated, an aircraft was shot off the catapult before everybody was ready; only the observer survived. The ship had to be docked for repairs when a heavy wire got caught round the starboard screw and docked again after a collision with a U-boat.[1] But Hüffmeier remained in place until October 1943, when it was belatedly decided that this most incompetent of seamen would be better employed on land. On arriving in the Channel Islands and eager to make his mark, he was quick to decide that von Schmettow was altogether too accommodating to the islanders and to his own men. Poldi was determined to add muscle to the German administration.

His first move, in October, was to get himself appointed chief of staff, a role that allowed him to voice his opinion on every aspect of the occupation. This was not to von Schmettow's liking. Having objected in vain to an officious naval officer trying to tell him what to do, the Commander-in-Chief did his best to avoid Hüffmeier's company. 'They don't even speak to each other now,' noted a fellow officer.[2] Hüffmeier then moved in for the kill. He reported to his superiors that not only was von Schmettow too inclined to listen to sob stories from troops and civilians alike but that he was planning to surrender the islands as soon as opportunity allowed.

The solution was obvious: the navy, with Hüffmeier at its head, should take on the responsibility for holding Hitler's prized possession against all comers. Initially this was seen as a step way too far. Naval personnel in the garrison were outnumbered almost ten to one, and the prestige of the Wehrmacht demanded that a soldier should head the administration. Hitler prevaricated until reports of sinking morale persuaded him to turn to the one officer he believed he could trust. The official announcement was made in the *Deutsche Inselzeitung* for 3 March 1945.

As from 12 noon on 28.2.45. I have taken over as Commander-in-Chief, Channel Islands, and Fortress Commandant, Guernsey, from General-leutenant Graf von Schmettow, who has returned to Germany for health reasons.

I have but one aim. To hold out till final victory.

I believe in the mission of our Leader and our People, and I will serve them with unswerving loyalty.

Hail to our beloved Leader.

(signed) HÜFFMEIER.

Vice-Admiral and Commander-in-Chief.

With von Schmettow went his chief of staff Colonel Helldorf, described by a member of the Jersey Superior Council who dealt with him on a day-to-day basis as 'one of the German officers who has shown us the greatest consideration'.[3] The excuse for von Schmettow's retirement fooled nobody. Though he had lost a lung in the 1914–18 war, he appeared in robust spirits and had not seen a doctor in over a year. According to the Dame of Sark, who spoke to von Schmettow after the surrender, he fully expected that his 'lack of zeal' would put him on the wrong side of a firing squad. He credited von Rundstedt with saving his life. For von Aufsess, the general's strongest supporter, his removal came as 'shattering news'. Reflecting on other changes in the command, he commented, 'the whole business smacks of a putsch or coup d'état', suspecting 'a move long since carefully planned'.[4] To von Aufsess' surprise he held on to his job, on the understanding that he would take 'a more ruthless line with the civilian population',[5] starting with a further reduction in rations. Given a free choice Hüffmeier would certainly have disposed of a colleague he rightly suspected of defeatist tendencies, but von Aufsess was a good administrator and, aside from Major-General Rudolf Wulf, one of the few senior army officers left standing. The navy was now in charge.

Hüffmeier was no sooner appointed than he launched into a hectic round of morale-boosting speeches and inspections. A daily guard of honour, taken in turn by the three services, was mounted outside his headquarters. Everywhere he went there were clicking heels and Nazi salutes. 'Two things strike me about him,' wrote von Aufsess,

> his round shoulders, typical of the bookman rather than the man of action, and his high forehead, typical of the thinker. The army officers must find him a puzzlingly alien being. He belongs to that category of Nazi who are so carried away and bemused by their own oratory that they can never be reckoned to be dealing honestly either with themselves or with others. The Admiral would not be out of place as an evangelical pastor speaking from the pulpit. Certainly he could not proclaim his political, as against his religious, beliefs with more fervour or conviction.[6]

It was a shrewd assessment. After the war Hüffmeier found God and turned to the church.

The effect of this adrenaline rush on servicemen who were used to two hours' afternoon nap can be easily imagined. For all those loyal servants of the Reich who felt inspired by Hüffmeier's oratory there were others who were less enamoured with the ravings of a fanatic. Unlike von Schmettow, the new man was no conciliator. By throwing the two sides into sharp relief, Hüffmeier created dissension in the ranks.

Those of his troops who tuned into the BBC – and many did – knew only too well that outright victory was a mirage. The Battle of the Bulge had cost Germany 80,000 to 120,000 of the Wehrmacht's finest, not to mention the destruction of vast quantities of military hardware blown to bits by Allied bombers as armour and trucks queued nose to tail on icy roads. In the east, the Soviet offensive was renewed on 12 January. On a twenty-five-mile front, 7,000 guns shattered the German defences. Warsaw was taken a week later. But most devastating of all was the news of towns and cities lost to blanket bombing. As one example, Cologne suffered 262 air raids. Over 90 per cent of the city was laid waste, half a million citizens were evacuated and 20,000 died. It was the same story across Germany. On 3 February it was Berlin's turn for annihilation. Close on 1,500 bombers took part in the raid, and estimates of the number of civilian deaths started at 25,000. By the end of the month Berlin had registered four hundred visits by mass formation bombers.

With all this as common knowledge across the garrison, Hüffmeier would have been well advised to tone down his rhetoric. A negotiated peace with the western allies based on a fear of communism sweeping across Europe was the best that Germany could expect and, indeed, was being talked up by Hitler's inner circle. But Hüffmeier refused to compromise. He continued to hold to his fantasy of victory come what may. There were those for whom his intransigence was a provocation.

Even as Hüffmeier was preparing to take over, there was in circulation an incitement to mutiny. Printed on flimsy notepaper and passed from hand to hand until the type was barely legible, the message was nonetheless clear.

> The Russians are on the doorstep of Berlin. The Anglo-Americans stand on German soil in the West and daily their planes lay more and more German towns in ruins, daily kill more of our women and children. Why?
>
> Hitler wanted to conquer the world. Hitler began this war. He wanted to pulverise English towns. He wanted to exterminate whole populations. The entire guilt of this insane visionary and his accomplices has been avenged. Even the most unintelligent begins by degrees to see that all Hitler's promises were nothing but pie-crust. We have only him and his Nazi clique to thank for the immeasurable sorrow that has been cast over the whole world, and above all, over the German people.[7]

For anyone who had read thus far, the conclusion was surely inescapable.

> Soldiers in Jersey. How long do you intend to take part in this, the biggest deception of all time? How long do you want to stay here and starve? The war is lost. We can do nothing to alter our common fate. On the contrary, through stubborn holding out we are spoiling our last chances of an assured future. We call upon

you to surrender. Raise your voices with us against the helpless officer clique and their accomplices. A large part of the garrison is preparing for insurrection against its tormentors. . . . You will not be alone. An experienced officer is on our side. . . . Do away with Nazism, and then Germany will be a free country.

The identity of the 'experienced officer' remains a mystery. Maybe he was a figment of hope. What has emerged over the years is the central role played by Paul Mülbach. A graduate of Hanover University, a linguist and industrial chemist, Mülbach was outside the ordinary run of army recruits. His father was Christian Mülbach, a socialist trade-union leader who had ended up in Dachau. Imbued with anti-fascist ideals, Paul had fought with the International Brigade in Spain. Returning home, he was offered the choice between the army and a concentration camp. He chose the best of a pair of bad options, serving in Russia, where frostbite left him with a severe limp, and in France. He arrived in Jersey in April 1944.

Some time towards the end of the year, Norman Le Brocq and Leslie Huelin, the leading lights of the Jersey Democratic Movement, got to hear of a German soldier who was looking to start a mutiny. It took a while to establish mutual trust. If Mülbach might easily have been an undercover agent there was no guarantee that Le Brocq and Huelin were not also playing a double game. After several meetings each side decided to take a chance. Their joint venture started with subversive literature written by Mülbach for the JDP to print. The job was handled by Warren Hobbs who had a home-made press, nothing sophisticated but it served its purpose.

There was no problem in finding readers. All the signs were of an occupation force falling apart. By 10 March the *Vega* had made three round trips. The civilian population was still short on necessities, but their troubles were nothing compared to what the Germans were having to put up with. 'The baker shops looked well today with bread displayed on the shelves,' recorded Leslie Sinel. 'The Germans gazed on this in wonder.'[8]

Robberies increased in number and in violence. Even more

ominously, the losers' anger began to show. Von Aufsess reacted furiously when, one night in late February, buildings all over Jersey were daubed with tar in the shape of swastikas.

> This idiotic prank had been carried out on an organised basis. Two German officers were responsible for . . . this infamous act. Entirely on their own initiative and without the knowledge of the fortress commander, they had issued orders to two companies of men to do the job. They claim that their motivation for this 'political protest' was their National Socialist principles. It was such criminal fools who plotted the 'crystal night' in 1938, which triggered off the storm of hatred against the Jews.[9]

After the initial shock, the islanders took it all philosophically.

> On liberation day these swastikas will show what cultural barbarians the Germans were. One humorist has hung an empty picture frame round 'his' swastika; another has written 'England for ever' alongside his; a third has converted the swastika into the type of cross used for British decorations for valour and merit.[10]

More worrying for Hüffmeier were the thousands of anti-Nazi leaflets scattered across the countryside and the growing evidence of a rebellious faction in the garrison. Knowing that he was under suspicion and fearing imminent arrest, Mülbach went on the run, helped by his friends in the JDP who dyed his hair and provided him with civilian clothes, lodgings and a bicycle. But if Mülbach was out of the action, others were ready to lead an insurrection.

Shortly before midday on 7 March, The Palace, Jersey's premier hotel, used exclusively by German officers, was set alight. In an effort to stop the fire from spreading, Lieutenant Hans Kiegelmann was ordered to use explosives to create a breach in the buildings. He was altogether too successful. The detonation set off charges in an adjoining ammunition store with the result that the entire hotel was gutted along with nearby houses.[11] Eight soldiers were killed and many injured.

How much of this was the result of planned sabotage is impossible to say, though subsequent rumours of hotel staff being warned to stay clear and of a time-bomb being put in a conference room used by senior officers would seem to be the stuff of war fiction. The likelihood is that the fire was deliberate and that happy accident did the rest. The assumption that an arsonist was at work gained credibility when that same day another fire damaged German stores and, a week later, a petrol dump was set ablaze.

Hüffmeier stamped hard on dissidents, sending several before a firing squad. One of the saddest cases was described by Joe Mière, whose prison cell was next to that of a German deserter whose name was Nicolas Schmitz. He was seventeen years old.

This particular chap had thrown away his uniform and went to live with this girl Alice Thaureaux and her family, and they sheltered him, but in the end somebody told on them; they were all arrested and then Alice was tried and sentenced to death, but the Bailiff intervened so she was sentenced to ten years imprisonment and her brother had six years. The day that this German had been sentenced to death, they brought him over from the military side and put him in the cell next to us. You were trying to get to sleep and he cried all night, 'Meine Mutter' [he said], he went on and it really affects you. He didn't mention his father, but he must have felt a lot for his mother. To think that a week later they took him out; we saw him go through the gate with his chains. The Germans used a dog chain with a 'T' piece so they could break your wrist if you made a move. It wasn't locked [as such]. There were two of them each side of him and an officer behind with a machine pistol [MP40] and as he got to the first inner lodge gate he pulled back because his girlfriend Alice called out 'Nicki, Nicki' from the bars. Two friends of mine, Belza Turner and Evelyn Janvrin, they were in the same cell as her and they lifted her up to the bars. He shouted something 'Liebe' or something, and a little dirty handkerchief came out and waved. They pushed him through the gate and that was it; they took him up to Fort Regent and they shot him that morning. The Germans are strange because they allowed her to come to his funeral with her mother that same day, under escort, to see him buried.[12]

But fear of retribution was no more than a negative force. Hüffmeier yearned for a success that would inspire his men if not for victory, at least for a grand finale. Letting his finger wander over the map, he settled on Granville for his valediction.

A plan to attack the French port, now in American hands, had been on the drawing board for some time. Just before Christmas five German prisoners of war had managed to escape to Jersey on an American landing craft. They brought with them details of the military layout at Granville, which was used as an unloading bay for coal coming in from Falmouth. Given the fuel shortage in the Channel Islands, the capture of a coal ship or two was tempting enough. But for von Schmettow and his then second in command, Admiral Hüffmeier, there was the added incentive of demonstrating solidarity with the troops leading the counter-attack in the Ardennes.

In the event, bad weather forced a cancellation and then, with the changes in the senior command, the raid was again put on hold. It was not until early March that Hüffmeier was ready to try his hand. His assault force consisted of around 750 men carried in a mixed flotilla including six minesweepers, three artillery carriers, two converted landing craft and three motor torpedo boats. Their objective was to put Granville harbour out of action, capture the coal ships and destroy any other vessels, together with the radar station. An attack on the Hotel des Bains to the north of the harbour was to create a diversion.

The assault force set off from St Helier after dark on the evening of 8 March. When they reached Granville at 1.0 am they saw that the harbour lights were burning, which suggested that there was some activity there. The three artillery carriers had taken up position between the Ile Chausey and St Malo to cut off any Allied patrols in that area, and two of the minesweepers stationed themselves between Jersey and the Cotentin Peninsula for the same purpose. Another two of the minesweepers were to be the spearhead of the attack. Their plan was to sail straight into the harbour, and when challenged by the signal station, simply to flash back the same challenge in the hope that this would throw the defence momentarily off their guard and allow them to get safely in.

This indeed is how it turned out.

Before anyone in the harbour realised what was happening, the two minesweepers were secured alongside the quays. The third pair of minesweepers was left outside the harbour to provide covering fire, the three motor torpedo boats made straight for the beach by the Hotel des Bains to land their party, the tug moved slowly towards the harbour entrance to give the leading minesweepers time to secure themselves. Before this was completed the assault parties were ashore and had established themselves in positions from which they could control the approaches to the dock area. For an hour and a half they remained in command of the situation in spite of fierce counter-attacks by the Americans.[13]

On board a patrol vessel offshore, Jack Yeatman saw only confusion around him. At 0130:

Granville called us, then went off the air. We have no idea what is happening, or which side is which in the exchanges of fire ashore. Hell let loose there – heavy small-arms fire. Looks like a commando raid! All navigation lights have been shot out, including Pointe du Roc lighthouse. . . . Some shells and tracer have come uncomfortably close in to the shore as there isn't enough water for us now, and it's a maze of unlit rocks and skerries. Anyway, we have no means of knowing what to fire at.[14]

The attackers made one serious mistake. It was low tide when they entered the harbour, meaning that three of the coal ships were aground and the radar station was out of range. The only coal carrier afloat was hurried away while dynamite put paid to everything on the dockside – cranes, wagons and fuel dumps. An American patrol boat that came in close to investigate was sunk while the diversionary assault on the Hotel des Bains led to the capture of several American officers. German casualties were limited to one officer killed and five men wounded.

The Granville raid was audacious and bravely executed but it achieved little of substance, except to provide the Channel Islands with an extra delivery of coal. It made no contribution to the German attempt to hold the Allies at its borders until a peace deal had been brokered, and while a boost to garrison morale was badly needed, there is no suggestion that it won over any of those who doubted Hüffmeier's sanity. However impassioned his appeals for 'spiritual and material' preparation for the great test and however sincere his determination to hold out until 'the Fatherland has won back the lost ground and the final victory is wrested', most of his listeners knew very well that their only priority was survival.

Talk of insurrection gave way to weary resignation. A call to action by Lieutenant Lindner, who described himself as 'a close associate of General von Schmettow', lost its impact when, two days before the meeting was set to begin, he was removed from his power base, such as it was, in Jersey and packed off to Guernsey.

As for the islanders, though disappointed once, this time they could not help but believe that the day of liberation was close at hand. 'We have certainly seen the decline of the German army,' wrote Leslie Sinel. 'The swag bag has been substituted for the swagger.'[15] He noted men in uniform picking up cigarette ends and when, on 8 April, the *Vega* was in port, carrying among other provisions 350,000 kilos of flour, 'German soldiers accompanied each trolley to the Red Cross depot equipped with spoons to scoop up flour and put it in their billy cans.'

Two small but significant advertisements appeared in the *JEP*, one for a Union Jack, the other for an American flag. There were no prizes for guessing why they were wanted. The confidence of the would-be flag waver was well founded. By 25 March, Allied forces had crossed the

Rhine in strength. Even German newspapers recognised what was coming. 'It is very difficult to be an openly declared, courageous Nazi today and to express one's faith freely,' conceded a leading article in the *Völkischer Beobachter*, adding, 'We have no illusion now.' The Swedish newspaper *Expressen*, which had a correspondent in Berlin, reported that 'panic has struck military circles'. Field Marshal Kesselring, who had taken over from von Rundstedt as commander-in-chief of German forces in the west, found his immediate prospects 'anything but pleasing'.[16] The rate of desertion was so high that Kesselring resorted to using some of his best men to round up the fainthearts who flooded to the rear whenever a battle started.

There was no question that the war on the western front was into its last phase. In the third week of April the British Second Army was closing around the North Sea ports of Hamburg and Bremen while the US First and Ninth Armies were up to and over the Elbe between Magdeburg and Halle. But the news everyone was waiting for was of the beginning of the Russian attack on Berlin. It came on 20 April, Hitler's fifty-sixth birthday, when the first shells began falling on the city centre. The Führer had ten days to live.

16

LIBERATION

The *Jersey Evening Post* for Thursday, 3 May 1945 was a sell-out. What attracted the readers was not the announcement that Syd Britten and his band were to appear at the Plaza Ballroom the following Saturday, or the article on bee-keeping for pleasure and profit, or the news that wooden clothes pegs could be bought in King Street for one mark a dozen. The stampede for copies had one objective: to savour the story headlined 'Adolf Hitler Falls at His Post'.

Few details were given. Readers were left to guess how he had fallen, although by now, three days after the event, it was common knowledge that the Führer had shot himself. Most of two columns was given over to a syrupy tribute to one who had 'met a hero's death' in 'his fight against the Bolshevist storm flood' and to the plans of his successor, Admiral Dönitz, to save Germany from communism while restoring 'tolerable living conditions for our brave women, men and children'. To support him in this task, he demanded 'discipline and obedience'.

What Dönitz really wanted was to strike a deal with the Anglo-Americans that would allow for an orderly withdrawal from the east. To achieve this he traded on what he assumed to be a shared aversion to Stalin and all that he stood for. But though neither London nor

Washington was charmed by the Soviet model there was no question of ratting on an ally who had done so much to defeat the greater evil. By the time the Channel Islands had been let in on the news of Hitler's death, Dönitz was facing up to the inevitable. Unconditional surrender meant just that. There were to be no concessions.

The second of May 1945 was the blackest day of the Admiral's career. Berlin succumbed to a frenzy of street-to-street and house-to-house fighting. The death toll was over half a million. German forces in Italy surrendered. Meanwhile, on Lüneberg Heath, Field Marshal Montgomery told a party of senior German officers that he had no intention of discussing terms. Having reported back to Dönitz, they returned on 4 May to accept capitulation in the west. Representatives of the US, Britain, France and Russia now began to make their way to Reims for the formal signing of total surrender.

In these last hours, seemingly divorced from reality, Admiral Hüffmeier made a desperate attempt to reinvent himself as the protector of the Channel Islands, soon to be working alongside his new best friends to defeat Bolshevism. On 6 May he was in Jersey for consultation with Coutanche, who was puzzled by a turn in the conversation.

> We discussed the situation from our different angles and then the Admiral suddenly said 'Of course, everything has changed. I don't know how much you know, but the fact is that your country and the Americans are going to join forces with us and we are all going to fight the Russians. Therefore, we have got to make suitable arrangements for this new turn of events.'[1]

Parroting what had come through from Dönitz, Hüffmeier was unaware that the policy of realliance was already in the dustbin. But, as Coutanche acknowledged, the delusion was helpful since it 'certainly had the effect of making it easier to conclude the necessary arrangements for the transfer of power'.

Leaving Coutanche to issue a pacifying message (islanders were urged to maintain their calm and dignity in the days ahead) and to set up loudspeakers in public places for Churchill's victory speech, Hüffmeier returned to his headquarters in Guernsey, where he had to decide what to do about two messages from the British Army's Southern Command setting out the terms for an immediate surrender. His response played for time: 'The Commander in Chief, Channel Islands, receives orders only from his own Government.' With the naivety of desperation, Hüffmeier could not bring himself to believe that there would not be a last-minute reprieve. He was to be disappointed. In the early hours of 7 May, Dönitz authorised the surrender of all German forces on all fronts.

By now, Hüffmeier appeared to be the only German on the islands not to realise that the game was well and truly up. His rank and file were under no delusions.

The Germans were very dejected, because they knew that their days over here were finished. And in any case they were in a worse state than us, and they were not a fighting team here any longer, they were old men. They were going round trying to barter with their rifles and pistols for our Red Cross parcels. I know two who were approached by a German, he was going to hand over his revolver for a Red Cross parcel. They had no food, nothing, so they were glad for it. So about a fortnight before, we really knew that this was nearly the end. And of course the day before was unbelievable. Flags were coming out. Where they got the Union Jacks from, I don't know, but they got them. I don't think there was any work done that week, we were just walking around waiting for the news. And then when we were told that Mr Churchill would be broadcasting in the afternoon, we all went in the square. It didn't hold a lot of us. We were all hanging around and there wasn't a German to be seen. Nobody slept that night. We were all waiting for the British boats to appear. It was a marvellous, terrific scene.[2]

In the event, the boats were a long time coming. The first British forces to approach the islands in any strength in five years were led by

Brigadier A.E. Snow. Late of the Somerset Light Infantry, Snow was a regular soldier of a certain age, formal and straight-backed with a neatly clipped moustache, who believed in doing things by the book. Based in Plymouth, his Force 135 consisted largely of former coastal artillery gunners. For three months they had been in training for a possible assault on the Channel Islands. This required them to adapt to the ways of the infantry, including lessons in street fighting carried out in the bombed districts of Plymouth.[3]

When it came to the point none of this hard graft was necessary, though one suspects Brigadier Snow would have loved to crown his military career with a charge into action. Instead he had to make do with a modest show of force put on by two destroyers, HMS *Bulldog* and HMS *Beagle*, each carrying a landing party of two officers and twenty men.

They reached Guernsey at midday on 8 May, being met four miles off St Peter Port by a German mine-sweeper bearing not Admiral Hüffmeier but a junior officer, Captain Lieutenant Armin Zimmerman, who proceeded to make a fool of himself by giving the Nazi salute. It then turned out that he was not there to accept defeat but to discuss terms. Snow soon put him right. Zimmerman was sent packing with a message for his chief that unconditional surrender was the only offer on the table. His compensation was to disconcert Snow with a warning that the continued presence of the British ships so close to shore would be regarded as 'an unfriendly act'. Having in mind the heavy shore batteries, Snow thought it prudent to withdraw.

The next confrontation took place soon after midnight. This time Zimmerman was accompanied by Major-General (until recently Colonel) Heine. Raymond Rees watched them come over in a dinghy: it 'was very degrading because their coat tails were dragging in the water and the sea was running a bit rough'.[4] Heine was, like his chief, a hardliner who now faced the humiliation of putting his signature to the formal article of surrender, the document, it was reported, resting on an upended rum cask on the *Bulldog*'s quarterdeck. According to von Aufsess, Hüffmeier had only submitted following a direct order from Dönitz. Presumably, his plan to blow up all the arms and ammunition on Guernsey as a final act of defiance was not well received by his now-deposed supreme commander.

On the morning of 9 May Coutanche heard that the *Beagle* was on its way to Jersey. He was told to go to the Pomme d'Or Hotel at noon 'and from there proceed with the German commander [Major-General Wulf] to HMS *Beagle* for the surrender'. Coutanche replied, 'I have never in my life received an order with which I shall have greater pleasure in complying.'[5]

After these formalities, the *Bulldog* and *Beagle* returned to Plymouth, where there was a disappointment in store for the ships' crews. 'When we got back there was nobody to meet us. Everyone had gone mad in Plymouth and all the pubs were dry.'[6]

*

Back in Guernsey it fell to von Aufsess to preside over the formal return of the island to the States:

This was effected briefly if worthily enough in the single sentence I spoke in English: 'The war is over; we herewith hand back the islands to you'. All the members of the States were assembled. We faced each other with polite but wordless bows like so many Chinese mummers.[7]

The collective memory of the early days of liberation is of unfamiliar sights and sounds. The first excitement was the arrival of Brigadier Snow with his Force 135.

We'd never seen anything like these landing craft coming up the beach, and the front opening and jeeps pouring out. The troops were no longer wearing forage caps which they wore when we last saw them. They were all now wearing berets. One of my lasting memories is the noise of the British car tyres; they all seemed to have new tyres and made the most wonderful noise along the tarmac. All through the occupation we'd had bicycle tyres made of rope or hosepipe and there were no cars about, or very few, so it was the most wonderful evocative noise.[8]

That and the ringing of church bells, banned throughout the occupation. Reg Langlois remembers:

> It was very noisy with people calling out to each other, the music of gramophones coming from the houses, the blowing of our horn and the noises made by our exhaust silencer which had begun to split open. I do not know how we managed to get through to the area by the Victoria Harbour, but I do remember looking on, fascinated, at the sight of the boats coming out of the water on wheels and driving up the slipway by the lifeboat station. We spent many hours cheering and watching the soldiers bringing equipment ashore. I had never heard such a cacophony of sound as I did that day from the crowds of people and the vehicles. We moved to the front of the Pomme d'Or Hotel on the Esplanade where the crowds were at their noisiest. They were calling out to the British troops 'throw more sweets' and every so often, as a shower of sweets was thrown into the air and over the crowds, there would be more cheering. The people had not seen sweets for over four years.[9]

As a Guernsey schoolgirl, Margaret Le Cras was worried by the appearance of so many men in uniform. What was more, her parents were happy to speak to them. Up to then, anyone in military outfit had been studiously avoided. It was all very strange. Stranger still was the chewing gum she was given.

> I remember distinctly putting it in my mouth and swallowing it, and being told that that was not what you did with chewing gum; you had to chew it. I never liked it then, and I still don't like it now.[10]

The advance party of the British army, who had done little but fall in as ordered, were greeted as heroes.

The crowd simply mobbed the soldiers. There was cheering, there was laughter, there were tears, weeping, hugging, embracing, smiles, grins and hand-shaking, and the British Tommy, characteristically, emptied his pockets of all his rations and distributed them among the crowd. I suppose the walk up the Pier – the march up the Pier, but it couldn't be called a march any more – should have taken about ten minutes. It probably took more than half-an-hour, and I remember how Colonel Robinson had to be lifted shoulder-high and appeal to us of the civilian population to let his troops get through! There was so much joy and rejoicing.

Having reached the top the troops raised the flag at the Pomme d'Or Hotel which had been the German naval headquarters. Then they went up to Fort Regent, climbing the old long steps, followed by masses of us, and the Union Jack was raised over the Fort by a Jersey officer, serving with the liberating forces, Captain Le Brocq. The Union Jack was flying too over the States' Building in the Royal Square, along with the American flag.

This was Dixie Lambert speaking at Liberation Day ceremony in 1989. Nearly half a century later, a rather more sobering thought came to his mind.

I suppose we should, young as we were some fifty years ago, have paused at that stage to reflect how much misery there had been in Europe and in the world generally, and of the sad and dreadful loss of life to reach that moment, but we were overcome with the feeling of joy and freedom after five years. I hope we can be forgiven for not at that moment falling down on our knees or having spiritual thoughts of deliverance. We were just full of happiness to think that there would be no more curfew that night, and that all our forbidden radios could come out. The popular music that was now being played was a bit of a change from the military band music which had been heard in the Royal Square when the Germans gave a concert, and it was also a change from the German marching songs when the troops had paraded through St Helier![11]

The emotional release that came with the end of isolation can be easily understood. In Guernsey ten days after the liberation, a reporter from the London *Evening News*, interviewing Marion Hamel, discovered at first hand what it must have been like to feel cut off from the world.

A week before she and her husband had been hungry; she did not know where the 17-year-old son, who had gone to England in 1939 to join the Services, was. She had had only two 25-word messages in five years from her twin daughters in school in England when the Germans invaded the islands. Yesterday she had had letters, real letters, gossipy and chatty letters from her daughters and her sister in England. And 20 snapshots taken over the five years. Pictures of the girls, pictures of her son, now 23, somewhere in the world, safe, so far, after six years in the Merchant Navy.[12]

Among the many emotional scenes, one of the unlikeliest was at the *Jersey Evening Post*, where the German editor and censor, Sonderführer Hohl, had served throughout the war, keeping the faith and forever confident that he was right. On the day before the surrender he published his last German-language paper to appear in the Channel Islands. It carried the programme for the Forum, the Soldiers' Cinema, scheduled for 12 May. Leslie Sinel and his colleagues were planning to tell Hohl just what they thought of German journalism but 'when the great day came, we couldn't do it. Hohl was a broken man, his entire world had collapsed. He came to say goodbye to me and his eyes were full of tears. To be honest, there were a few in mine as well.'[13]

For youngsters there was the adventure of rediscovering their own country. Leo Harris was fifteen when the occupation ended. He and his brother and father went out to Noirmont Point. It was five years since they had last been there.

The gun positions were just as the Germans had left them. There were hand grenades and other weapons lying about. The tables still had food on them. It felt like a German could enter at any moment and ask what you were doing there.[14]

The big surprise for Philip Le Cuirot was finding that his family was the proud owner of a brand-new Dodge truck and a top of the range Humber. He was too young to remember the vehicles being hidden in a barn behind bales of straw.

We put some petrol in, charged the batteries and off we went. After five years, that's all it took to get them running. Of course, everybody was flabbergasted.[15]

Owners of requisitioned vehicles were not so lucky. By the time their former possessions had been identified they had invariably been visited by fellow islanders in pursuit of spare parts. Bargain hunting was all the rage. For many, the treats were found in the billets lately occupied by German troops.

Small groups of ill-clad civilians, equipped with hessian shopping bags, wandered about opening cupboards, turning out drawers, gathering up folding chairs and unscrewing lamps and other electrical fittings. Long-life food such as dried vegetables and biscuits were quickly snapped up though there was less demand for the hundreds of bottles of Vichy water which materialised. It appeared that some German officers lived by a curious order of priorities.[16]

Another of the oddities of the last days of the war was the number of German outposts that held on after the surrender, either because they wanted to be the last to give in or because there was no one on hand to tell them what to do. Having been bypassed by the invasion, Dunkirk was German-controlled until 9 May, St Nazaire and Lorient until 10 May. In the Channel Islands, the seven-strong German observation post on the Les Minquiers reef was still in place on 12 May. When a French fishing boat called by, the forgotten men were only too happy to be taken to Jersey. For some years this was thought to be an occupation record but it now seems that this distinction must go to Schiermonnikoog, the Frisian island in the northern Netherlands, where German troops held out until June.

For the islanders who had spent up to three years in German internment camps, liberation was on a delayed fuse. Conditions had begun to ease early in the new year. With the senior military having much else to worry about, the camp guards were left to manage their own affairs. Their inclination was to make life as easy as possible, for themselves and for the inmates.

At Bad Wurzach, the sixteen-year-old Michael Ginns went into the village every day to collect bread and milk. One day there was no guard on the gate. Internees had been wandering about but were now drifting back into the camp to enjoy afternoon tea, courtesy of the Red Cross. Shepherding them along was a flustered elderly German who was clearly overstretched with responsibilities. Spotting Ginns with his cart waiting to set off, he saw the solution to his problem. 'I must get back to the guardhouse. When the last one's in, lock up and bring me the key.'[17]

Also at Bad Wurzach, when the mayor was troubled by looters breaking into the bakery and the coal store, he went to the camp to ask for volunteers to support the communal interest. Internees, equipped with German rifles, took it in turn to stand guard.[18]

With the sound of guns getting closer, their biggest fear was of being run over in the Allied advance. There was no reason to suppose that the camps were clearly identified on army maps. It was just as likely that the internees would be taken to be legitimate targets, part of the last-ditch defence of the fatherland. The risk was all the greater at Bad Wurzach, which had a Hitler Youth centre nearby where the occupants were sworn to fight to the last man. Laufen was another danger point since it was so close to the Southern Redoubt, centred on Hitler's mountain hideaway at Berchtesgarten. The rumour was of a devastating attack to shift the SS from this last Nazi stronghold. In the event, the part of Hitler's entourage that had taken refuge in his Eagle's Nest gave up without much of a fight. This brought a sigh of relief from the occupants of Laufen, who had been planning their own last stand after the commandant had promised free access to the armoury should the SS decide to use them as hostages.

It was the Free French who did most of the liberating. At Biberach, the youngest internees went to meet their saviours.

> We started cheering and waving. They thought we were Germans, 'bad people'. But we were only youngsters. One of the tanks stopped, and the officer got out and he spoke to us. He asked what we were. Of course we spoke to him in English and some of us with what French we had. We made ourselves understood and we told him. Well they jumped out of the tanks and they were kissing us. In the end they put us up on the tanks and took us back down into the village.[19]

Less rashly, a group from Bad Wurzach went out to meet the arrivals carrying a Union Jack painted on to a bed sheet.[20] This had one desired effect but was no help to the guards, who were assumed to be running a concentration camp. The French troops 'were hugely indignant to find civilians in prison and immediately lined all the guards against a wall. It took great persuasion and assurances that we had not been treated brutally, before they put away their guns.[21]

Laufen was liberated on 8 May. Edward Fox remembers the heavy rain that fell that day.

> There was one chap in the camp who was good at painting and he painted two flags – one Union Jack and one stars and stripes. They hoisted them up to the top of the building and then all of a sudden, down came the rain and turned the flags into a right mess. I don't know how the Americans recognised it when they turned up in their tanks and jeeps.[22]

When Edward was warned that it might be several months before they could return home, he and a friend decided to make it on their own.

Having found an autobahn used by American convoys they hitchhiked their way out of Germany.

Nearly all the internees were free by the end of April, though apart from increased rations their circumstances did not change much until well into June, when transport was found to carry them home. When John Green got back, he felt very lucky.

Jersey was lucky too. We got to England and saw the effect of the bombing in London. We'd already seen France after the war and realised what had happened there. Not only from the fighting around the coast – the landing beaches – but the villages outside where there's been resistance. Terrible things had happened. We were isolated from it in Jersey, and certainly in camp. We weren't badly treated. We were prisoners – but the Red Cross got to us, and the Germans stuck by the rules of the Red Cross and the Geneva Convention. In a lot of ways we were lucky.[23]

Today, Bad Wurzach is twinned with St Helier.

17

A VINDICTIVE POST-MORTEM

Along with the celebrations came the recriminations. The risks of a breakdown of law and order were severe, as anyone who witnessed the outpouring of emotions on 8 May could recognise. Relief that it was all over was quickly followed by outrage that the five years under German rule had been made harder by those who had sided with the enemy.

Appeals for calm went unheeded. With authority in abeyance, gangs of youths who, for five years, had been taught that delinquency was acceptable as long as it was in a good cause, felt free of all restraint. Unconscious of their imitation of the Nazi thugs they professed to hate, they screamed for summary justice. That the same happened in every former satellite of the Reich makes the record no less disturbing.

The girls who cuddled up were the first to feel the wrath of the mob.

Boots' doorway had an arcade in those days; all of a sudden a young girl rushed past – she was only about fifteen or sixteen with not a stitch of clothes on, blood running down her face where they had, like they did in France, cut her hair off and she got in the corner and bent down. I don't know why I carry this old military mack, I still do, and I went up to her to say 'it's all right my love', and she put her arm up; she thought that I was going to hit her. I made her stand up and put this old mack on her and asked her where she lived; she pointed up the road towards La Motte Street. I don't know who she was; on Liberation day she must think of the young chap who gave her his raincoat; she must be a grandmother now.[1]

What troubled Joe Mière the most was the ease with which cruelty was visited on the defenceless.

If a German had come round the corner unarmed they would have run. Those people who did that [to collaborators] didn't do a thing against the Germans whilst they were here, but as soon as the war ended they were very patriotic, waving the flag and hitting these girls about.

Joe Berry was a Jersey policeman.

We had trouble at Snow Hill. We're going up Queen Street, a woman came running down Snow Hill, and all she had on was a skirt. It was dark, but a crowd were running after her. She ran down Bath Street, we turned and I jumped out the car, opened the door, and as I got level there, put my hand down and pushed her in.[2]

They called them Jerrybags. The violence against them had less to do with patriotism than with the frustration and sexual inhibitions of a buttoned-up society. The prurience of the British media has kept the Jerrybags in the news for more than half a century along with the unspoken assumption that, had the Germans landed on the mainland, stout-hearted girls would have stood firm against the wave of Teutonic charm. But, as they say, anyone who believes that will believe anything.

During the occupation there were 184 illegitimate births in Jersey, twice the level of the same period up to 1940. In Guernsey, the figure was 285, four times that of the previous five years. This was nothing out of the ordinary. Across Europe the stories are tediously familiar. When Allied forces entered Germany the rule against fraternisation proved impossible to enforce, though it is surely no coincidence that attempts to repress normal relationships coincided with an increase of crimes against women. In the last weeks of the war court-martials for rape by British soldiers against German girls were around eighty a week in the Second Army area alone. After the surrender, it was a standing joke that every maternity hospital in western Germany should have a statue to the unknown soldier. What happened in the Channel Islands fitted a well-established pattern.

Of course, there were women who used sex for financial or other gains, sometimes very cleverly. The von Aufsess diary records the exploits of a Miss Langlois who 'may well be described as the most active and experienced girl in the island in the field of amorous adventure'. An attempt by an anonymous informer to put a stop to her activities by accusing her of possessing a revolver backfired when the German police discovered not only the suspected weapon but also a collection of letters from a high-ranking officer. This 'most delicate and embarrassing affair' was hushed up and Miss Langlois continued to entertain the troops.[3]

On the other side of the scale were genuine love affairs such as that between Werner Rang, a medical orderly on Sark, and Phyllis Baker, a farmer's daughter. Having attended German classes at the Seigneurie, she acted as the interpreter for the army doctor when he visited his civilian patients.

> One day Phyllis Baker fell ill herself, staying for a day or two in bed. Werner Rang happened to be the orderly who brought the doctor's pills to her house but, as he knew no English, he was unable to make himself understood by Mrs Baker at the door. Phyllis called to her mother from above, telling her to send the young man up. It was the beginning of a serious relationship. After the war when Werner Rang finally left the prisoner of war

camp in England he married Phyllis Baker and they settled down in Sark to live out their lives together.[4]

One relationship ended if not with marriage then with at least one good joke. When a friend of Pauline Fisher had to name her illegitimate son by a German soldier, she decided to call him Winston. 'We thought that was very funny.'[5]

There were no jokes attached to the blatant collaborators, the few who betrayed their fellow islanders for financial gain or for the satisfaction of destroying lives happier than their own. Easily identified, they were an early target for revenge. Had not the army intervened, it is likely that murders would have been committed. As it was, several of the more notorious German sympathisers spent weeks in prison, not for punishment but for their own protection.

The demonstrations of anger in the Channel Islands were no way exceptional. Elsewhere in Europe the bloodletting was severe. In France alone, up to 10,000 died in the occupation aftermath. A much smaller, and largely united society, was easier to manage, but Brigadier Snow was surely right to advise against an early evacuation of the military. Continuing signs of social volatility were all too evident. Within a fortnight after the liberation letters were appearing in the press denouncing those who had thrived on the black market or who had made a living working for the Germans. Thus, almost immediately, debate was joined on what, precisely, constituted collaboration.

The articles of war ruled that civilians could not be compelled to carry out work of a military nature, but in an island community, where the influence of the occupying force was all pervasive, it was impossible to draw a firm line between military and non-military activity. At an extreme a farmer could be seen to be giving comfort to the enemy if the food he produced found its way into a German kitchen. At first glance the case against those who played any part in building or maintaining fortifications would seem to be rock solid. But what was a family man to do if other work was unavailable? The conflict of loyalties was all the more acute when, eager to recruit labour, the occupiers imposed a low ceiling on wages paid on civilian projects while those who signed up for the Organization Todt could earn twice as much. With the ever-increasing cost of necessities, it was only to be expected that in families where there were several mouths to feed, the pressure to opt for the highest reward proved irresistible.

Money was not the only consideration. The Germans were not above bending the rules to suit their objectives. Early experience of this came when it was decided to allow for more air traffic. As head of Jersey's department of labour, Edward Le Quesne recorded 'a day of depression and anger' when he was ordered 'to send an architect and men to enlarge the airport'. He had no doubt that this amounted to 'assistance to the enemy to prepare a base for action against my own country'.[6] When he protested against this and other instances where he was called upon to support the military, he was told that a failure to co-operate 'would mean the conscription of our younger men and the sending of many of them to France'.[7] One way or another, the Germans usually got their way. Was Le Quesne therefore a collaborator? Unquestionably not. In all the records of the occupation it is hard to come across another civic leader who fought harder for his principles.

Many islanders, probably the majority, came to share with Le Quesne the realisation that refusing to have anything to do with the occupying forces could cause more harm than good. As a garage mechanic, John Bouchere found himself working on German as well as civilian vehicles.

> One had little choice; there was a simple rule – if we wanted spare parts to repair the dairy trucks, which were an essential part of our life, we had to go to a German work station to get them. If we chose not to do German work, there were no spare parts for the dairy lorries. It was as simple as that. It was a matter of 'Hobson's choice' I suppose.[8]

Working alongside Germans did not mean that you had to be overtly friendly with them. But then again, was fraternisation at any level also collaboration? If so, how old did you have to be for blame to be attached? Cyd Le Baile readily admits that as a small boy he and his friends went out of their way to be friendly with the Germans.

I do remember on one occasion stealing pears with my cousin – from his own garden – and going down to Greve de Lecq where the Germans were billeted, and swapping these pears for what we thought was lemonade. It turned out to be Vichy water, that's the first time I saw a Vichy water bottle. On another occasion, probably prompted by hunger, me and a friend sang outside a house occupied by a German colonel. After we had sung a song or two, he came out and gave us custard and prunes, which I'd never tasted before, or had forgotten having tasted. And then, something which has remained with me for the rest of my life, he began to show us photographs of his family. And I remember, child as I was, thinking to myself that my father might be doing the same thing somewhere in the world, showing photographs of his family. That was my first intimation of war and the stupidity of human nature.[9]

With no prospect of a consensus on degrees of collaboration, those who felt themselves to be the prime victims of wartime profiteering and an overzealous bureaucracy vented their frustration in print and on the streets. There had to be somebody to blame. Easy targets were the Irish itinerants, neutrals who were free to choose their friends; likewise the conscientious objectors, imported in 1939 under the auspices of the Peace Pledge Union to help out with the harvest. These minorities were seen as outsiders and therefore culpable, though in both camps there were opponents of Nazism. It may have been naïve of a vocal element among the conscientious objectors to discuss the war as a capitalist conspiracy but it was these same people who took great risks by giving refuge to Russian fugitives from the OT work gangs.

But all this was incidental to the big question. By co-operating with the occupiers, to what extent were the civilian leaders culpable in supporting German war aims?

For Churchill the islands were an aberration, a hard-to-account-for exception to the myth he was already creating of Britain alone against the fascist dictators, a stalwart nation that, come what may, would have brooked no compromise in its mission to restore the world to sanity. How then to account for the occupation of the Channel Islands other than by justifying compromise?

It did not help Churchill that demilitarisation was signed off at his desk. Everything that happened in the Channel Islands between 1940 and 1945 could be said to have been rubber-stamped in Downing Street. Matters were further complicated by conflicting advice from the Home Office and the intelligence services, the former hoping that a softly, softly approach would avoid unpleasantness, the latter eager to root out collaborators without too much account of island sensitivities.

When, in his victory day speech, Churchill went out of his way to refer to 'our *dear* Channel Islands' he appeared to be adopting the Home Office line. A visit by the Home Secretary on 14 and 15 May resulted in a report to the War Cabinet that positively glowed with superlatives. Herbert Morrison had nothing but praise for the island authorities who had 'discharged their difficult responsibilities . . . in exemplary fashion and had succeeded to a remarkable extent in getting the best possible treatment from the Germans commensurate with the avoidance of any semblance of collaboration'. Moreover, 'There appears to be no evidence of anything which could be regarded as a war crime as far as the Germans on Jersey and Guernsey were concerned.'[10]

Morrison's two-day visit was like a royal progress. He was received rapturously and, being a good-hearted politician who enjoyed a party, he was receptive to the best-possible interpretation on events. A harsher critic might have said that he was naïve. It would not have taken much to detect the underlying tensions in a society disrupted by years of trauma. While Morrison was assuring his colleagues that everything in the garden was lovely, exchanges between islanders were of unprecedented bitterness. The ill feeling intensified as servicemen and evacuees returned home, often to find that their homes had been desecrated.

Josephine Ginns was one of many. Her father reacted angrily to the absence of any official welcome for demobbed servicemen while her mother and grandparents were distressed to find an empty and derelict house. The Irish tenant had sold just about everything on the black market. It was the same with the family business, an antiques shop which now had nothing to sell. There was no compensation, though the family was given a voucher entitling them to a roll of lino.[11]

As the de facto ruler of the islands, albeit by temporary appointment, Brigadier Snow was well aware of widespread disaffection but was determined on a peaceful transition to civilian rule, an aim which called for a tactful handling of complainers. He stayed close to the Home Secretary on his tour of the islands and no doubt made sure that Morrison was fed the views of the civil-affairs unit which accompanied the military.

> There has been a certain amount of criticism of so-called collaboration with the enemy from time to time, but the fact is that during five years of occupation such as these people have undergone, when there was always one German for every three islanders and sometimes many more, it is impossible to avoid some degree of apparent collaboration. . . . It is important that people at home in England should realise the tremendous burden which these small communities bore under German occupation. Houses in hundreds of cases – much worse in Guernsey than in Jersey – have been damaged, gutted or completely destroyed. Furniture and household goods are in an almost inextricable tangle. The Germans often took what they fancied in one house and used it somewhere else.[12]

In characteristically blunt language, Snow declared that his civil-affairs officers were working closely with local police to 'sort out the very few solid facts from the froth of gossip'. Reporting to the War Office and Home Office on social unrest, particularly in Jersey, Snow suggested that military government should be extended beyond the scheduled ninety days. This was refused but pressure was put on the refugee societies to avoid a rush of homecomings until conditions were more settled.

Another Morrison ally was Theobald Mathew, the Director of Public Prosecutions, said to be a lawyer of 'common sense and great humanity'. Reporting on his own visit to the Channel Islands, he pointed out that the occupation was the first experienced by Britain in many centuries and that consequently there was no recognised 'code of conduct for the civil population under these conditions'. Mathew set out clearly the context in which the administration had to operate.

> During the years 1940 and 1941 it must have appeared to the islanders as a whole that England herself was likely to be occupied and, knowing little of events in the outside world except what was told them by the Germans, the prospects of liberation seemed extremely remote until D-Day. So far as I can judge from my talks with them, the morale of the islanders was probably at its lowest in the autumn and winter of 1944. They had watched with their own eyes the battle of the Cherbourg peninsula and had come home and toasted their own liberation. As weeks and then months went by without the expected relief and with the conditions in the islands becoming increasingly serious, it is easy to appreciate that even the most loyal and courageous might well have been daunted.

Furthermore, he added, the Germans appeared to have behaved well and islanders were unaware of atrocities committed in other countries.

> Any crime of violence by the Germans against the civil population was severely dealt with and there was very little crime committed by the occupying troops until food and fuel became desperately short in the last few months of the occupation. . . .
> [In Guernsey] where at one time [German] troops out-numbered the civil population and were at no time less than one in three, active resistance was out of the question. Individual cases of alleged positive collaboration, which are now being

investigated, can be offset by individual cases of heroism in helping secret service agents and allied airmen and in arranging escapes.

It was 'unfortunate', he admitted, that Bailiff Carey, 'elderly, charming but not of strong character', appeared on occasion to have given way to German pressure. Far from being disloyal, however, 'there is abundant evidence that . . . the Bailiff did his best to protect the civil population and to stand up to the Germans'. He and others in the administration were 'entitled to praise rather than censure'.

As for Jersey:

In my opinion not only are there no grounds for suggesting that the administration was disloyal or collaborationist, but all the evidence that I have seen goes to show that the Bailiff and the Attorney-General, who were mainly responsible for the conduct of negotiations with the occupying authorities, were remarkably successful in securing every possible advantage for the islanders. In particular Mr Coutanche appears to have carried out his extremely difficult duties with exceptional ability and skill. Considering that he was in effect carrying out the duties of Lieutenant Governor, Prime Minister and Lord Chief Justice, it is remarkable that the complaints against him personally are confined to those of a few individuals with grievances.

Mathew concluded, 'there is no prima facie case for complaint or criticism either of the conduct of the islanders as a whole or of the administration in their dealings with the occupying forces in either island'. That said, he recognised the need for reform, conceding:

no report on the present condition of the islands can ignore this question. There is undoubtedly a general feeling that this matter is ripe for immediate consideration. The provision of a more democratic governing body, the separation of law making from law enforcement, and the provision of proper appeal courts are all questions of active discussion amongst responsible islanders from the Bailiffs downwards.

He warned that it would be 'gravely detrimental to the success of any reforms if their consideration were to be linked up with the conduct of the administration during the occupation'.[13]

Though this eminently sensible analysis was welcomed by the Home Office, there was one Whitehall department where it was not well received. The intelligence services, as has recently come to light, were committed to an entirely different version of events. Convinced that the Channel Islands were the weakest point in an otherwise rock-solid line of British resistance to Nazism, MI5 was eager to lead the hunt for collaborators. As early as February 1944, Major J.R. Stopford, charged with preparing a security brief for the return of the Channel Islands to British jurisdiction, was urging the immediate appointment of a representative to work alongside the military. His preferred candidate was Major d'Egville, a former Port Security Officer in the Channel Islands who 'knows local conditions well'.[14] What little was said to the Home Office was not put in writing but Brigadier Snow was told to expect an MI5 Liaison Officer who would set up a 'small security unit' that would stay on 'after the military phase is over'.[15]

By now Charles Markbreiter, who was still the overseer of the Channel Islands at the Home Office, was agitated by the MI5 tendency to rock the boat. While raising no objection in principle 'to the idea of the attachment of an accredited representative of the Security Service to the Civil Administration', he argued against premature decisions while the shape of the peacetime administration had still to be determined. MI5 did not find this helpful from one who 'as usual [was] rather woolly and uninterested'.[16] But Markbreiter had every reason to fear that MI5 would make trouble where it was least needed. He did not have long to wait to find out where clumsy meddling would lead.

Some documents in the MI5 files are still held back or have words obliterated, but it is clear that soon after liberation Stopford gave up pressing for d'Egville to stay on long term after the end to military government. Now a man in a hurry, d'Egville lost no time in delivering the worst-possible construction of the wartime records of island officials.

> In Guernsey the attitude of the Bailiff, Victor Gosselin Carey, towards the Germans was friendly and co-operative. We have seen articles in the Guernsey newspapers written by the Bailiff, one of which condemned in no uncertain terms the maliciousness of a Guernseyman for the cutting of German telephone wires and extolled the virtues of the Germans for their kindliness and gentlemanly behaviour, while the other article recommended the inhabitants to attend a German musical concert, saying how pleasant it would be and making quite unnecessary complimentary remarks about the Germans.

In addition to press warnings of severe punishment for those who infringed occupation edicts which appeared over Carey's signature, d'Egville drew attention to a drinks party given by the Bailiff for senior German officers. Carey was also accused of giving tacit support to anti-Jewish measures and, even more bizarrely, doing 'everything possible to protect the Masons of which he himself is the Senior Representative'. To avoid the implication that the Masons had somehow done better than the Jews as a result of Carey's intervention, d'Egville might have added that the Masons were nonetheless proscribed. A stronger protest against anti-Semitism would have been welcomed as a sign of unity with the persecuted but d'Egville should have asked himself if anything of practical value could have been gained.

D'Egville's lack of imagination and understanding regarding what had happened in the islands was demonstrated by his apparent shock at discovering that 'not the slightest attempt had been made by any official whatsoever to accumulate any information which might have been of value to the Force, nor to prepare the ground in the way that might have been expected if they had been wholeheartedly zealous British officials'. Leaving aside the fact that he was not dealing with British officials as such, the idea that the administrations could have acted as intelligence-gathering bodies, given everything else they had to cope with, was laughable.

Jersey fared a little better under d'Egville's scrutiny; he grudgingly conceded that Coutanche 'does not seem to have been so gratuitously friendly', but concluded that the latter's conduct was 'very far from being satisfactory', arguing that the Bailiff had been too ready to supply names and addresses of subjects born on the mainland who were marked for deportation and that members of the States abused their position by 'obtaining commodities not available to the general public'. D'Egville did at least acknowledge that these allegations were based on hearsay, although he also made a sideswipe at the Dame of Sark, who apparently was 'guilty of friendly and ingratiating behaviour towards the Germans'.[17]

While no court would have taken these charges seriously without solid evidence or at least hearing the other side of the story and probably not even then, d'Egville's report was readily accepted by Stopford as an adequate basis for mounting a prosecution. Ever the diplomat, the Director of Public Prosecutions tried to let him down gently, explaining that since the Defence Regulations did not extend to the Channel Islands, the only relevant legislation was the Treason and Treachery Acts, which carried the death penalty.[18]

It is likely that Theobald Mathew was being less than absolutely straight with Stopford. If the charges had had substance, there was surely enough flexibility in the law to bring actions that would have stopped short of the scaffold. All over Europe, collaborators were facing penalties based on the thinnest legal precedents, while objections to retrospective legislation did not seem to bother the judges at Nuremburg. However, the DPP's dampener was sufficient to force Stopford to rethink his position. He now took comfort in the knowledge that two islanders who had broadcast for the Germans while interned in Germany might be prosecuted under the Defence Regulations. How this would have looked if for political reasons Sherwill had to be let off the hook did not appear to worry this intelligence expert, whose grasp of detail was such that in one memo he named Carey as Bailiff of Jersey.[19]

But if Stopford felt thwarted, there were those attached to the liberating force who were ready to adopt his cause as their own. Captains Palmer and Blake, reporting from Guernsey and Jersey respectively, made known how 'upset' they were that nothing was being done to punish collaborators.[20] Casting about for a means of working off his own frustration and that of his friends, Stopford hit on the idea of a semi-official vendetta. His partner in conspiracy was Captain J.R. Dening, MI5's contact on Brigadier Snow's staff. Stopford wrote to Dening on the last day of May:

> The policy as I see it at the moment is that we are unlikely to be able to bring prosecutions against most of these people or in fact any of them, unless there is direct evidence of their having been of active assistance to the enemy against the United Kingdom. Therefore, it seems to me the best way to deal with the women, and possibly also the men, is to have them up before you, grill them thoroughly, take down what they say, and make pretty public the fact that they have been seen and why, so that their fellow-citizens can make their lives as unpleasant and uncomfortable as possible. The way these girls have behaved is a perfect disgrace and the more people who know about it the better.[21]

For good measure, Stopford suggested 'it would be a good thing if the local papers got hold of the names of these people and published them for everyone to see'.

That, on his own initiative, this gatherer of supposed intelligence should have assumed the right to foster social unrest, even to encourage violence, in British territory challenges credibility. Was he mad or merely deluded? Almost certainly the answer is buried in the National Archives in documents 200A and 197A, 'retained in Department under the Public Records Act, Aug. 99'. It is generally assumed that certain files are locked away to save domestic embarrassment in the islands but it is just as likely that the embarrassment of the British government is the real issue.

What is clear from the available records is that Stopford had no intention of calling a stop to his meddling. He told Dening that he was planning a long-term investigation:

> We wish to keep a record of the people who have been friendly or who have collaborated with the Germans. We want their names, addresses, personal particulars, and such details of their collaboration or of their friendship as will provide an efficient record of what has happened, so that in time to come we may know who is likely or susceptible to assist the enemy and why.[22]

Stopford had contacts in high places who were prepared to listen to him. In late June he managed to corner the Cabinet Secretary, Sir Edward Bridges, the most powerful man in the political establishment after the senior ministers. Stopford had got wind of a Home Office recommendation that honours should be awarded to leading islanders. According to Stopford, the two of them agreed 'that he [Bridges] would defer the award of any decorations and use the opportunity to goad the Home Office into taking some action about the punishment of collaborators'.[23]

But the Home Office was not to be goaded. Dening was aggrieved to be studiously avoided by Home Office representatives in the islands who did not relish his myopic preoccupations. But allowing his prejudices to show, Dening had no one but himself to blame for his failure to win confidence and co-operation. His reports to Stopford deteriorated to rants against all islanders.

> It was generally agreed that the majority of the inhabitants of the island – Norman peasants with all their limitations of character and outlook – view German and Englishmen with almost equal indifference as long as their material prosperity is unaffected. Throughout the occupation they enjoyed an administration which faithfully protected their parochial interests and which to achieve its ends was quite willing to discard a loyalty to Britain which appears to be merely nominal.[24]

At this point a more objective observer of the scene might have recalled that the islands' wartime administration was in place at the behest of the British government. If anyone was guilty of 'merely nominal' loyalty it was the politicians and their military advisers in London who had rarely thought beyond the islands' strategic value or lack of it.

If Dening was vexed by his lack of progress what must it have been like for Major Alan d'Egville, the star turn of MI5, who wandered between Jersey and Guernsey to discover that 'everyone accused the next man of collaboration only to have the same accusation made against himself'? Why this should have come as a surprise to him is hard to understand. A little knowledge of human psychology might have been of help, though he did have enough awareness to concede that 'the population is so small and so concentrated that a man's business may easily suffer unless he keeps in with everyone, so that he is forced to wink at a good deal, if only to be winked at in return'.[25]

Stopford urged him on, and with Dening's help d'Egville put together a list of suspected collaborators who qualified for prosecution. The file handed down to researchers has been doctored, presumably to exclude sensitive names, but those that are listed include so many minor offenders or characters who were plainly dotty that the entire catalogue must be suspect. Typical was the Reverend F.G. Waterbury, Rector of Castel in Guernsey, whose co-operation with the Germans in pointing out 'unreliable elements' in his parish secured for him an exemption from deportation. In the parade of congenital liars, first place went to John Latham alias John Dyball, who claimed to be a double agent but appeared to have sided most often with the Germans. The possibility of a prosecution was irrelevant since Latham had disappeared without trace.[26]

As his general observations on the wartime behaviour of the Channel Islands indicate ('incompetence of the men at the top . . . widespread collaboration with the enemy by the civilian population'[27]), Stopford was not deterred in his crusade. In mid-August he told the Home Office that he had 'approximately eleven cases where the evidence already accumulated seems to warrant consideration by the Director of Public

Prosecutions'. That left 180 cases (profiteers, informers and 'women who consorted with German troops') where there was insufficient evidence to mount a prosecution but where the perpetrators 'deserve some form of punishment'.[28]

A hostile reaction from the Home Office was no more than Stopford expected, but what may have taken him by surprise was the roar of disapproval from Brigadier Snow. He rubbished the MI5 report as a 'rehash of the tittle tattle prevalent in the islands but which nobody is prepared to come forward and substantiate', concluding that the main charges were 'mountains out of molehills . . . imputing the worst motives to people on every occasion'.[29] Exposed to the Brigadier's wrath, Dening put up a feeble defence which nobody but Stopford appreciated.

> The evidence is irrefutable and I cannot see how the present embarrassment of the Home Office can be alleviated in a major degree by any extenuating circumstances which the Force Commander may see fit to put forward. Even when all allowances are made, the character of the Administration of the Islands during the occupation remains pusillanimous – particularly so in Guernsey.[30]

With Snow on side, the Home Office felt able to press ahead with its policy of reform and reconciliation. James Chuter-Ede, who had succeeded Morrison as Home Secretary when Labour came to power in 1945, announced to the House of Commons that collaboration was a dead issue. This did not put an end to press exposés based on stories told by the man in the pub or to the activities of the Jersey Loyalists, a small but vocal lobby which took sanctimonious pleasure in casting the first stone. There was disappointment among those such as Norman le Brocq who favoured a commission of inquiry,[31] but for the most part there was a sense of relief when the files were locked away and MI5 told to stand down.

Secure in his arrogance, it is unlikely that Stopford ever recognised the fault in his logic: that the evidence of collaboration, such as it was, could never be proved beyond doubt in the context of demilitarisation. Resistance was legitimate for those who wished to resist but there was no moral imperative to oppose an occupation that had been wished on the islands by the British government.

18

WAR CRIMES

There remained the question of what action, if any, should be taken against the Germans. It was a curiosity of the liberation that while it set off a flurry of accusations and counter-accusations among islanders, there is little evidence of rancour against the former occupiers. In large measure this was thanks to the restraint of Hüffmeier's senior officers, who, fortunately for all concerned, paid no heed to their chief's call for a death and glory last stand. In contrast to most of western Europe, the Channel Islands handover was smooth. The anecdotage is of both sides playing out the last act in ways that would make it easy for all concerned. In the days before liberation, Leo Harris's father, owner of the Marina Hotel on the seafront at Havre-des-Pas, was visited by a German officer. The two men were a sartorial contrast, Mr Harris in a threadbare suit which hung loosely on bony shoulders, the German in riding boots and elegant cloak, fastened at the throat by bronze lion-head clasps.

'Are you the owner of this house?' he asked in perfect English and in a polite tone of voice. 'I am' my father replied. 'Then may I ask you, Sir, as one gentleman to another, to take down the flag. The ordinary soldier does not know how near the war is to ending and has not heard of the fall of Berlin. Already they are asking why the British flag should be flying and to save bloodshed I have come to ask you personally to take it down' and after a moment's pause he smiled, inclined his head, bowed slightly and added, 'please'.[1]

The request was granted. If others were less amenable, the taunts and provocative V signs soon gave way to what von Aufsess praised as the British sense of fair play. Or, as Coutanche commented, 'You don't kick a dog when it's down'. The quayside queues of once-proud young men waiting to board the ships that would carry them off to prisoner-of-war camps on the mainland were watched in silence. Last impressions were bittersweet.

On the first Sunday after the liberation, I recall walking to St Joseph's Church for the 5 a.m. service. As I approached, I could hear singing and the closer I got, the stronger it became. I had no idea that I was about to witness the church full to bursting with what must have been as many as four hundred German soldiers all standing and singing with booming voices. It really was an impressive sight to behold and a powerful sound to remember. I shall never forget that moving experience![2]

Bob Le Sueur holds the memory of a barricade on the Trinity road outside St Helier. 'On one side there was a Tommy smoking and on the other side there was a German smoking. He could only have got the cigarette from the Tommy but there they were.'[3]

Some of the first hesitant steps towards reconciliation were taken on the tiny island of Herm.

My family lived on the island. When the Germans finally surrendered a young German soldier who was on the island at the time helped my mother to put a small Union flag on the top of the harbour crane. My mother, whose opinion of the Germans was not very high, was speechless![4]

While most of the former garrison were taken off the islands in the days after the liberation, there was a contingent that stayed on until the following summer to help clear the islands of mines and military equipment. The job was not without its risks. Most dangerous were the roll-bombs hanging from cliffs. They were supposed to deter landing parties but, once in place, they were hard to recover except by releasing them to explode on the beach below. On Sark their removal had fatal consequences.

> The fishermen told me that the roll-bombs hanging over our harbour were held by such rusty wire that they might crash down when our troops arrived, so I gave an order that they were to be removed, and was slightly taken aback when the Commandant telephoned to say that two of his soldiers had been killed while obeying this order. The only reply I could think of at that moment was, '*Ach, so?*' There was a pause and then he asked if the soldiers could be buried in our cemetery.
>
> 'Yes, but our grave-diggers are to make their graves.'
>
> Another long pause and then the tentative voice enquired, 'Would it be permitted to fire a volley over their graves?'[5]

The Dame sought the advice of Brigadier Snow, who gave his consent. But if, by and large, islands took a tolerant view of their one-time masters, opinion in Downing Street was harder-edged. While Churchill held aloof from delivering judgement on the wartime administration of the Channel Islands, he was keen to demonstrate that the German command was not so decent and honourable as feedback suggested. He made no secret of his view that von Schmettow and his senior officers should be designated war criminals for failing to keep islanders decently fed. But he was also keen to follow up on what he saw as specific breaches of the rules of war. In early September 1944, he was harrying Combined Operations for details on Commando raids early in the war.

> The Prime Minister wishes to obtain particulars about a raid on the Channel Islands some two-and-a-half years ago when two of

our men, natives of the Channel Islands, were left behind and afterwards received into their homes. These men were shortly afterwards betrayed to the Germans by a Channel Islander (a police constable) and were shot. Mr Churchill thought there might well be other cases such as this, and considers it important that the guilty parties should be brought to trial.[6]

A search of the archives revealed that the Prime Minister had been misinformed. The report was read by Churchill who scribbled in the margin, 'Leave it'. He might have added, 'for the time being'. With the surrender, he was keen to restart inquiries.

There were two parallel investigations, one conducted by the Office of the Judge Advocate General in the person of Major Francis F. Haddock, the other by MI19, the department chiefly responsible for investigating war crimes, represented by Major Theodore Pantcheff. Both were short on basic information, being ignorant even of the whereabouts of such as Baron von Aufsess, who was in a mainland prisoner-of-war camp, and Colonel Knackfuss, who was living out his last days as a prisoner in a Yugoslavian camp and who died in October 1945.[7]

From the very start Haddock was unhappy with his role. Taking his lead from the two bailiffs and their senior officers, he began by collecting testimony on German activities that were thought to cross the boundary of acceptable behaviour, ranging from the cuts in the bread ration as a reprisal for the sinking by Allied forces of food ships on their way to the Channel Islands to the deportation of English-born subjects. Somewhere along the line it must have occurred to him that given the horrors of the war in Europe such actions were no more than par for the course, that far worse had been sanctioned by the Allies in pursuit of victory or greater good. Haddock then turned to specific cases where islanders protested against cruel treatment. Somehow the genuine cases eluded him. The poor major was beset with claims that turned out to be fanciful or patently false.

With regard Anita Gomez . . . I hear from the Island Attorney General downwards that her character is such that no reliance can be placed on any of her statements, which when I interviewed her I found to be chiefly concerning a Russian doctor who, she alleges, behaved in a sadistic manner to his OT patients. Consequently I have taken no statement from her, but I enclose a garbled account of her experiences typed by herself.[8]

Equally frustrating was the testimony of Paul Gourdan, who claimed to have been sent to a concentration camp. However,

> he admitted that his newspaper article was an exaggeration for the purpose of impressing the girls of Jersey (including his wife) who had consorted with Germans. His description of Buchenwald was different in many respects from that given me by Emile Dubois, and on three occasions during my interview with him he gave me a different number as being his in the camp. I came to the conclusion that in all probability he had never been to Buchenwald, but I took from him an exercise book which he assured me contained his actual experiences, and I enclose a copy of the contents of this book, which is freely illustrated with gruesome drawings by Gourdan.[9]

Haddock then discovered that, before the occupation, Gourdan had been convicted of forgery (three times), false pretences, housebreaking and burglary. 'The Field Security Police are interesting themselves in his activities while in Germany.'[10]

It might be thought that Major Pantcheff of MI19 would have had an easier task in Alderney, where war crimes against the OT's East European workforce were widely acknowledged. But since the chief culprits had departed when the labour camps were demolished in 1943, Pantcheff was left with unreliable witnesses who were only too happy to tell what they thought they knew but too often were reporting stories that had travelled some way along the grapevine, gathering drama with every retelling. One of the few of the Alderney residents to stay on the island after the mass evacuation claimed that mass shootings and other atrocities had taken a thousand lives. Yet even those who thought the worst of the Germans found this hard to accept. Where were the bodies? Thrown into the sea, said one; buried in the concrete of the fortifications, said another. Then why were no bodies washed up on the shore? As to the concrete internment, this was surely reserved for the more credulous of the rumour mongers.

That there had been inhuman treatment of the slave workers there could be no doubts. Arbitrary beatings were commonplace, rations were woefully inadequate for men on heavy work for long hours, clothing was pitiful and illness ignored until the sufferer collapsed. Pantcheff did not have to go far for reliable documentation of persistent brutality. The Reverend Ord, a Guernsey clergyman, testified how on a fine sunny day in June 1944, he was at his door chatting with the milkman when:

we heard a curious shuffling sound as of many feet in sabots. We went down the drive to the gate and there we saw a dreadful sight. Coming down from the harbour was a column of men in rows of five. All were in striped pyjama suits of sorts and their footgear varied from wooden sabots – hence the sound so familiar to me from my own days of being a prisoner of war – to pieces of cloth bound round the feet. Others were barefoot. There were more than 1,000 of them – political prisoners brought away from Alderney and being fetched down by their guards to an open field at Blanc Bois. They were shaven-headed and in varying degrees of weariness or lameness. Scattered through the column among men of subhuman criminal type were others obviously intellectuals, men of superior calibre who had offended the brutal Nazi regime. It tore the heart to see the effects of this systematic and deliberate degradation of human beings. At the head of the column marched five evil-visaged SS men armed with automatic guns. At the rear of the column and along its flanks on both sides and at a distance of about a dozen feet from each other were more of these brutes, similarly armed, and all on the alert for any attempt at a breakaway. I have never seen such brutality written on human countenances. Occasionally there have been individuals of whom this could be said during the past four years, but here we had, gathered together, a number of the same type, and the ensemble was horrifying. The leading guards marched with deliberation but those on the flanks just slouched by, accompanied by Alsatian hounds which, fierce as they were, did not look quite so wicked as their human associates.[11]

Statements from those working for the Germans on Alderney, the few who could be traced, told of deaths by what the medics called 'undernourishment' and random torture. Karl Janetzkv was a Russian interpreter who questioned a seventeen-year-old boy accused of breaking into a church and stealing food.

He protested his innocence. The next day his face was badly swollen. They gave him a cigarette to mock him but he could not put it in his mouth. They made him sit on a stove which they stoked. The heat was unbearable seven feet away. They kept him there half an hour. He was crying.[12]

When the inquiry looked to be stuck on horror stories without resolution, Major Haddock was drafted in to give support. He was accompanied by Major Cotton, formerly a police inspector with the Sheffield force. The two did not get on. With his legal training Haddock did not take well to reports 'typed in a great hurry and, being typical police statements, full of irrelevant matters'.[13] On the other hand, Cotton did manage to put a few names to serious charges, though where these individuals could be found was a question no one could answer. The frustrated Haddock then had to report that his corporal, having returned home to Jersey for a short leave, had found his wife living with another man. It was the last straw. Haddock was heartily sick of the islands and all who lived there. 'Why people used to come here for their holidays is quite beyond me.'[14]

Major Pantcheff also had problems that went beyond his investigative duties. In early June he had visited on him a Major Gruzdev of the Soviet Military Mission in London. Accompanied by an interpreter from the Royal Canadian Artillery, Gruzdev was on hand, ostensibly, to inquire into allegations of atrocities against his fellow countrymen. In fact, his purpose was to act up to Stalinist paranoia by ensuring that no Soviet citizen should be allowed to settle in the iniquitous west. In this, despite spending much of his time sleeping off vodka binges, he succeeded one hundred per cent. Such was the affection for Uncle Joe that Jersey States recorded its congratulations on hearing that all the surviving Ukrainian slave workers had been dispatched to Mother Russia – where they almost certainly ended up in the Gulag, charged with having collaborated with the Germans.

In May 1965 the Soviets awarded twenty gold watches to those islanders who had fed or sheltered escaped Russian labourers. Nobody knows how many died in Alderney. Pantcheff reckoned that the probable number of foreign workers buried there was 337, a figure arrived at by counting the death certificates signed by German doctors. No one was ever brought to trial.

19

A NEW LEAF

That the British Communist Party should have shown an interest in the Channel Islands must seem an unlikely proposition. Yet it was so. As the war ended, the comrades on the mainland decided that Jersey and Guernsey were ripe for revolution. The idea was not entirely fanciful. The occupation and its aftermath had left a society that was unhappy with its present and confused about its future. Neighbour had been set against neighbour and there had been violence in the streets. For the first time in generations the bailiffs and their executive colleagues were uncertain as to their status.

In Jersey there was even a communist cell, led by Leslie Huelin and Norman Le Brocq. The Jersey Communist Party, a spinoff from the Jersey Democratic Movement, was a mere six strong and of that number, Huelin was the only genuine Marxist revolutionary. Having spent his pre-war days in Australia, where he had been a communist official, Huelin looked forward to the liquidation of the Channel Islands establishment as a necessary component of the transition to a workers' dictatorship. But while his friends distanced themselves from his extremism, they were hot in their condemnation of the civil authorities who were seen as a self-serving oligarchy. They had a point.

The island administrations, a law unto themselves without a credible opposition to urge a rethink of hastily contrived policies, were overdue for reform. Spotlight on the Channel Islands, a special report by the *Daily Worker*, the Party mouthpiece, scored heavily on some sensitive issues.

Supporting the call from the Jersey Democratic Movement for a Commission of Inquiry, the article, reprinted as a brochure, began by fastening on to archaic practices in government. The island constitutions, haloed by tradition and a conviction that it was good to be different fell way short of the democratic ideal. In Jersey, voting was restricted to ratepayers and those in the income-tax bracket, a rule which disenfranchised close on half the population who either had no property of their own or who were too poor to cross the tax threshold. Moreover, of the fifty-seven members of the States Assembly, only seventeen were popularly elected. Twelve jurats were returned by the ratepayers of each parish. Once in they were there for life. The rest held office either by virtue of other appointments or by royal command.

If it had been the communists alone pressing for change there might well have been strong establishment resistance. Certainly, not much quarter was given to the Jersey Democratic Movement. But other voices were raised. Interviews with escapees, all young and bright, revealed dissatisfaction with the prevailing civil order not because it was too German-leaning but because it was anachronistic, a system of government that was tied to the previous century. Typical were the comments of an eighteen-year-old male nurse.

> He had very pronounced ideas on reforms which he considered overdue on the island. He believed that many young people thought as he did. Some thought such views might be regarded as 'Communistic' but they certainly had nothing in common with the Russian type of communism. They might also be regarded as advanced socialistic or as a kind of idealism. Asked to explain what he meant by this, informant said that it was really equality of opportunity which people of the island wanted. In his own case his father had died young and he was left with his mother and

sister. It had not been easy to make ends meet and lack of money had denied him the education which the children of richer people could enjoy.[1]

There was praise for the Jersey Democratic Movement though the suspicion was voiced that the Germans had made more of it than was warranted to scare the States into clamping down on subversive movements. Letters brought over by escapees, mostly from Jersey, expressed hostility towards the Bailiff and the States, described by one correspondent as a 'weak livered lot . . . quislings of the first water'.[2] That they should continue in office after the war was beyond comprehension.

The most vociferous calls for reform came from the Channel Island refugees centred on the north of England. Before the evacuation, most of them had never strayed far from their island homes. Now, having experienced another way of life, they could not help but wonder if some things were not ordered better on the mainland. As early as November 1941, the *Channel Islands Monthly Review*, published in Stockport, was giving space to the challenges of post-war reconstruction when those returning must 'resolve to take up the burdens of citizenship in a different spirit to the slack and apathetic ways of old'.[3]

In the new year, there were calls for setting up a Channel Islands government in exile on the lines of those for France, Norway, The Netherlands, Poland and Czechoslovakia, all based in London. Social welfare, housing, education, public health and transport were on the proposed agenda along with an extension of democracy including the possibility of House of Commons representation for the Channel Islands. With nearly fifty refugee societies spread out across the country, the setting up of a government in exile proved to be too ambitious but the leading groups based in Cheshire, Lancashire and Yorkshire did come together in a federation which set about lobbying the national government.

The message was simple. After the war the status quo would be unacceptable. 'The old order should make room for a better way of life for the greatest number. Privilege, class, the possession of the world's goods or influence should no longer be considered sufficient of itself as a credential for rule and authority over the lives and destinies of others.'[4]

The radical tone may have acted as a warning signal to those of a more conventional stance. In any event, by 1944 a Channel Islands Study Group of some twenty islanders, 'most of whom at the outbreak of war were following with distinction professions in Britain',[5] had produced a series of papers which pointed the way to greater transparency and accountability in island affairs. Another moderating influence was the accommodation reached between the evacuees and the long-standing Refugees Committee to form a Central Advisory Committee for Channel Island Affairs. This grand-sounding body brought together those who were dealing with current problems, mostly financial, with the advocates for a fresh start.

Was it by design that the first post-war elections were held before the democratic reforms were in place? Probably. Still, constitutional amendments take time and an expression of the will of the people, however imperfect, could not be long delayed. What had happened on the mainland, with Churchill voted out of office to make way for socialism, set a powerful precedent.

Predictably, in the Channel Islands, the unamended electoral system weighed against the left. (The British Communist Party soon lost interest.) But the traditionalists did not get it all their own way. Everyone recognised that the days of paternalism were over. Even if the old guard had wanted to hold back the new bloods in politics, many of them, returning servicemen who had seen something of the world, knew that there could be no going back. In any case, proposals for more direct representation were already on the table. So it was that less than a year after the end of the war, it was agreed that unelected members of the States should either be excluded or lose their voting rights. Alderney, starting again from base, was, in effect, merged with Guernsey while Sark alone remained a feudal outpost.

But democracy was no easy cure-all. What with the loss of export revenue during the war years and the costs of the occupation, the islands were loaded with debt. Then there was the reconstruction to pay for. Repairing the damage caused by the German military was expensive enough but there were also legitimate demands for half-decent social services. The tourist image of the Channel Islands as havens of peace and plenty, an offshore Shangri-La, was far from reality. Here is Josephine Ginns on life as a schoolgirl from an ordinary home in early post-war Jersey.

> I went to St Luke's School, which was very rough. Some of the children didn't even have underclothes and a lot of them had plimsolls with the toes cut out because their feet were growing, and that was summer and winter. . . . We were given milk out of a big can and it had bits in it and there were rather disgusting enamel chipped mugs. At age six, I was a finicky child. I didn't like to share the same cup with lots of other children. The other thing was the nits; the nit lady used to come round – she used to pull your hair about and she had a big comb. A lot of children, most children, had nits. I don't understand what they say about nits only going into clean hair because a lot of the children there had remarkably dirty hair. I mean they couldn't help it; there was a lot of poverty after the war – it was really bad. I can remember queuing up with my grandmother for one garment. We were told that if there was anything we urgently needed, they had some second-hand clothes. I can remember a brown coat that I had to go and queue up for; it was very humiliating.[6]

After lengthy discussions, not always amicable, with the British Treasury, the Channel Islands economy was given a kick-start after the war with a £7.5 million grant – £4.2 million to Jersey and £3.3 million to Guernsey. There was some surprise at Westminster that the islands could not do more to help themselves, most obviously by raising taxes to create a welfare state on the British model. The counter argument, that high taxes would drive the economy into the ground, has a familiar ring to those currently preoccupied with reducing a massive national debt without taxing out of existence the entrepreneurs on whom recovery depends.

Whatever the strength of the case for retaining the islands' status as a low-tax refuge, it was a policy that made it harder to bridge the gap between the haves and the have-nots. The impression, justified or not, that certain people in high places had done well out of the war incensed those who were refused compensation for possessions that had either been requisitioned or purloined.

But the chief cause of continuing discontent was the British government's failure to state plainly how it judged the wartime conduct of the Channel Islands. It was in Churchill's power to resolve the issue but, instead, he chose to remain silent while the Home Office and the intelligence services fought it out. It was a failure of leadership that allowed rumour and false witness to flourish. Churchill made no effort to visit the islands – that job was handed on to Buckingham Palace – and left no clear directions for his successor in Downing Street. As a result, Clement Attlee was understandably confused when the Home Office delivered its recommendations for occupation honours. A knighthood for Coutanche might be justified but for Carey too? The Guernsey bailiff had played a relatively minor role in dealings with the Germans and by general consent was no more than a figurehead.

The Prime Minister wanted to know how the Home Office squared its generous recognition of the bailiffs' wartime services with the views of MI5. 'As you will see, their report contains most adverse comment on both these gentlemen.'[7] In response, the Home Secretary reprised the commendations of the Director of Public Prosecutions and of Brigadier Snow, adding that the recently appointed lieutenant-governors agreed that 'the criticisms directed in certain quarters against the bailiffs and the administration were largely due to ignorance and misunderstanding'.[8]

Allowing for errors of judgement (how could they be avoided in circumstances beyond precedent?) the conspiracy theorists had little to go on save for a few examples where civilian officials had appeared to bend over backwards to pacify the occupiers. The Sherwill broadcast was a prime example. Others were Victor Carey's notice of £25 reward leading to the conviction of anyone marking up 'the letter V or any other sign or word calculated to offend the German authorities' and, in

Jersey, the outburst of John Leale when, as attorney-general, he took a 'very serious view' of a case in which an Irishman had punched a German soldier: 'I wish it to be clearly understood by the public that to assault a German officer or soldier . . . is a grave offence which will not be tolerated.'[9] Yet in all such cases the natural tendency to opt for accommodation over confrontation, to 'hold on to nurse for fear of getting someone worse' was a defence not easy to dislodge.

Joining the chorus of approval was Lord Justice du Parcq, a Jerseyman privy councillor and appeal judge who was Chairman of the Channel Islands Refugee Committee. A long-time adviser to the Home Office, du Parcq had voiced reservations about Carey but appears to have concluded that singling out one senior islander for public admonition would cause more trouble than it was worth. In any event, he went along with the Home Office recommendations for awards.

There remained the problem of striking some sort of balance of recognition between those who had tried to modify the effects of the occupation with those who had set themselves against German rule. The simple answer was to give equal acknowledgement. But the Home Office could not accept this. To shower praise on the resistance would be to imply that those who had taken the more conventional route, and were already under heavy criticism, had failed in their duty. That the converse was also true, that failure to acknowledge the risks taken by brave islanders in giving refuge to slave workers, for example, or helping escapees, would necessarily denigrate their efforts does not seem to have occurred to anyone. There may have been those on the islands who were happy for this to happen. Who knows what pressure was put on the Home Office not to give too much credit where it was due?

When the honours were announced in late 1945, knighthoods went to Coutanche, Carey and Leale. Sherwill had to make do with a CBE but was knighted four years later, after he succeeded Carey as bailiff. Duret Aubin also garnered a CBE. Of the thirteen OBEs handed out, not one went to an islander who had actively opposed the occupation. In fact, the only nod in the direction of the resistance was an award from the lowest rank of the honours list to Bill Bertram who had risked much to help escapees. He was presented with the British Empire Medal.

From this cack-handed attempt to dispose of an embarrassing issue stems one of the great ironies of the war. Everywhere else in occupied Europe, the part played by the resistance in overthrowing Nazism was quickly recognised, celebrated and, before long, promoted as a symbol of national pride, a security blanket to smother the shame of defeat. In the Channel Islands, by contrast, memories of resistance were seen by its establishment as an aggravation to the post-war settlement, a reminder that the British had not handled matters too cleverly.

In an attempt to draw a thick red line under the collaborative issue, the DPP virtually dictated what the island administrations should release for public consumption. There were to be no prosecutions, there being no 'method whereby those persons who have been found guilty of reprehensible conduct can properly and fairly be punished'.[10] But the controversy would not go away. Even if islanders were ready to forgive and forget, interest on the mainland remained strong. The reason is not hard to find. The war as it touched the Channel Islands is the only indication of what might have happened across the whole country had the Germans made the leap across the Channel. It is like a mirror in which we see ourselves as we might have been. The reflection is not welcomed by those schooled in the myth of the impregnability of the British character. It was certainly not welcomed by Churchill who created the myth. Hence the frequent efforts to depict islanders as a race apart whose loyalties were suspect. A fairer image is of ordinary people responding as best they could to extraordinary circumstances. No more could have been asked. Not everyone finds this easy to accept but that does not make it any less than the truth.

20

REFLECTIONS

'Most of us were glad to surrender. We longed for the end. It was a question which concerned our own existence. . . . This eternal hunger and this eternal tiredness, the weakness . . . we never knew for sure what the effect would be afterwards. We couldn't stand it, we had older people who were getting weak and already showing the first symptoms of malnutrition. There was oedema in the legs from starvation, and sunken stomachs, and God knows what. Hearing defects and sight defects, and difficulties in moving, and we watched it happen. . . . And we heard the English news as well as the German news . . . it wasn't promising, not when you heard that, for example, on the 19th of March, Hanau was bombed by the Americans. They were already in my home town. What hope was there left? Better to have an end with horror than a horror without end.' *Hans Kegelmann*[1]

*

'I learned a great deal from the Occupation. I learned to speak German. I learned to communicate with people of other nationalities. How else would I have talked to a Russian boy? I learned a lot about human nature, about how people can be kind to each other. It brought out the best and the worst in people, that period, but all in all I felt that it just showed that human beings are the same the world over.' *John Boachere*[2]

*

'I think I lost my teenage years without the normal amount of fun. It was just solid hard work but I think it did a great deal for me. There were so many things that you had to get on and do and I think it makes one a better human being. So that although it was a sad time in our lives, a long time in our lives, a worrying time, with hindsight you realise that I made a great deal of myself, and I'm sure that's what a lot of other people [would say].' *Betty Thurban*[3]

*

'On a warm summer's day in 1995, the Mayor of Bad Wurzach, a little town in southern Germany, led my husband and me to the town's imposing Schloss. As we approached the gates I struggled to adjust my fifty-year-old memories of a grim grey building, surrounded by rolled barbed wire and patrolled by soldiers with guns and fierce Alsatian dogs, to this fine renovated castle, gleaming with fresh paint. Here were colourful, cheerful gardens where I remembered a bare compound, iron-hard from soldiers' boots. My mental picture was of a prison camp, grey and black and hard and bare. This was a grand baroque castle, shining in the August sun. But the same guardhouses were still there at the gates.

My last view of these gates had been when they were flung open for the American lorries to tear through, throwing up clouds of dust, as they carried the inmates out of their prison to the airport. It was a hot day and the American soldiers drove at tremendous speed over bumpy roads; I wasn't the only child being sick over the tailgate. But the speed and the vanishing view of Wurzach could not have been more welcome; after two years and nine months behind barbed wire, these men, women and children, from babies to teenagers, were at last going home.' *Sylvia Diamond*[4]

*

From: Hptwm. Hubert Schmitz D681370, 70 G.P.W. Working Goy, Great Britain

To: Mrs Brouard, Guernsey
England
20.8.46

Dear Mrs Brouard

Having been here in this country for practically more than a year I shall finally forward the promised letter. I am quite well and I hope you are also in a good state of health. August last year I had an accident which occurred at my working place maiming my left hand for a very long time. Today I work in my trade in the camp. Unfortunately my hand isn't quite in shape yet – but I expect it to be alright soon again. Luckily I do get good news from my folks especially from my dear wife. They all await my repatriation rather impatiently. Once I wrote to O. Le Cheminant without, however, receiving an answer, perhaps I used the wrong address!? Would you have the kindness as to forward a note to her? I sincerely hope you have resettled again in your former home & forgotten all the misery in the meantime. Very often my thoughts abide at this pleasant spot over which God held his protecting hand.

Hoping that these lines will reach you in best of health. I remain with all my best wishes & greetings to all of you

Yours truly, Hub Schmitz[5]

*

'We were in St Helier for a week and were staying at the Norfolk Hotel. One evening when we were taking a stroll on the beach we came upon a man sitting on a rock. We started chatting and I told him that I had been here during the war, as a German soldier. And he said, well, he'd never imagined he'd meet another German soldier at his ripe old age. As we said goodbye he said, would you let me give you a hug? Because before, during our conversation he'd asked me what Germany was like now, was there still a chance of the Nazis getting to power again? And I was able to convince him that there was absolutely no chance of that, that we were a democracy now and didn't have parties like the Nazis anymore. And he was very happy and he hugged me and my wife, too. And off he went, looking very happy. He had also told me that during the hunger months, when the population was fed by the International Red Cross, he had taken parcels in his small car, which he had been allowed to keep since it was too small for the Wehrmacht's requirements, to the people who lived out of town. And so we ended our chat . . . And I was very happy about it. It was like a reconciliation. "Encounter on the beach" would be a good title.' *Willy Worner*[6]

ACKNOWLEDGEMENTS

For every book there is someone (rarely the author) who fires the starting gun. In this case it was Richard Lewis, who argued passionately for a fresh look at the German occupation of the Channel Islands. When Richard retired, his directorial responsibilities on behalf of the owners of the Jersey War Tunnels Museum were taken on by Roger Colyer and Debbie Lang, who have given unstinted support to the project. I owe them all a huge debt of gratitude.

For research gems that might otherwise have gone unnoticed, full credit goes to Chris Addy, archivist at Jersey War Tunnels, who has built up a valuable collection of first-hand experiences of the occupation, and to Samantha Wyndham, whose delvings into the National Archives have supported the reinterpretation of much that passes for standard history. I was also fortunate in being able to draw on the unrivalled knowledge of Jersey historian Michael Ginns. For responding, ever helpfully, to a flurry of inquiries, I thank the staff of the London Library, the Imperial War Museum, the Liddell Hart Centre for Military Studies at Kings College, London, the National Archives and, most particularly, the Société Jersiaise and the Priaulx Library, Guernsey.

My assistant, Jill Fenner, has saved me from many literary sins of omission and commission. Whatever errors of fact or judgement that remain are mine alone.

ENDNOTES

INTRODUCTION

1 Brian Harrison, *Seeking a Role: The United Kingdom 1951–1970*, Clarendon Press, 2009, p. 533
2 Bunting, *The Model Occupation*, 1995

CHAPTER 1: A SHOCK TO THE SYSTEM

1 Arthur Kent's daily record of the occupation, Jersey War Tunnels Collection, JWT/2004/131
2 E.V. Clayton, *Channel Islands Occupation Review*, No. 28, June 2001
3 'Strategic Importance of the Channel Islands', Report by the Chiefs of Staff, 11 June 1940, PRO/CAB 66/8/27
4 *Ibid.*
5 War Cabinet Conclusions (vol. V) May–June 1940, 162(40)PRO/CAB 65/7/57
6 Memorandum by Chiefs of Staff, 18 June 1940, PRO/CAB 66/8/38
7 Alanbrooke, *War Diaries 1939–1945*, p. 36
8 War Cabinet Conclusions (Vol. V) May–June 1940, 172(40) PRO/CAB 65/7/67
9 Leslie Harding, Folkestone's People's History Centre, *Financial Times*, 2 February 2008

10 Arthur Kent's daily record of the occupation, Jersey War Tunnels Collection, JWT/2004/131

11 Read, *No Cause for Panic*, p. 13

12 Sherwill, *A Fair and Honest Book*, p. 76

13 Reg Blanchford, Imperial War Museum, IWM MISC 189/2(2826)

14 Journal of Dr Alistair Rose, written 1944, published in *Channel Islands Occupation Review*, no. 28, June 2001

15 Jill Harris, BBC WW2 People's War, Article ID 01/a3847601

16 Malcolm Woodland, BBC WW2 People's War, Article ID A3992349

17 Frank Hubert, 'Occupying My Mind 1940–45', *Channel Islands Occupation Review*, no. 28, June 2001

18 Durand, *Guernsey under German Rule*, p. 14

19 Mahy, *There is an Occupation . . .*

CHAPTER 2: AWAY FROM HOME

1 Betty Harvey, BBC WW2 People's War, Article ID A2871939

2 Polly Burford, BBC WW2 People's War, Article ID A2034578

3 Mahy, *There is an Occupation . . .*

4 Zilma Roussel, BBC WW2 People's War, Article ID A1998147

5 Maurice Hill, interview, 2000, Jersey War Tunnels Collection, JWT/2008/494

6 *News Chronicle*, 1 July 1940

7 Josephine Ginns, interview, 2000, Jersey War Tunnels Collection, JWT/2008/495

8 Ada Willmot, BBC WW2 People's War, Article ID A3158075

9 Bob Le Sueur, interview, 2004, Jersey War Tunnels Collection, JWT/2007/857

10 Read, *No Cause for Panic*, p. 38

11 Gwenda Smith, BBC WW2 People's War, Article ID 10/a3913210

12 Margaret le Poiderin, BBC WW2 People's War, Article ID 29/a3943929

13 Antoinette Duperouzell, BBC WW2 People's War, Article ID 14/a4045114

14 Mr Warren, interview, 2000, Jersey War Tunnels Collection, JWT/2007/1025

15 Read, *No Cause for Panic*, p. 64

16 *Ibid.*, p. 66

17 *Ibid.*, p. 59

18 *Ibid.*, p. 128

19 Parliamentary Debate, Fifth Series, vol. CXVI, House of Lords, 9 July 1940,

20 *Ibid.*

21 Parliamentary Debate, Fifth Series, vol. CXXVI, House of Lords, 18 March 1943

CHAPTER 3: UNWELCOME STRANGERS

1 Hans Grah, diary, *Channel Islands Occupation Review*, no. 28, June 2001
2 Presumably bomb racks lowered under the belly of a plane.
3 Malcolm Woodland, BBC WW2 People's War, Article ID A3992691
4 Frank Hubert, 'Occupying My Mind 1940–45', *Channel Islands Occupation Review*, no. 28, June 2001
5 McLoughlin, *Living with the Enemy*
6 Pocock, *The Memoirs of Lord Coutanche*, p. 18
7 Imperial War Museum, IWM MISC 189/2 (2826), Tapes 4394–6
8 *Jersey Evening Post*, 1 July 1940
9 Report by Major Albrecht Lanz, published in translation in the *Channel Islands Occupation Review*, no. 28, June 2001
10 Hathaway, *Dame of Sark*, p. 117
11 Lanz, Report published in *Channel Islands Occupation Review* no. 28, June 2001
12 Hathaway, *Dame of Sark*, p. 117
13 *Ibid.* pp. 117–18

CHAPTER 4: CHARM OFFENSIVE

1 Pocock, *The Memoirs of Lord Coutanche*, p. 20
2 *Ibid.*
3 *Ibid.*
4 *Ibid.*
5 Sherwill, *A Fair and Honest Book*, p. 183
6 *Ibid.*
7 Pocock, *The Memoirs of Lord Coutanche*, p. 112
8 Sherwill, *A Fair and Honest Book*, p. 188
9 *Ibid.*, p. 91
10 *Ibid.*, p. 109
11 *Ibid.*, p. 99
12 *Ibid.*, p. 109
13 The total number of messages sent during the occupation was over half a million.
14 Sherwill, *A Fair and Honest Book*, p. 104
15 *Ibid.*
16 *Guernsey Evening Press*, 2 August 1940
17 Pocock, *The Memoirs of Lord Coutanche*, p. 26

18 *Ibid.*, p. 27

19 Sherwill, *A Fair and Honest Book*, pp. 144–5

20 *Ibid.*, p. 143

21 Imperial War Museum, Werner Grosskopf, IWM MISC 189/1(2826), Tape 4488/4489

22 Imperial War Museum, Karl Urban, IWM MISC 189/1(2926), Tapes JT4

23 Imperial War Museum, Hans Constable, IWM MISC 189/1(2826), Tape 4439

24 Imperial War Museum, IWM MISC 189/1(2826), Tape 4444

25 Hathaway, *Dame of Sark*, p. 138

26 Saunders, *The British Channel Islands under German Occupation*, p. 182

27 Sherwill, *A Fair and Honest Book*, p. 244

CHAPTER 5: LIVING WITH THE ENEMY

1 Michael Ginns, interview, 2000, Jersey War Tunnels Collection, JWT/2009/1022

2 Leslie Ricou, interview, 2004, Jersey War Tunnels Collection, JWT/2009/1012

3 John Boucheré, interview, 2000, Jersey War Tunnels Collection, JWT/2008/516

4 Reg Langlois, BBC WW2 People's War, Article ID 46/a3403946

5 Jean Budden, BBC WW2 People's War, Article ID 96/a4008296

6 Margaret Le Cras, BBC WW2 People's War, Article ID 78/a4008278

7 Ruth Walsh, BBC WW2 People's War Archive, Article ID 50/a4013650

8 Bob Le Sueur, interview, 2000, Jersey War Tunnels Collection, JWT/2009/61

9 Fred Hockey, escapee from Guernsey, interviewed by the *Daily Herald*, 17 October 1940

10 Malcolm Woodland, BBC WW2 People's War, Article ID 60/a4013560

11 Michael Ginns, interview, 2000, Jersey War Tunnels Collection, JWT/2007/1022

12 Cortvriend, *Isolated Island*, p. 84

13 Le Quesne, *The Occupation of Jersey Day by Day*, p. 10 (entry for 16 August 1940)

14 Joe Mière, interview, 2003, Jersey War Tunnels Collection, JWT/2007/929

15 Arthur Kent's daily record of the occupation, Jersey War Tunnels Collection, JWT/2004/131

16 Leo Harris, interview, 2003, Jersey War Tunnels Collection, JWT/2007/1001

17 Fred Gallienne, BBC WW2 People's War, Article ID a3992970

18 *Ibid.*

19 Longmate, *If Britain Had Fallen*, p. 176

20 Imperial War Museum, interviews with German Soldiers, IWM MISC 189/1(2826), Tape 4444

21 Jean Budden, BBC WW2 People's War, Article ID 63/a4013263

22 Harris, *A Boy Remembers*, pp. 66–7

23 Cortvriend, *Isolated Island*, p. 150

CHAPTER 6: MAKING DO

1 Sinel, *The German Occupation of Jersey*, p. 14

2 Fred Hockey, escapee from Guernsey, interviewed by the *Daily Herald*, 17 October 1940

3 Hathaway, *Dame of Sark*, pp. 128–9

4 Wyatt, *Jersey in Jail*, p. 20 (diary entry for January 1941)

5 McLoughlin, *Living with the Enemy*, p. 94

6 Daphne Breton, BBC WW2 People's War, Article ID 76/a4013876

7 Hathaway, *Dame of Sark*, p. 137

8 Reg Langlois, BBC WW2 People's War, Article ID 46/a3403946

9 Grace Buttery, interview, 2004, Jersey War Tunnels Collection, JWT/2005/34

10 McLoughlin, *Living with the Enemy*, p. 88

11 *Ibid.*, p. 144

12 Kenneth Podger and Roger Fauvel, interview, 2003, Jersey War Tunnels Collection, JWT/2007/1015

13 Bob Le Sueur, interview, 2004, Jersey War Tunnels Collection, JWT/2007/857

14 Arthur Kent's daily record of the occupation, Jersey War Tunnels Collection, JWT/2004/131

15 Reg Langlois, BBC WW2 People's War, Article ID 46/a3403946

16 Kaye Le Cheminant, BBC WW2 People's War, Article ID 28/a4014028

17 Ken Podger and Roger Fauvel, interview, 2003, Jersey War Tunnels Collection, JWT/2007/1015

18 *Ibid.*

19 Arthur Kent's daily record of the occupation, Jersey War Tunnels Collection, JWT/2004/131

20 Bob Grant, BBC WW2 People's War, Article ID 72/a3623672

21 Graham, *A Separate Peace*, p. 93

22 Bob Grant, BBC WW2 People's War, Article ID 72/a3623672

23 Jeanne Michel, interview, 2000, Jersey War Tunnels Collection, JWT/2008/465

24 Wyatt, *Jersey in Jail*, pp. 23–4 (diary entry, January 1942)
25 Myrtle Tabel, BBC WW2 People's War, Article ID 79/a5461779
26 Kaye Le Cheminant, BBC WW2 People's War, Article ID 66/a4013966
27 Fred Gallienne, BBC WW2 People's War, Article ID 63/a4007963
28 Brian Le Conte, BBC WW2 People's War, Article ID 34/a4008034

CHAPTER 7: CHURCHILL'S FIASCO

1 War Cabinet Conclusion, 2 July 1940 PRO CAB 65/8/3
2 Durnford-Slater, *Commando*, p. 18
3 Wood and Seaton Wood, *Islands in Danger*, p. 68
4 Imperial War Museum, Tom Mansell, interview, IWM MISC 189/2(2826)
5 Sherwill, *A Fair and Honest Book*, p. 138
6 Philip Martel, quoted in McLoughlin, *Living With the Enemy*, p. 29
7 Durnford-Slater, *Commando*, p. 21
8 *Ibid.*
9 *Ibid.*, p. 23
10 *Ibid.*, pp. 26–7
11 Sherwill, *A Fair and Honest Book*, p. 119
12 Philip Martel, quoted in McLoughlin, *Living with the Enemy*, p. 29
13 Hathaway, *Dame of Sark*, p. 123
14 Wood & Seaton Wood, *Islands in Danger*. p. 76
15 Sherwill, *A Fair and Honest Book*, p. 146
16 Cruickshank, *The German Occupation of the Channel Islands*, p. 92
17 Wood & Seaton Wood, *Islands in Danger*, pp. 106–7
18 Imperial War Museum, interview with Channel Islanders, IWM MISC 189/2(2826), Tape 4425
19 Sherwill, *A Fair and Honest Book*, pp. 146–7
20 *Ibid.*, p. 146
21 *Ibid.*, p. 147
22 *Ibid.*, p. 158
23 *Ibid.*, p. 167

CHAPTER 8: PROPAGANDA WAR

1 Hiram Warren Johnson, US senator
2 Falla, *The Silent War*, p. 30
3 *Ibid.*

4 Arthur Kent's daily record of the occupation, Jersey War Tunnels Collection, JWT/2004/131

5 *Ibid.*

6 Sinel, *The German Occupation of Jersey*, p. 13

7 Fred Hockey in the *Daily Herald*. 23 October, 1940

8 *Ibid.*

9 Imperial War Museum, John Blampied, IWM MISC 189/2 (2826), Tapes 4394–6

10 Journal of Dr Alistair Rose, published in *Channel Islands Occupation Review*, no. 28, June 2001

11 Alfred Pipon, interview, 2003, Jersey War Tunnels Collection, JWT/2007/1016

12 Mr Birch, interview, 2004, Jersey War Tunnels Collection, JWT/2007/1000

13 Arthur Kent's daily record of the occupation, Jersey War Tunnels Collection, JWT/2004/131

14 Recalled by Arthur Linthorn Le Masurier's daughter Margaret Hull, BBC WW2 People's War, Article ID 58/a3942858

15 Bertrand, *A Record of the Work of Guernsey Secret Press 1940–1945*, pp. 7–8

CHAPTER 9: INTO EXILE

1 Bob Le Sueur, interview, 2000, Jersey War Tunnels Collection, JWT/2009/61

2 Longmate, *If Britain Had Fallen*, p. 193

3 Reg Langlois, BBC WW2 People's War, Article ID A3403946

4 Harris, *Islanders Deported*, part 1, p. 4

5 Home Office file on collaboration in the Channel Islands, PRO HO 45/22399

6 Pocock, *The Memoirs of Lord Coutanche*, p. 30

7 *Ibid.*, pp. 32–3

8 Mière, *Never to Be Forgotten*, pp. 54–5

9 Imperial War Museum, Joe Berry, IWM MISC 189/2(2826), Tape 4482

10 Sinel, *The German Occupation of Jersey*, p. 89

11 Victor Graham, *Both Sides of the Wire* (unpublished memoir)

12 Imperial War Museum, Michael Ginns, IWM MISC 189/2(2826), Tapes 4448 & 4479

13 Arthur Kent's daily record of the occupation, Jersey War Tunnels Collection, JWT/2004/131

14 Harris, *Islanders Deported*, part 1, p. 17

15 Hathaway, *Dame of Sark*, p. 140

16 Frank Stroobant, quoted in Harris, *Islanders Deported*, part 1, p. 41

17 Harris, *Islanders Deported*, part 1, p. 42

18 BBC WW2 People's War, Article ID 55/a3546155

19 Graham, *Both Sides of the Wire* (unpublished memoir)

20 Maisie Plain, née Poster, interview, 2006, Jersey War Tunnels Collection, JWT/2007/977

21 Victor Graham, *Both Sides of the Wire*

22 Pat Holt, interview, 2006, Jersey War Tunnels Collection, JWT/2003/1789

23 Michael Ginns, interview, 2006, Jersey War Tunnels Collection, JWT/2007/1024

24 John Green, interview, 2006, Jersey War Tunnels Collection, JWT/2007/973

25 *Ibid.*

26 *Ibid.*

27 Cortvriend, *Isolated Island*, p. 239

28 *Ibid.*

29 Maurice Hill, interview, 2000, Jersey War Tunnels Collection, JWT/2008/494

30 Sherwill, *A Fair and Honest Book*, p. 193

31 *Ibid.*, pp. 192–3

CHAPTER 10: FORTRESS ISLANDS

1 Saunders, *Hitler's Atlantic Wall*, p. 1

2 *Time*, 18 August 1941

3 Saunders, *Hitler's Atlantic Wall*, p. 17

4 Cruickshank, *The German Occupation of the Channel Islands*, p. 198

5 Van Grieken, *Destination 'Gustav'*, 1992

6 Cruickshank, *The German Occupation of the Channel Islands*, p. 215

7 Sinel, *The German Occupation of Jersey*

8 Michael Ginns, *The Organization Todt and the Fortress Engineers in the Channel Islands*, Channel Islands Occupation Society Archive, 1994

9 Le Quesne, *The Occupation of Jersey Day by Day* (entry for 12 August 1942)

10 Keiller, *Prison without Bars*, p. 96

11 Joe Mière, interview, 2003, Jersey War Tunnels Collection, JWT/2007/929

12 Keiller, *Prison without Bars*, p. 96

13 Ginns, *The Organisation Todt and the Fortress Engineers in the Channel Islands*, p. 90

14 PRO 199/2090A55851

15 Ginns, *The Organization Todt and the Fortress Engineers in the Channel Islands*, p. 93

16 BBC WW2 People's War, Article ID 99/a4419399

17 Pancheff, *Alderney Fortress Island*, p. 13

18 *Ibid.*

19 *Ibid.*, p. 14

20 Imperial War Museum, interview with Paul Markert, 4485/4486 IWM MISC 189/1(2826)

21 *Ibid.*

22 Pancheff, *Alderney Fortress Island*, p. 55

23 Imperial War Museum, interview with Paul Markert, 4485/4486 IWM MISC 189/1(2826)

24 McLoughlin, *Living with the Enemy*, p. 179

CHAPTER 11: RAISING THE STAKES

1 Speidel, *We Defended Normandy*, p. 67

2 *Ibid.*

3 Cabinet Papers, Channel Islands, February 1941–May 1950, PRO CAB 121/367

4 *Ibid.*

5 PRO, PREM 3/8/87, ff. 145–6

6 PRO, Cabinet Papers, PREM, 3/87/ f. 143

7 PRO, Cabinet Papers, CAB 121/367/G.14A

8 PRO, Cabinet Papers, CAB 121/367/G20

9 Public Record Office, PRO CAB 121/367 f. 21

10 Alanbrooke, *War Diaries 1939–1945*, p. 357

11 *Ibid.*, p. 383

12 Public Record Office, PRO CAB 121/367 f. 24

13 Public Record Office. PRO CAB 121/367 f. 28

CHAPTER 12: RESISTANCE AND RETALIATION

1 Admiralty Files, PRO ADM 223/697

2 *Ibid.*

3 *Ibid.*

4 Arthur Kent's daily record of the occupation, Jersey War Tunnels Collection, JWT/2004/131

5 Mahy, *There is an Occupation . . .*, p. 39

6 *Ibid.*

7 Norman Le Brocq lecture to the Channel Islands Occupation Society, 4 April 1988

8 McLoughlin, *Living with the Enemy*, p. 71

9 Harold Carter, quoted in McLoughlin, *Living with the Enemy*, p. 72

10 Len de Poidevin, interview, 2006, Jersey War Tunnels Collection, JWT/2007/994

11 Sherwill, *A Fair and Honest Book*, p. 234

12 *Ibid.*

13 Bob Le Sueur, interview, 2000, Jersey War Tunnels Collection, JWT/2009/61

14 Fraser, *The Jews of the Channel Islands and the Rule of Law, 1940–1945*, p. 1

15 Chapman, *The Profession of Government*, p. 275

16 Imperial War Museum, MISC 189/1(2826), Tape 4494

17 *Ibid.*

18 Von Aufsess, *Occupation Diary*, pp. 61–2 (entry for 28 October 1944)

19 Maurice Green, interview, 2004, Jersey War Tunnels Collection, JWT/2007/1003

20 *Jersey Evening Post*, 1 November 1982, quoted in Knowles Smith, *The Changing Face of the Channel Islands Occupation*, p. 192

21 Arthur Kent's daily record of the occupation, Jersey War Tunnels Collection, JWT/2004/131

22 *Ibid.*

23 Bernard Baker's diary, quoted in Hillsdon, *Jersey Occupation Remembered*, p. 113

24 *Ibid.*

25 Imperial War Museum, IWM MISC 189/1(2826), Tapes JT2

26 Joe Mière, interview, 2003, Jersey War Tunnels Collection, JWT/2007/929

27 Fred Gallienne, BBC WW2 People's War, Article ID 35/a4013335

28 *Hitler's British Islands*, p. 47

29 Martin Falle, interview, 2003, Jersey War Tunnels Collection, JWT/2007/990

30 Arthur Kent's daily record of the occupation, Jersey War Tunnels Collection, JWT/2004/131

31 Imperial War Museum, MISC 189/1(2826), Tape 4494

CHAPTER 13: BEGINNING OF THE END

1 Leo Harris, interview, 2003, Jersey War Tunnels Collection, JWT/2007/1001

2 *Jersey Evening Post*, 6 June 1944

3 Michael Ginns, interview, 2000, Jersey War Tunnels Collection, JWT/2009/1022

4 Arthur Kent's daily record of the occupation, Jersey War Tunnels Collection, JWT/2004/131

5 *Jersey Evening Post*, 9 June 1944

6 *Jersey Evening Post*, 11 July 1944

7 *Ibid.*

8 John and Carette Floyd, interview, 2004, Jersey War Tunnels Collection, JWT/2007/1017

9 Von Aufsess, *Occupation Diary*, pp. 1, 4

10 Admiralty Files, PRO, ADM. 223/697

11 Imperial War Museum, IWM MISC 189/2(2826), Tapes 4396–7

12 Sinel, *The German Occupation of Jersey*, pp. 222–3

13 Quoted in *Hitler's British Islands*, p. 53

14 John and Carette Floyd, interview, 2004, Jersey War Tunnels Collection, JWT/2007/1017

15 George Houghton, interview, 9 June 2005

16 Keiller, *Prison without Bars*, p. 49

17 McLoughlin, *Living with the Enemy*, p. 99

CHAPTER 14: THE HUNGER WINTER

1 Horace Wyatt, unposted letter no. 8, January 1945, pp. 72–3

2 Von Aufsess, *Occupation Diary*, p. 51

3 Arthur Kent's daily record of the occupation, Jersey War Tunnels Collection, JWT/2004/131

4 Tim Rogers, interview, quoted by Michael Ginns

5 Public Record Office, PRO CAB 121/367

6 *Ibid.,* f. 58

7 *Ibid.*, f. 60

8 Cruickshank, *The German Occupation of the Channel Islands*, p. 284

9 Public Record Office, PRO CAB 121/367, f. 74

10 *Ibid.*, f. 79

11 *Ibid.*, f. 80

12 *Ibid.*, f. 81

13 *Ibid.*, f. 82

14 *The Times*, 5 December 1944

15 *Ibid.*

16 Pocock, *The Memoirs of Lord Coutanche*, p. 38

17 Von Aufsess, *Occupation Diary*, p. 25

18 *Ibid.*, p. 29

10 *Jersey Evening Post*, 10 January 1945

20 Sinel, *The German Occupation of Jersey*, p. 254

21 *Ibid.*

22 Arthur Kent's daily record of the occupation, Jersey War Tunnels Collection, JWT/2004/131

23 Imperial War Museum, IWM MISC 189/1(2826)

24 Higgs, *Life in Guernsey under the Nazis*, p. 63

25 Imperial War Museum, IWM MISC 189/1(2826)

26 Frank Hubert, 'Occupying My Mind 1940–45', *Channel Islands Occupation Review*, no. 28, June 2001

27 Kay Houiellebecq and Vivienne Amy, BBC WW2 People's War, Article ID 03/a3886103

28 Imperial War Museum, Hans Glauber, IWM MISC 189/1(2826), Tape 4428

29 Elizabeth Doig, unpublished diary, Priaulx Library

30 Ruth Walsh, BBC WW2 People's War, Article ID 16/a4014316

31 Imperial War Museum, Frank Browning, IWM MISC 189/1 (2826), Tape 4424

32 Arthur Kent's daily record of the occupation, Jersey War Tunnels Collection, JWT/2004/131

33 Imperial War Museum, Werner Grosskopf, IWM MISC 189/1(2826), Tape 4490

34 Captain Ralph H. Covernton, MC, *Fifty Odd Years of Memoirs 1893–1945*, Liddell Hart Centre for Military Studies 1946

35 Kaye le Cheminant, BBC WW2 People's War, Article ID 88/a4014488

36 Public Record Office, PRO CAB 65/49/26

37 Public Record Office, PRO CAB 66/63/38

38 Ruth Walsh, BBC WW2 People's War, Article ID 05/a4014505

39 Kaye le Cheminant, BBC WW2 People's War, Article ID 74/a4042874

CHAPTER 15: A LAST STAND?

1 Winton, *Death of the* Scharnhorst, p. 3

2 Cruickshank, *The German Occupation of the Channel Islands*, p. 297

3 Le Quesne, *The Occupation of Jersey Day by Day*, p. 226

4 Von Aufsess, *Occupation Diary*, p. 144

5 *Ibid.*, p. 144

6 *Ibid.*, p. 158

7 Translation in R.C.F. Maugham, *Jersey Under the Jackboot*, Coronet, 1992

8 Sinel, *The German Occupation of Jersey*, p. 281

9 Von Aufsess, *Occupation Diary*, p. 141

10 *Ibid.*

11 Michael Ginns, interview, 2000, Jersey War Tunnels Collection, JWT/2009/1022

12 Joe Mière, interview, 2003, Jersey War Tunnels Collection, JWT/2007/929

13 Jack Yeatman, diary, BBC WW2 People's War, Article ID 52/a4041352

14 *Ibid.*

15 Sinel, *The German Occupation of Jersey*, p. 287

16 Kesselring, *Memoirs*, p. 253

CHAPTER 16: LIBERATION

1 Pocock, *The Memoirs of Lord Coutanche*, p. 45

2 Imperial War Museum, John Blampied, IWM MISC 189/2(2826), Tapes 4394–6

3 Lamerton, *Liberated by Force 135*, p. 76

4 Raymond Rees, interview, 2006, Jersey War Tunnels Collection, JWT/2009/71

5 Pocock, *The Memoirs of Lord Coutanche*, p. 48

6 Raymond Rees, interview, 2006, Jersey War Tunnels Collection, JWT/2009/71

7 Von Aufsess, *Occupation Diary*, p. 190

8 Ruth Lewis, interview, 2000, Jersey War Tunnels Collection, JWT/2008/468

9 Reg Langlois, BBC WW2 People's War, Article ID 46/a3403946

10 Margaret Le Cras, BBC WW2 People's War, Article ID 96/a4043396

11 L.A. Landick, 'Do You Remember Liberation Day?' *Channel Islands Occupation Review*, no. 23, May 1995

12 Marion Hamel, interviewed by Eileen Travis, *Evening News*, 22 May 1945

13 Quoted by Michael Ginns

14 Leo Harris, interview, 2004, Jersey War Tunnels Collections, JWT/2007/989

15 Philip Le Cuirot, interview, 2004, Jersey War Tunnels Collection, JWT/2007/936

16 John Boucheré, 'The Day Peace Broke Out', *Channel Islands Occupation Review*, 1975

17 Imperial War Museum, IWM MISC 189/2 (2826), Tape 4448

18 Graham Hawley, interview, 2006, Jersey War Tunnels Collection, JWT/2007/1027

19 Masie Plain, née Poster, interview, 2006, Jersey War Tunnels Collection, JWT/2007/977
20 John Green, interview, 2006, Jersey War Tunnels Collection, JWT/2007/973
21 BBC WW2 People's War, Article ID 55/a3546155
22 Edward Fox, interview, 2005, Jersey War Tunnels Collection, JWT/2009/64
23 John Green, interview, 2006, Jersey War Tunnels Collection, JWT/2007/973

CHAPTER 17: A VINDICTIVE POST-MORTEM

1 Joe Mière, interview, 2003, Jersey War Tunnels Collection, JWT/2007/929
2 Imperial War Museum, IWM MISC 189/2(2826), Tapes 4481–2
3 Von Aufsess, *Occupation Diary*, p. 61
4 McLoughlin, *Living with the Enemy*, p. 109
5 BBC WW2 People's War Article ID 14/a4045114
6 Le Quesne, *The Occupation of Jersey Day by Day*, p. 9
7 *Ibid.*
8 John Bouchere, interview, 2000, Jersey War Tunnels Collection, JWT/2008/516
5 Cyd Le Baile, interview, 2000, Jersey War Tunnels Collection, JWT/2008/647
10 War Cabinet Memorandum, 24 May 1945, PRO CAB 66/65/74
11 Josephine Ginns, interview, 2000, Jersey War Tunnels Collection, JWT/2008/495
12 War Office Statement No. 7, 18 July 1945
13 Home Office File on collaboration in the Channel Islands, PRO HO 45/22399, 9 July 1945
14 MI5 Files, PRO KV 4/78
15 *Ibid.*, 20 July 1944
16 *Ibid.*, 5 August 1944
17 *Ibid.*, f. 356a
18 *Ibid.*, f. 351a
19 *Ibid.*
20 *Ibid.*, f. 355b
21 *Ibid.*, f. 192a
22 *Ibid.*
23 *Ibid.*, f. 239a
24 *Ibid.*, f. 254a, 3 July 1945
25 *Ibid.*, f. 264a, 8 July 1945

26 *Ibid.*, f. 315f

27 *Ibid.*

28 *Ibid.*, f. 333a, 17 August 1945

29 PRO, HO 45/22399

30 PRO, KV 4/78 f. 346

31 Imperial War Museum, IWM MISC 189/2(2826), Tapes 4392–4

CHAPTER 18: WAR CRIMES

1 Harris, *A Boy Remembers*, p. 133

2 Frank Hubert, 'Occupying My Mind 1940–45', *Channel Islands Occupation Review*, no. 28, June 2001

3 Bob Le Sueur, interview, 2004, Jersey War Tunnels Collection, JWT/2007/857

4 BBC WW2 People's War, Article ID 33/a2129933

5 Hathaway, *Dame of Sark*, p. 171

6 PRO, Premier, 3/87/ f. 137

7 Imperial War Museum, Channel Islands War Crime Papers, IWM MISC 172/2640

8 *Ibid.*

9 *Ibid.*

10 *Ibid.*

11 Priaulx Library, diary of Rev. Ord, 1 May to 25 October 1944, pp. 804–5

12 Imperial War Museum, Channel Islands War Crime Papers, IWM MISC 172/2640

13 *Ibid.*

14 *Ibid.*

CHAPTER 19: A NEW LEAF

1 Admiralty Files, PRO ADM 223/697

2 Censorship Report on the Channel Islands, PRO, KV4/78, f. 136B

3 *Channel Islands Monthly Review*, vol. 2, November 1941–April 1942

4 *Channel Islands Monthly Review*, February 1942

5 Cruickshank, *The German Occupation of the Channel Islands*, p. 347

6 Josephine Ginns, interview, 2000, Jersey War Tunnels Collection, JWT/2008/495

7 PRO HO 45/22399

8 PRO KV 4/78, f. 356a

9 *Jersey Evening Press*, 5 July 1940
10 PRO HO 45/22399

CHAPTER 20: REFLECTIONS

1 Imperial War Museum, MISC 189/1(2826), Tape 4440
2 John Boachere, interview, 2000, Jersey War Tunnels Collection, JWT/2008/516
3 Betty Thurban, interview, 2000
4 Sylvia Diamond, Patricia Vibert, William and Alice Butler, Edward Helie, BBC WW2 People's War, Article ID 55/a3546155
5 Family of the late Mrs L.E. Brouard, Guernsey, private papers
6 Willy Worner, interview, 2005, Jersey War Tunnels Collection, JWT/2008/467

BIBLIOGRAPHY

The German Occupation of Jersey, 1940–45: Notes on the General Conditions: How the Population Fared, Société Jersiaise

Histoire et Mémoire de la Résistance à Anderlecht, project piloté par la Fédé des Groupements patriotiques d'Anderlecht et le Musée national de la Resistance, October 2007

Histoire et Mémoire des Juifs d'Anderlecht, Années 20–40

Hitler's British Islands: The Channel Islands Occupation Experience by the people who lived through it, Channel Island Publishing

Alanbrooke, Field Marshal Lord, *War Diaries 1939–1945*, ed. Alex L.E. Danchev and Daniel Todman, Weidenfeld & Nicolson, 2001

Bertrand, L.E., *A Record of the Work of Guernsey Secret Press 1940–1945*

Bunting, Madeleine, *The Model Occupation: The Channel Islands under German Rule*, HarperCollins, 1995

Carlton, Eric, *Occupation: The Policies and Practices of Military Conquerors*, Barnes & Noble Books, 1992

Casper, Wilhelm, *Britische Stimmen über die deutsche Besatzungszeit auf den britischen Kanalinseln*, R. v. Decker's Verlag, G. Schenck, 1963

Chapman, Brian, *The Profession of Government*, Allen & Unwin, 1959

Cobb, Matthew, *The Resistance: The French Fight against the Nazis*, Simon & Schuster, 2009

Cortvriend, V.V., *Isolated Island*, Guernsey Star Ltd, 1947

Cruickshank, Charles, *The German Occupation of the Channel Islands*, Sutton, 2004

Durand, Ralph, *Guernsey under German Rule*, Guernsey Society, 1946

Durnford-Slater, Brigadier John, *Commando: Memoirs of a Fighting Commando in World War II*, William Kimber, 1953

Evans, Alice (ed.), *Guernsey Under Occupation: The Second World War Diaries of Violet Carey*, Phillimore, 2009

Falla, Frank, *The Silent War: The Inside Story of the Channel Islands under the Nazi Jackboot*, Frewin, 1967

Forty, George, *Channel Islands at War: A German Perspective*, Ian Allan Publishing, 1999

———, *Fortress Europe: Hitler's Atlantic Wall*, Ian Allan Publishing, 2002

Fraser, David, *The Jews of the Channel Islands and the Rule of Law, 1940–1945*, Sussex Academic Press, 2000

Fuykschot, Cornelia, *Hunger in Holland: Life During the Nazi Occupation*, Prometheus Books, 1995

Gavey, Ernie, *A Guide to German Fortifications on Guernsey*, Guernsey Armouries, 2001

Graham, Victor, *A Separate Peace*, unpublished memoir

Harris, Leo, *A Boy Remembers*, Apache Guides, 2000

———, *Boys Remember More*, Apache Guides, 2002

Harris, Roger E., *Islanders Deported*, part 1, Channel Islands Specialists Society, 1980

———, *Islanders Deported*, part 2, Channel Islands Specialists Society, 1983

Hathaway, Sibyl, *Dame of Sark: An Autobiography*, Heinemann, 1961

Hawes, Stephen & White, Ralph (eds), *Resistance in Europe 1939–45*, Pelican Books, 1976

Higgs, Dorothy Pickard, *Life in Guernsey under the Nazis, 1940–45* (originally *Guernsey Diary*), Toucan Press, 1979

Hillsdon, Sonia, *Jersey Occupation Remembered*, Jarrold Colour Publications, 1986

Holmes, Richard (in association with the Imperial War Museum), *Churchill's Bunker: The Secret Quarters at the Heart of Britain's War Victory*, Profile Books, 2009

Keiller, Frank, *Prison without Bars: Living in Jersey under the German Occupation 1940–45*, Seaflower Books, 2000

Kesselring, Field Marshal Albert, *Memoirs*, William Kimber, 1953

Knowles Smith, Hazel R., *The Changing Face of the Channel Islands Occupation*, Palgrave Macmillan, 2007

Lamerton, Mark, *Liberated by Force 135: The Liberation of the Channel Islands, May 1945*, ELSP, 2000

Le Quesne, Edward, *The Occupation of Jersey Day by Day*, La Haule Books, 1999

Le Ruez, Nan, *Jersey Occupation Diary: Her Story of the German Occupation, 1940–45*, Seaflower Books, 1994

Longmate, Norman, *If Britain Had Fallen*, Arrow Books, 1972

Lund, Joachim (ed.), *Working for the New Order: European Business Under German Domination 1939–1945*, University Press of Southern Denmark & Copenhagen Business School, 2006

McLoughlin, Roy, *Living with the Enemy*, Starlight Publishing, 1995

Mahy, Miriam M., *There is an Occupation . . .*, The Guernsey Press, 1993

Meehan, Patricia, *A Strange Enemy People: Germans under the British 1945–50*, Peter Owen, 2001

Mière, Joe, *Never To Be Forgotten*, Channel Island Publishing, 2004

Money, June, *Aspects of War: The German Occupation of the Channel Islands 1940–1945*, 1995

Moore, Bob (ed.), *Resistance in Western Europe*, Berg, 2000

Ousby, Ian, *Occupation: The Ordeal of France 1940–1944*, John Murray, 1997

Pantcheff, T.X.H., *Alderney Fortress Island: The Germans in Alderney, 1940–45*, Phillimore, 1981

Pocock, H.R.S., *The Memoirs of Lord Coutanche: A Jerseyman Looks Back*, Phillimore, 1975

Read, Brian Ahier, *No Cause for Panic: Channel Island Refugees 1940–45*, Seaflower Books, 1995

Rivett, Peter J., *A Tiny Act of Defiance*, Planetesmal Publishing, 2001

Saunders, Anthony, *Hitler's Atlantic Wall*, Sutton, 2001

Saunders, Paul, *The British Channel Islands Under German Occupation 1940–45*, Société Jersiaise, 2005

Sherwill, Ambrose, *A Fair and Honest Book*, lulu.com, 2006

Sinel, L.P., *The German Occupation of Jersey: A Diary of Events from June 1940 to June 1945*, *Evening Post*, Jersey, 1945

Speidel, Lieutenant General Hans, *We Defended Normandy*, Herbert Jenkins, 1951

Tremayne, Julia, *War on Sark: The Secret Letters of Julia Tremayne*, Webb & Bower, 1981

van der Zee, Henn A., *The Hunger Winter: Occupied Holland 1944–1945*, Bison Books, 1998

van Grieken, Gilbert, *Destination 'Gustav'*, Guernsey Press, 1992

von Aufsess, Baron Max, *The von Aufsess Occupation Diary*, ed. & trans. Kathleen J. Nowlan, Phillimore, 1985

Winton, John, *Death of the* Scharnhorst, Cassell, 1983

Wood, Alan & Wood, Mary Seaton, *Islands in Danger*, Evans, 1955

Wyatt, Horace, *Jersey in Jail*, diary

INDEX